Soft Skills

That

Make or Break

Your Success

12 Soft skills to master self, get along with, and lead others successfully

Assegid Habtewold

Success Pathways Press
Web: www.successpws.com

ISBN- 13: 978-1-947524-01-9
ISBN- 10: 1-947524-01-1

Printed in the United States of America

Published July 2017

Copyright © 2017 by Assegid Habtewold
P.O. Box 10136
Silver Spring, MD 20914

Email: assegid@successpws.com and assegidh@gmail.com
Tel: (703) 895- 4551

TABLE OF CONTENTS

Preface

Research shows that soft skills play the lion's share of success than technical skills. Sadly, many professionals over depend on their expertise. And thus, neglect to develop their soft skills proactively and in turn pay dire prices individually and cause havoc in their organizations. Common complaints such as high turnover, conflict, lack of synergy, and low levels of productivity in many of today's organizations come down to lack of certain soft skills.

This book is based on the story of a successful professional, Dan Murphy who works for a multinational research organization- Global Health Research (GHR). Dan was promoted to lead a multimillion dollar project because of his superb technical skills as a researcher. Unfortunately, due to lack of certain soft skills, problems started to surface. He couldn't get along with his peers and lead his team members.

After several attempts to help, verbal warnings, and then a written one for his file, his immediate boss- Susan Jeffrey, decided to remove him from leading the project. However, since Dan was one of the superstar researchers at GHR, this caused havoc and forced the CEO- Paul Gray, to intervene. Finally, Paul negotiated a deal, which required Dan to attend a three-part Soft Skills Development program and to work with a mentor to continue leading the project.

The book narrates how the problem began, the negotiations, and the main discussion points from the mentoring sessions. The first section of the book covers the discussions among Dan, Susan, and Paul. Introductions of the remaining three parts (Mastering Self, Getting Along, and Leading Others) narrate the talks between the trainer and attendees of the program. The 12 chapters recount Dan's one-on-one mentoring sessions with his mentor- Rafael Arthur.

The main discussion points of each mentoring session include:
1. Four key lessons he learned;
2. Some of the assessments, processes, models, and tools he found helpful; and
3. Immediate actions he plans to take as a result of attending that particular workshop.

The story of GHR and its staff in this book is fictional but realistic. GHR and its employees serve as an illustration of common challenges many companies around the world may face because of lack of certain soft skills. As a former researcher and workshop facilitator for scientific and research organizations, the examples are based on my experiences though the identifying details have been changed.

The program Dan attended is composed of 12 interactive workshops necessary to master self, get along with, and lead others. These 12 soft skills are industry and culture neutral. In whichever industry and country you may belong, they empower you to achieve extraordinary success in your personal life, career, and business.

Speaking of extraordinary success, by default, we all strive to succeed. It's within our DNA. By hook or by crook, every one of us goes the extra mile to succeed- to achieve more, and to go to the next level. We all, individually and collectively, have a desire to succeed.

Of course, success is subjective. It's in the eye of the beholder. What you consider a success may not be recognized as a success by someone else, and vice versa.

To achieve the success that you're pursuing, you need personal mastery; you need to get along with and lead others successfully. And, this book contains great insights, tools, and processes that empower you to develop the 12 soft skills that make or break your success in life, career, and/or business.

Introduction

Research conducted by Harvard University, the Carnegie Foundation, and Stanford Research Center revealed, *"85% of job success comes from having well-developed soft and people skills, and only 15% of job success comes from technical skills and knowledge (hard skills)."*[1] Unfortunately, many inventors, technocrats, business owners, new hires, supervisors, and managers from diverse industries over depend on their expertise. Accordingly, they neglect to develop their soft skills proactively and in turn pay dire prices individually and cause havoc in their organizations.

Lack of soft skills denied Tesla benefiting from his inventions
In our history, we've witnessed many technically genius individuals struggling to succeed because of lack of some essential soft skills. Nikola Tesla was one of such individuals. Tesla invented AC electrical system and coil, which is recognized for laying the foundation for wireless radio technology. On top of these two inventions, Tesla was also a pioneer in discovering technologies such as X-ray, remote control, radar, dynamos, and so on.

Sadly, Tesla lacked the necessary soft skills that could have complemented his technical skills. He was unable to communicate- both in writing and verbally, his inventions. He came short of promoting and marketing his discoveries. Tesla failed to hold patents for all of his inventions. He was also unable to negotiate to benefit from his ideas fully. At the end of the day, regrettably, his technical genius couldn't save him from dying poor in solitary.

Wozniak wouldn't have pulled off Apple
As of 2016, Forbes acknowledged that Apple outshines its tech peers such as Microsoft and Samsung. It's one of the most valued companies in the world. Behind the formation of Apple were two outstanding individuals- Steve Jobs and Steve Wozniak.

However, without the supplement of Jobs' soft skills, Wozniak- regardless of his off chart technical genius, wouldn't have pulled off Apple. Even if he could, he wouldn't have launched it to become a worldwide phenomenon without Jobs' excellent soft skills. In short, millions around the globe wouldn't have enjoyed the amazing products of this leading company if the two didn't come together and complemented one another.

Both Tesla and Wozniak had outstanding hard skills. Unfortunately, these were not enough to attain extraordinary achievement. Only 15% of success comes from technical expertise.

The difference between the two gentlemen, nonetheless, was that Wozniak teamed up with soft skills genius Jobs who articulated, promoted, and marketed Apple and its products; selected, empowered, and continually inspired Apple's leaders and team members; negotiated, formed coalitions, and more. Tesla wasn't lucky to have such a partner. He paid the dire prices of lack of soft skills. Accordingly, he died lonely and in debt.

The vast majority of startups fail as a result of lack of soft skills
The same is also true when it comes to entrepreneurship. When some technical professionals see that they are amazingly good at what they do, they are tempted to start a business (or encouraged by well-meaning people to become their boss). They quit their job and open their own business thinking that their hard skills alone are enough to excel in the business world.

Disappointingly, it's widely believed that *nine out of ten new startups end up unsuccessful.* There are many reasons why new startups fail. What you won't find in the list of reasons why the overwhelming majority startups die is the lack of technical skills. If you sum up all the reasons, however, they boil down to one thing- the lack of certain soft skills.

The majority of new hires keep getting fired due to lack of soft skills
Not just in the field of invention and entrepreneurship, everywhere, the lack of soft skills is affecting every industry. Let's just pick the corporate world. There is no shortage of employees. For every position they announce, businesses receive hundreds and sometimes thousands of submissions from overly qualified, technically excellent, and highly experienced applicants. The common challenge all companies face is selecting that one right employee who has the qualification and experience plus the soft skills to fit into the corporate culture and get along with the already existing team members.

Despite carefully selected criteria, background checks, and contemporary screening approaches, the majority employers often end up disappointed in their choices. In the majority of the cases, this is not usually an issue with technical abilities. Mark Murphy- author of Hire For Attitude said, *"Forty-six percent of new hires fail in the first 18 months, and 89 percent of them failed for attitudinal reasons. Only 11 percent failed due to a lack of hard skills."*[2] The expertise that brought the new hires through the door was unable to help them stay there longer and flourish. Companies let go of many of their new hires regardless of their superb technical expertise due to the absence of certain soft skills.

Millions are quitting because of managers who don't have soft skills

Of course, it's not just new hires that disappoint because of lack of soft skills. Look around you. Many existing employees, supervisors and managers also struggle due to lack or poorly developed soft skills.

Higher-level positions frequently involve supervisory duties that require having excellent soft skills. Unfortunately, many companies don't pay close attention to soft skills when they promote their super achievers. When the latter demonstrate outstanding technical abilities and outperform their peers, they get promoted to lead their team. And, as a result, they cause havoc.

Common workplace complaints such as high turnover, conflict, lack of synergy, and low levels of productivity many companies are experiencing today come down to lack of certain soft skills by supervisors and managers. For instance, *"A Gallup poll of more than 1 million employed U.S. workers concluded that the No. 1 reason people quit their jobs is a bad boss or immediate supervisor…People leave managers not companies...in the end, turnover is mostly a manager issue."*[3]

GHR isn't exceptional, one of its managers caused havoc

A couple of years ago, Global Health Research (GHR) faced a valuable opportunity for growth when one of its managers- Dan Murphy, entered into conflict with his boss due to lack of certain soft skills. Dan is an excellent researcher. He is intelligent and creative when it comes to his scientific work.

He had first joined GHR as a doctoral student. He completed his dissertation and later joined GHR as a staff member. His publications, while still working on his thesis and following his graduation, brought him both admirations and promotion.

To Dan's dismay, nevertheless, he was unable to negotiate the promotion without supervisory duties. He wanted to lead the project. But, he didn't like the accompanying supervisory responsibilities that come with the new title.

Alas, not long after he was promoted, Dan stumbled. He couldn't successfully get along with his peers and lead his team due to lack of certain soft skills. His immediate boss got grievances from a few of his team members and peers. She investigated the complaints and found them true.

Susan tried her best to help Dan understand the importance of getting along with others. Unfortunately, he refused to admit that he is the problem, let alone to make changes and address the issue. The problem persisted. For that matter, some key researchers from his project and a few managers from departments that provide support to his project threatened to quit because of Dan's unacceptable behaviors.

Finally, after trying her best, she decided to remove Dan from leading the project. She didn't want to 'lose all' to retain one. This decision, however, caused havoc and forced the CEO of GHR to intervene.

In the next part, I'll narrate for you the following:
- The genesis of the problem
- The involvement of the CEO to rescue one of his best superstars
- The negotiation to break the deadlock
- The soft skills development program Dan finally agreed to attend to tackle the problem.

Lack of soft skills is a universal phenomenon
One thing to note here is that though this story occurred in a research company in the US, almost all organizations in every industry around the world face the same kinds of challenges. The good thing is that some companies have come to realize the significant roles soft skills play. Accordingly, they are willing to invest millions of dollars every year in enabling their people to develop the necessary soft skills.

You too should consider empowering yourself and your team regardless of in whichever industry and country you may be right now. Your people need to develop certain soft skills to master self, get along with, and influence others. And, this book is a great starting place.

This book contains the twelve soft skills that are critical to achieving success in your life, relationships, career, and so on. These soft skills are industry and culture neutral. They are vital to succeed in whichever industry and country you may belong.

The 12 soft skills make or break your success
Remember that without these soft skills one may still:

- Find a job,
- Open a business,
- Get promoted, and
- Even take a key leadership position like in the case of Dan.

Nonetheless, it's unlikely to succeed, serve one's organization, community, and society extraordinarily without developing these essential soft skills. These 12 soft skills make or break your individual and/or collective success. They are mandatory to attain impactful, lasting, and sustainable success.

These soft skills aren't just for people like Dan who are struggling
By the way, these soft skills aren't relevant just for people who are struggling like Dan. They are very critical to all professionals, entrepreneurs, and leaders in any industry around the world who aspire to succeed. Of course, the success you desire to attain may differ from someone else's. Regardless, you need to develop, at least, these 12 soft skills if your desire is to succeed in what you do continually.

With whom do you relate?
In this book, you may relate to:

- **Dan**. You may relate with Dan and say, "That's me! I'm Dan." Up until now, you might not have realized how much the lack of some soft skills has prevented you from succeeding in your personal life, profession, social life, business, and leadership. Now, as you read this book, you may be able to see yourself in Dan and relate with his story. This is my hope that, as a result of reading this book, you may start to invest your time and energy to work on those soft skills that you need to succeed in your personal life, at work, and in the marketplace.

- **Dan's team members and peers**. You may already know one or more people in your life, organization, community, and business who are creating havoc because of the lack of one or more of these soft skills covered in this book. The story of Dan and the changes he demonstrated following attending the soft skills development program may inspire you to help your friends and colleagues understand the significance of soft skills. You may even decide to empower them to develop these soft skills. Or at least, you may give them this book as a gift with the hope that they may relate with Dan and take the courage like he did to work on their soft skills.

- **Susan or Paul.** I'm sure that in every organization, there are individuals like Dan. As a leader of your team, as you read this book, you may relate with Susan or Paul. You may have professionals like Dan. They have excellent technical expertise, and you don't want to lose them. At the same time, they're unable to get along and lead others, and causing havoc. Till now, you might have been thinking either letting them go while feeling sad or tolerating them regardless of the damages they are causing to your team. Now, as you read the transformation of Dan once he passed through the program, it may give you the hope that it is possible to transform your supervisors and managers from being liabilities into assets. This book may also provide you some insights on how to approach such leaders. It may also assist you to select the right soft skills they need to develop to master self, get along with, and influence others successfully, and in turn succeed individually and also contribute their share toward meeting the company's bottom line.

Lack of soft skills wreaking havoc at GHR

1. The genesis of the problem

Dan manages a multimillion dollar research project. He reports directly to the program manager, Susan. Though she supervises other managers, he is one of her best producers.

The employees who report to Dan need his help. But, they also fear him. After speaking with him about it several times, two of them scheduled a private meeting with Susan. They acknowledged his expertise, but they accused him of making the environment hostile. After carefully listening and asking follow-up questions, Susan promised to work with Dan. She was confident that he would come around once she made it clear how critical it was for him to build appropriate relationships with his team.

To her disappointment, Dan responded defensively. Later, half-heartedly consented to work on it. After several verbal warnings and then a written one for his file, his behaviors are the same. Dan had made the mistake of assuming that his fantastic research outputs and celebrity status due to his publications make him untouchable.

Marshall Goldsmith was right when he said, *"The trouble with success is that...our previous success often prevents us from achieving more success."* Our past success sabotages our current and future success unless we are careful. If what we have been working in our favor, why change? *'If it's not broke, why fix it?'* It seems fair, isn't it? It looks like a no-brainer. But, it's not. Those competencies, behaviors, decisions, and actions that have brought us this far will get in the way and prevent us from achieving the next level success unless we take proactive measures to upgrade ourselves continually.

Before taking this supervisory role, his lack of some soft skills hadn't been that much a problem (at least not one that he's noticed). Dan had been succeeding and achieving project milestones with relative ease. This success prevented him from realizing the need to make some changes following his new role as manager of a mega project. Dan's behavior wasn't strange to

Susan. She worked with other high-achieving researchers. In most cases, the desire to advance had made them take their supervisory roles more seriously.

Susan is an excellent communicator. She tried everything she could think of in order Dan to take her specific feedback seriously. Finally, she gave him a last warning. "If you don't build rapport with your team in the next couple of weeks, you will no longer be the lead on this project."

Despite her assurances, she was serious, Dan smirked at her. "You'd never do something like that. No one knows this research better than I do. Doing that would result in a guaranteed failure. I mean, have you met my team?"

Finally, Susan realized that Dan isn't going to change nor quietly give up his managerial position without a fight. Considering his high profile status and Paul's high regard for him, she didn't want to take a unilateral decision without first consulting Paul.

She wanted Dan to succeed. But, she didn't see how he could continue in his current role without working on his:
a) Personal growth,
b) Ability to get along with others, and
c) Leadership competency to influence others.

2. The CEO intervened to rescue one of his superstars

a) Lack of self-mastery as a stumbling block

Susan had kept Paul updated on her hopes for Dan and a couple of weeks ago on her concerns that he wasn't taking her feedback seriously. Following her latest disappointing conversation with Dan, she reached out to Paul and requested for a quick meeting to talk about Dan. The next day, they met in his office.

After exchanging quick greetings and inquiring about Susan's recent family vacation, Paul shifted his attention to business. "How are things going with Dan?" He asked. Susan pulled herself at the edge of the sofa, cleared her voice, and explained. "Dan has delivered more than our expectations when it comes to his project's milestones. He is hard working, with extraordinary self-discipline, and time management skill. But, Dan does things the way he wants, and when others point out better ways of doing things, Dan gets frustrated, lashes out and unable to control his emotions and anger. He is incapable of resolving problems before they escalate and cause damages. Dan also makes decisions without involving key stakeholders."

Paul listened attentively and probed. "What you're saying is that he doesn't have personal mastery. Am I correct?" "Exactly!" Susan consented. And further elaborated, "Dan thinks that he has all that it takes to do the job by himself. He couldn't see his limitations. Dan isn't self-aware about some of his shortcomings. Even if some of his team members and myself mentioned some of his blind spots, he wasn't willing to acknowledge and work on them."

"We had hoped for better. But, I'm not surprised. Too many of these situations end up with someone leaving the organization." Paul expressed his disappointment. "Do you have any suggestion on how we can work toward a win-win? I know you don't want to lose Dan. Neither do I. Things have to change if he's going to stay, though." He solicited her advice.

Susan wished if these were the only failings of Dan. And therefore, she remarked, "Paul, these are the tip of the iceberg." When Paul heard this statement, he knew that he was there for a long ride. Hence, he leaned back on the sofa, sat comfortably, and signaled Susan to continue.

b) Unable to get along with others causing trouble

Once Susan got his attention, she continued. "Dan also failed to get along with others. He is a loner, finds himself productive when he works alone.

Dan spends a lot of time in the lab. He firmly believes that spending time with others to know their needs, aspirations, and also the challenges they face is a distraction from his busy schedule."

Knowing these behaviors Susan just mentioned are common among scientists, he interrupted Susan politely. "He is a scientist for God's sake, Susan!" He then asked her a rhetoric question. "What is wrong with seeking to be alone and spending time in his lab most of the time? Many researchers are introverts and prefer to stay within their world, and these behaviors come with the territory."

Unlike Susan whose background is MBA, Paul came from a science background. He had been a scientist for many years before he began taking a series of managerial positions in the last two decades.

"You're right, Paul, the majority of his time should be spent in the lab and alone for him to reflect, read, and write. But, as you already know, his new role as a project manager requires him to interact with both people within his project and outside more frequently." Susan felt Paul undermined her ability to understand what it takes to be a successful scientist. Even if she doesn't have a scientific background, Susan is a veteran project manager. Before joining GHR, she had been working with scientists and researchers successfully.

Paul read the facial expression of Susan, which apparently revealed her frustration. To ease the tension, Paul smiled big and clarified his point. "As far as he is communicating with the team using technologies, and conducting those mandatory in-person meetings and one-on-ones, I don't see the need for him to spend lots of time with others. You should understand his challenge. He must deliver his promises to our donors, interact with other scientists in his field, and also publish and present the results at scientific forums."

I worked for an international research organization while I was still back home in Ethiopia from 1999 till I came to the US in 2005. In this industry, you either publish or perish. You're constantly pressured to write proposals, aggressively seek funds, and also deliver your promises. It's a very competitive and high paced environment. Because of that many researchers are tempted to spend less time with their team members and other stakeholders to devote more time on surviving and thriving in this cutthroat environment.

Paul's attempt didn't work. Rather, it further irritated her. She is well aware that Dan should get enough time to do his job with minimal interruptions. She hadn't wanted to overwhelm Paul with details, but she didn't have any choice. "I fully understand his situation. But, if he invests a fraction of the time that he spends alone in his lab to communicate with his team properly, problems wouldn't have cropped up."

She further poured out her frustration. "Even those scant communications are mostly via email. Whenever Dan conducts meetings and one-on-ones, he doesn't provide enough info and context. Dan is disinterested listen to their opinions and concerns." She further pointed out that he is impatience as he interacts with people outside of his project. "Not only that he makes critical decisions without involving key stakeholders. Some of Dan's team members and peers also accuse him of being insensitive to their culture and religion. Conflict is rampant in his team, and Dan doesn't have the time, interest, and will to address them on time."

"What did he say about the conflicts?" Paul inquired. Susan groaned and rubbed her head. "He thinks that the conflicts are none of his creations. He blames others. Most importantly, Dan seems oblivious to all the resentment even though outsiders can feel it just walking into his department."

"That is the most common response in my experience. Since we can't see ourselves without bias, we tend to think that the conflicts we experience are everyone else's problem. I see that Dan needs to develop his people skills." Paul shared his observation and asked a follow-up question, "Have you suggested him attend some training courses to improve his people skills?"

While nodding her head, Susan answered, "Initially, yes but Dan was dismissive. I can't force him to attend training. And even if I could, what good will it do if he's not invested in improving and doing better?" "What are his reasons?" Paul wondered.

Susan couldn't hold back. "He is adamant about not having time. He's sure the project would fall way behind schedule and said he wouldn't do it even for something that seemed worthwhile to him."

After a few moments, Paul asked, "Do you agree with him?"

With a slight shake of her head, Susan replied, "It would be a lot of time away from the research, but I can't help wondering if his team won't be productive enough to make up for it. His borderline-abusive relationships with his staff certainly aren't helping the tight schedule."

Susan's mention of abusive relationships triggered Paul's memory. "I can't remember even seeing him chat with anyone. He always leaves team lunches and birthday celebrations as soon as he's done eating . . . Will you tell me more about his abusiveness?"

This question of Paul was difficult for her. Susan sighed. Not because she didn't have examples. Susan felt disloyal. But, did she have any choice?

Before continuing, Susan paused. "Dan hardly ever gives his team members all the information they need. I'm not sure if he knows he is doing it or not, but I suspect it's part of his belief that intelligent people can find answers on their own. Like a test, I guess? Later when they fail to meet his extremely high standards, he cuts them out of the most significant works. He doesn't demote them officially, but task assignments say otherwise. That way he doesn't have to address the matter at all."

Though Paul was satisfied with Susan's response, he decided to push it further. "And when they ask him about it?"

"He refuses to answer. He says things like, 'If you don't know, you're even worse off than I thought.'"

Paul wasn't about to let this thing go. He wanted to know. "Is he like this with his peers and donors too?"

Susan paused to think about her answer. "Dan does it with his peers. It's worse if anything, he doesn't hold back or leave it for them to ask. He tends to lay it out for them via email. I know some of his donors keep contact with him to a minimum, but no one has complained so far."

Bending his head down, Paul shook his head. Before he asked another question, Susan further elaborated, "When donors come to observe the progress of the project, he makes the time for them, but he is quick to dismiss them. He tells them to email him with any questions. That comes back to his work coming first, though. He does respond to the questions right away; he emails them in the evening once he's left the office. He doesn't seem to see the value of their active involvement."

"I see." Paul looked aggravated. "And how is your relationship with him lately? Have you found him to be receptive to anything you say?"

Another tough question. Regardless, without taking the time to think, Susan explained. "Occasionally, we can find some common ground. He's quick to remind me that my background is in business and his science. In general, though, he tells me that everyone is overreacting. He has accused me of trying to make him into someone he doesn't like. Someone who is more like me." Both laughed.

c) Failing to influence others getting in the way
Paul looked perplexed. He kept quiet for several seconds. The room froze.

"I see that he needs to improve his communication skills but what about his leadership? The project seems going very well as I've read from your reports." Paul was hoping to hear some encouraging reports.

Nonetheless, Susan had none. "Leadership, as you know is about influencing others to do what you want them to do even more. Unfortunately, Dan has limited influence both within and outside of his project. His team complains that he pressures them to deliver using various techniques such as some forms of fear and manipulations than motivating them to tap into their potential."

Paul chimed in. "That means he is using old school motivation approaches that don't work any longer." Both laughed loudly.

"Besides, some of his team members also criticized him for failing to invest in them. He expects them to over deliver his expectations without spending enough time to empower them." Susan agreed. There was a brief quiet moment. No one spoke.

Susan then added, "I also learned that rather than negotiating and building the coalition he needs to achieve what he wants, Dan prefers win-lose scenarios. He also barely participates in the companywide long-term transformation efforts since he is preoccupied in delivering quick and immediate project results."

To demonstrate that Dan failed to lead his team, Susan further gave Paul some incidents. These examples painted a clear picture concerning Dan's struggle to influence others. She shared, almost word-for-word, the argument she had with Dan that led her to believe that he wasn't going to change.

She then dropped the bomb. "I informed Dan that I'm going to remove him from managing the project unless he demonstrates a turn around in the next couple of weeks. I came here to give you a heads up since I know how much you value Dan and the hope you had for him."

Rushing to save one of the bests

Paul looked thwarted. Though he could hear from her voice that she was irritated when she called to set up this meeting, he hadn't anticipated she would go this far. Who blames him? This news is upsetting to him. He knows Dan's achievements and hard work. He was hoping that he continues to excel. However, he cannot undermine Susan. He knows that she is beyond reproach.

After asking a couple of more questions and listening carefully, he realized that Susan had strong reasons to reach this conclusion. Nonetheless, Paul felt that it wasn't a good idea to put a demand on Dan like this. And therefore, he expressed his concern, "He may not respond positively to your precondition. If you remove him from leading his project, he may overreact and may take some desperate measures that may not be good to our organization both in short and long term."

"Removing Dan at this point is going to be a big loss and substituting him with another person is even more challenging." Paul further argued. "Even if we get someone in his caliber, remember, his project just finished phase one, the donors have tremendous confidence in him, and if they know that he isn't the one leading the next phases, they may not continue to fund the project. And, I don't want to take that chance yet."

Accordingly, Paul suggested a three-way meeting in his office to find a middle ground to resolve the stalemate. He proposed that Dan should be given some growth opportunities before demoting him. Susan with a skeptic tone, "I've tried that. I asked him to attend some workshops, but he insisted that he doesn't have time. He is also cynical about workshops on themes that are non-technical."

Paul shared his resentment to attend these kinds of workshops as a scientist and then a junior manager, and asked Susan to give Dan one last chance. Susan gave in. "Paul, I'm okay if you decide to give it a try, and you may succeed to change his mind. But, you should know that some key scientists and managers threatened to quit if he continues with his unacceptable behaviors. We shouldn't lose all to retain one."

"I won't let that to happen. If Dan declines to accept my offer and fails to demonstrate improvements within a reasonable period, I'll let him go." Paul promised. Susan agreed to the compromise and left Paul's office. Right away, Paul called to Dan, talked to him briefly, and asked him to come to his office on Friday at 1 pm for a three-way meeting.

3. Negotiation to break the deadlock

That triple threat meeting arrived. Both Susan and Dan arrived at the CEO's office on time. The warm sunny weather was a stark contrast to what was happening in Paul's office. Two of GHR's best minds sat across from Paul's empty chair. Susan asked Dan about his plans for the weekend. His short answers ended the conversation quickly enough.

Short answers and limited eye contacts are typical for Dan. He doesn't see the point in small talks, something he had mentioned to his team many times. Dan was also holding a grudge against Susan over an argument they had earlier in the week. Dan hated Susan for having complained about him to the CEO. For that matter, she was the very reason why he was sitting in this office instead of working. He couldn't wait to be done with this nonsense and go back to his lab table. Unlike this meeting, that project was meaningful and was, in fact, where most of his attention was focused while sitting there waiting for Paul to arrive.

Paul was a little late as he was attending an important meeting outside. After apologizing for being late, he thanked both for coming.

He quickly moved to tackle the issue. Paul's plan was to directly go to the solution thinking that if he brings up what had happened between the two, things may go out of hand in an unexpected direction. Besides, he was out the whole morning; thus, he would like to finish this trio meeting quickly and go back to work.

Dan, however, wasn't ready to let go so fast. He jumped in. "Paul, before we move on to address the problem, you haven't heard my side of the story. I don't see any problem here. Why should we rush to fix a problem that doesn't exist at all."

Feeling guilty for not giving Dan a chance to share his side of the story, Paul nodded his head signaling Dan to continue. He said, "My bad! Go ahead." Dan complained. "I've met the milestones of the project, and things are going as planned. The complaints are unfair and personal. These people don't like my personality and style of management. I'm a researcher, what do they expect from me? I cannot please everyone. Susan should have known this."

Paul's fear just happened. Susan felt that Dan's last statement undermined her. Susan couldn't let that go without a comment. "Look, Dan! When you were working by yourself, your communication skill, style, and approaches weren't that much important. Now, you are leading a huge project. Two dozens of researchers are reporting to you. They look up to you. Not only that, your position requires you to interact with professionals from other departments cordially."

With a visible impatience, Dan responded immediately. "I have the ability to lead this project successfully, and things are going well, we are on track. I don't understand why you should listen to these people and bother me. We just met a significant milestone and celebrated the success with the main stakeholders. Everybody is happy with the results so far. We are on time and within budget. What else do you expect from me?"

Though he tried to control his emotion, appear calm, and friendly, his facial expression, gestures, and voice pitch betrayed him.

Dan is a victim of a psychological condition called cognitive dissonance. Goldsmith argues that cognitive dissonance is a result of *"the disconnect between what we believe in our minds and what we experience or see in reality."* Dan thought that he was successful in his very mind in his new role as a manager. Unfortunately, that wasn't what was happening. The reality on the ground painted a different picture.

He wasn't alone in blaming others for his predicament. It's counterintuitive and against our nature to first look inwardly and accept responsibilities. We point our fingers somewhere when something goes wrong. Very few people point their fingers inwardly and take responsibility to work on themselves until they master self.

The above were the same lines of arguments Susan had heard again and again. "You don't listen to anyone else but yourself." Dan's continual defensiveness disenchanted Susan.

Susan continued while still exasperated. "I've given you lots of feedback again and again. I expected you to make some changes in your interaction with your team and people from other departments. But, you ignored them all. You continued to irritate key people in our organization. These people are sick and tired of being bullied and disrespected. For that matter, you pushed some of them to the extreme. They threatened to quit if you continue to behave like this. You didn't give me any choice but to take you off from leading the project if you don't improve your approaches."

Mockingly, Dan said, "With all due respect, you don't know squat about research and what it takes to succeed in this field." Before Dan continued to utter words that he might regret, Paul jumped in. "Stop blaming one another. We are here to find a win-win solution."

While calming the two down, he realized in his mind that, unlike his original intention, things heated up and he lost control. He immediately decided to change his approach. He knew that Dan must be open to change in order his proposal to get acceptance.

Shifting his weight toward Dan, Paul zoomed in and confronted him. "Dan, we are here because we respect you and we want you to succeed. You should be part of this effort, not against it. You are working hard to make sure this project succeeds. You want to have a significant role in the management of this big project for which you have extreme passion."

"Unfortunately, it seems to me that you hate the accompanied leadership responsibilities, which require you to come out of your comfort zone. As a successful world-class researcher, you are succeeding by working hard in your lab and focusing on the quality of your project works. Esteemed journals have been publishing your papers. You have been over delivering and attracted millions of dollars funding. No one denies that. We are proud of you. The success you have achieved through your hard work alone, however, couldn't help you excel in your current managerial role."

To allow Dan process what he just said, Paul paused intentionally. He looked at Dan. To avoid eye contact, Dan looked away. Paul continued firmly. "We want you to succeed in this company. You're young. The sky is the limit for you in this organization. However, you need to grow in certain aspects of your life, particularly in your soft skills, and I have an offer." He set the tone before putting forward his proposal.

The room was quiet.

It seems Paul's approach worked. Dan listened carefully and realized that Paul supports Susan's position and expects him to make some changes. It finally dawned on him that his abilities such as writing winning proposals, designing outstanding experiments, flawless project execution and monitoring are not enough to keep leading the project.

Paul underscored, "The technical skills that propelled you to excel in the lab alone cannot enable you to succeed continually in your contemporary leadership position. We are here to help you overcome this challenge."

Both Susan and Dan remained silent. Hence, Paul propositioned, "My proposal requires a compromise from both of you." Paul looked at both and felt that they seemed okay if he proceeds. "Susan, let Dan remain in his position for awhile. We should give him ample chances before you take him off from leading the project."

"Dan, I want you to attend our popular soft skills development program. It's fantastic, especially for people like you and myself whose background is science. I've heard lots of great things from many scientists who attended the program thus far. You know Rafael Arthur, the program manager?"

"Yah, I know him." Dan nodded.

"He has been a mentor for some of our young scientists like you over the years. I'll ask him to mentor you. By the way, not only he has a scientific background and an excellent mentor, he had also attended this the same program some years back."

"Nonetheless, I don't want you to participate in this program out of pressure. It works if you are passionate about it and if you take it seriously. Continue to lead the project while attending the program. And later, we'll come back here again to assess your progress. In the meantime, if you may have any question or concern, feel free to stop by at any time." Paul explained further.

Though Dan wasn't convinced at all that attending a training program makes things better, considering the efforts Paul had made to resolve the conflict between him and Susan, he was obliged to accept the compromise.

However, the real difference maker for Dan to agree to the offer was the fact that Rafael attended that the same program. Rafael is a well-known scientist, who like Susan manages one of the programs at GHR. Paul paired the two knowing that they can quickly establish rapport as both have a science background.

The room froze. Both Paul and Susan waited for Dan's answer anxiously. He agreed half-heartedly. "Okay, Paul. I see that you're trying to help here. I'll join the program, and also work with Rafael."

Paul was happy that Dan took his offer positively, and said, "I'm not ambitious, Dan. I know that soft skills cannot be mastered in three months. However, this is my hope that you make efforts to work on your soft skills going forward. I don't anticipate you to demonstrate a turnaround within a

short period, but we hope that you would show some improvements."
Susan seemed content. She didn't say anything except shaking her head up and down to show her agreement with the proposal.

Paul thanked both for coming and agreeing to his proposal. He stood from his chair, shook their hands, and led them out of his office.

When he returned to his chair, Paul felt relieved knowing that Dan agreed to join the soft skills development program, and Susan accepted his proposal.

Both of these leaders are his superstars. He needs them to work out their differences.

Dan is young with lots of potentials. Paul believed that Dan would be convinced once he participates in the program and realizes the significance of soft skills. Paul was sure that, once Dan appreciates the vital roles they play in his success in his managerial role and future career aspirations, he would invest his time, energy, and make efforts to work on his soft skills continuously.

Rafael and Dan met before the start of the program. Rafael shared his experience and how much the program helped him in his managerial roles-first as a manager of a mega project and now as a program manager. He also answered Dan's questions and clarified his concerns.

They agreed to meet in Rafael's office the day after each workshop for an hour. They discussed the format and outline of the mentoring sessions. Below are the discussion points they agreed to cover. From each workshop:
1. Four key lessons Dan learned,
2. Assessments, processes, models, and tools he found helpful, and
3. Immediate actions he plans to take as a result of attending that particular workshop.

4. Soft skills development program to tackle the problem

Experiencing mixed feelings, Dan drove to attend the orientation session, just one week before the start of the program. In one hand, he was worried about being away from the project one full day each week for the next three months. Dan was concerned that the project team might not function properly in his absence. He was also wondering whether the project might fall behind schedule. On the other hand, Dan was excited since he had accepted the challenge to give this program a try.

Dan arrived at the conference room just before 9 am. While walking to sit at one of the tables in the back, Dan audited the room very quickly to see who else was attending the program. He saw some familiar faces. Some of the participants applied for this program while the rest either forcefully sent like Dan or recommended to participate in this program by their bosses.

Everyone was seated eagerly waiting for the orientation session to begin.

Patrick Young is the Senior Program Manager of GHR's professional development program. Sharp at 9 am, he opened the meeting. Pat has Ph.D. in Biochemistry and is a certified Project Management Professional (PMP). He is a scientist and has extensive experience as a researcher.

However, in his current position, Pat only spends 25 % of his time at GHR on research works. He welcomed everyone and briefly talked about:
- Why GHR decided to provide this program to its people,
- The selection criteria used to select participants, and
- The organization's expectations from each participant.

At the end of his opening remark, Pat encouraged participants to reach out to him if they may have any question or need support. Before stepping down from the stage, he briefly spoke about the training company that won the contract to deliver the program in the next three years. Next, he invited the facilitator of the orientation session, Karen James, to the stage.

Karen is a very charismatic, and articulate trainer. She briefly talked about her education, companies she worked for, and a few of her hobbies. With her sense of humor and playful personality, she immediately captured the attention of participants. Karen asked participants to introduce themselves briefly and share their expectations from the program.

In attendance, there were 15 people. Some of the participants were scientists like Dan while others were technical professionals working in the

IT, Engineering, and Accounting Departments while still others were department and section heads.

Participants of this program came from diverse cultural backgrounds. The majority of the participants were from the US. Some of the participants, nonetheless, were from Europe, Africa, South America, and Asia. Participants were also diverse regarding gender and age.

Many schools failing to equip their graduates

Once the introduction was over, still as friendly and warmly as when she opened the session, Karen smiled and continued, "I'd like to start by emphasizing the importance of soft skills." She gave them some statistics that showed how soft skills play the lion's share of success.

After sharing a few stories to highlight the critical roles soft skills play in individual and collective success, she then pointed out that soft skills haven't been given the attention they deserve. "Many schools fail to empower their students to develop certain soft skills while they are still with them before they go out to face the world following graduation. Though they equip their students to do their technical jobs meticulously, many of the contemporary education systems around the world don't recognize the pivotal roles soft skills play for career success of their students."

While speaking, she scanned the class. She observed that almost all participants nodded their heads concurring with her assessment.

I can testify to that. Whether when I was doing my veterinary degree or master's in computer science, I don't remember taking a single course or attending any workshop on soft skills.

Not just schools and colleges. For instance, American Society for Training and Development (ASTD) in its State of the Industry Report disclosed, "*U.S. organizations spent $171.5 billion on employee learning and development in 2010.*"[4] Nonetheless, "*While 72% of the expenses were allocated to hard skills, only 28 % of those training dollars went to soft skills.*"[5] If 85% career success comes from soft skills, the latter should have been given a proportionate amount of funding. But, the above statistics from ASTD shows the reverse.

Numerous organizations fail to invest in the soft skills of their people

After a very brief pause, Karen pushed on. "Once students are graduated, that is when the real challenge surfaces. As you have already experienced, most jobs require communicating with superiors, peers, and internal and external clients."

We communicate more than we would like to admit. I remember reading one of MIT's surveys. It reported that scientists and engineers spend the majority of their time communicating than actually doing their technical works in the lab and workroom, respectively. If professionals in technical fields devote the majority of their time on communicating, you can imagine how much professionals in other fields may spend.

"Our success in fulfilling our job description and meeting our personal and organizational goals requires developing certain soft skills." Karen further argued. "Unfortunately, many organizations are unaware of this fact. And therefore, they fail empowering their people to develop those critical soft skills necessary for their people to undertake their job, get along with, and influence others successfully."

Karen paused. No one interjected. She interpreted their silence as permission to continue. "The good thing is that GHR has made a serious commitment investing in the soft skills of its people. That is why we are here." Karen admired GHR's decision to invest in this soft skills development program.

After another long pause, she opened the floor to questions. "Any question, comment, or thought about the importance of soft skills?"

From her experience, Karen came to realize that many technical professionals struggle to accept the fact that the lack or under development of some soft skills may get in the way and prevent them from succeeding and advancing up the corporate ladder. She anticipated some resistances. That was why she opened the floor to questions before jumping to talk about the program and how it works.

However, the first question she got was nothing to do with soft skills.

Defining hard skills
Kelley Johnson is an African American who is recently promoted to lead the Human Resources Department. Before her promotion, she was the head of employee engagement section. Kelley has a sense of humor. Kelley always smiles even when she asks tough questions. She also provides tough feedback with ease.

Kelley wondered, "Karen, I heard you mentioning hard skills a couple of times. I'd like to be on the same page with you. What do you mean by hard skills?" Karen redirected the question to the class. A couple of participants ventured and defined hard skills.

For instance, Kofi Solomon- who is originally from Ghana and Facility Manager at GHR- defined, "Hard skills are tangible abilities and know how we use to accomplish a task, whether the task is in our backyard, workplace, or marketplace."

Antonio Raul, like Dan, is a project manager of another mega project at GHR. He defined hard skills as follows, "Technical skills are those abilities we use to perform hands-on duties."

Karen attentively listened to the definitions proposed by participants and acknowledged that these are great descriptions. But, she reminded the class that there is no one perfect definition we all must agree. Once the class was on the same page concerning the meaning of hard skills, she asked, "Any other question?" Participants seemed to be accepting the meaning.

Dan questioned the significance of soft skills

One of the things that have been bothering Dan since the issue of soft skills surfaced in his professional life was the importance they have been given. He felt that both Susan and Paul blew the significance of soft skills out of proportion. He couldn't take it any longer as he listened Karen glorifying soft skills over technical skills.

He firmly believed that technical expertise are more important than soft skills, especially in organizations like GHR. And hence, he expressed his skepticism. "From the recent discussions I had with some of my colleagues, and now from your presentation earlier, I cannot stop thinking that soft skills have been given more prominence than they deserve as if they are more important than technical skills. I disagree."

Some participants chuckled. Karen smiled big time and kidded. "Dan, what you're saying is that soft skills are overrated." Even Dan smiled while the rest laughed out loud. "Joke aside, you're right. Technical skills are critical. Without technical expertise, it's unlikely that one could fulfill his or her job description. Every team, business, and organization in any industry need some key set of hard skills to succeed and meet its mission."

Technical skills to set one's foot in, soft skills to succeed and flourish

Karen continued. "It takes hard skills to set one's foot in. It's unlikely to perform one's duties without technical know-hows successfully." She went ahead and further built her case:

- "An accountant without the hard skill of math knowledge is lame. No one hires such a handicap accountant.

- An IT help desk professional without hard skills such as disassembling and reconstructing a PC, installing software, antiviruses, and antispyware, and other technical expertise such as troubleshooting should not be at the desk at all.
- A surgeon without the necessary technical skills should not be allowed to pen anyone.
- A lawyer who doesn't know all the laws in the area where he represents his clients doesn't qualify to serve clients.
- The list continues…

But, we need to develop and hone certain soft skills if our desire is to enjoy success in what we do."

Defining soft skills

Krishna Anil is a scientist from India. He came to Karen's aid. "I concur. Though technical proficiencies in any field are mandatory to have, as far as we are working with others, hard skills are not enough to succeed in any career."

Lucas Arthur is Head of Logistics at GHR. He was curious. "What are soft skills?" As usual, Karen redirected the question to participants.

Many hands raised but most of these hands were from those who had been very active. Thus, Karen gave a chance to Natalia Kamil.

Natalia is a second generation Polish. She leads the social media section within the Marketing Department. She explained. "Hard skills are job-related knowledge and abilities that we have to fulfill our job description. Soft skills, on the other hand, are intangible and may not directly relate to the jobs that we are hired to perform but essential to succeed in our roles."

Some more participants shared their understanding of what soft skills mean to them personally. Some used interchangeable words such as human skills and interpersonal skills in place of soft skills. Others narrowly defined soft skills like communication skills, emotional intelligence, and mindfulness.

"Soft skills aren't just those abilities we need to communicate and get along with others. In this program, they've wider applications. They're competencies necessary to master self, get along with, and lead others. One can't do extraordinary things and become successful in any endeavor without developing and refining these soft skills. They complement technical competencies and result in undeniable success." Karen clarified.

Karen moved on and made a quick disclaimer. "By the way, the twelve soft skills we're going to cover in this program can't empower us to succeed unless we develop:

- Positive attitude,
- Optimistic outlook, and
- Hopefulness."

Soft skills for corporate success

It's impossible to meet our corporate goals by solely depending on our people's technical abilities. The workplace needs, more than ever, team members who have developed certain soft skills. The latter contribute toward more productive, harmonious, and fruitful work environment, which in turn leads to achieving irrefutable results collectively.

In response to NACE's Job Outlook 2016 survey, out of the ten skills employers look for when they hire, the top-five are soft skills. These soft skills include, *"Ability to verbally communicate with persons inside and outside the organization, Ability to work in a team structure, Ability to make decisions and solve problems, Ability to plan, organize and prioritize work, and Ability to obtain and process information."*[6]

Difficult to find team members with the right soft skills

James Brett is a senior grant writer and manager of the grant office that interacts with both internal and external clients as it provides grants to qualifying research proposals. James weighed in. "Some of us are challenged to appreciate the significant roles soft skills play because they are elusive. It's harder to quantify these skills compared to hard skills. But, we can quickly recognize when we see individuals who have developed and fine-tuned their soft skills. These are the ones who contribute the lion's share toward the overall success of their team, and organization. And it is not that hard to identify such individuals." Karen nodded her head in agreement. "I couldn't agree more with you, James. You nailed it!"

I've talked to many managers. The conclusion that I reached from my conversations is that if a manager must let go one of her team members who have more or less identical technical competencies, she lets go the one who doesn't have certain soft skills even if the latter graduated top of her/his class. We shouldn't be surprised. You can always quickly find someone with superb technical skills for almost most jobs. But, it's tough to find someone who has the necessary technical skill plus the soft skills essential to getting along with the existing team.

Does soft mean weak?

Dan remarked dryly. "In one hand, we're talking about how critical soft skills are, and how tough it's to develop them. On the contrary, we use a label like 'soft.' If you ask me, it's confusing."

Without waiting for Karen's reply, Dan asked skeptically. "Don't you think that the word 'soft' may be taken as 'weak'?" Participants looked at one another and shrugged as if to say, 'I don't.' Not Karen. She took Dan's question seriously.

Karen paused for several seconds, and clarified. "The word soft shouldn't diminish the significance and power of soft skills. People shouldn't take the word 'soft' literally. They shouldn't also assume that 'hard' means strong and tough. Developing soft skills is more difficult and tougher than developing hard skills." Dan looked unconvinced.

Karen continued. "By the way, there are soft things that are strong. Think about silk. Insects produce it. Yes, it's soft. But, it can be as strong and tough as steel."

However, she admitted that the term 'soft skills' has been controversial. "We had tried to find an alternative fitting name that could show a parallel between the two skills without success. We brainstormed and came up with some alternative names such as interpersonal skills, people skills, adjunct skills, non-cognitive skills, 21st C skills, and more. But, none of them seemed best fit for the purpose of this program. Though we recognized that some people might get confused with the word 'soft' and take it literally, we thought that the term 'soft skills' is universally known and can easily be used to make a comparison with hard skills."

Hard skills and soft skills complement one another

Karen looked at her watch and realized that she was running out of time. However, she didn't want to conclude the current discussion like this. And thus, she decided to give the class an example that demonstrates how soft skills supplement hard skills, and their critical roles. Though Karen's background is computer science, she chose to use a simple analogy everybody could understand.

Karen explained as simple as possible. "A computer may be packed with excessively powerful hardware such as a high-speed processor and a large memory chip. It cannot even boot without the aid of an operating system (software) let alone to function and execute your tasks properly. Similarly, hard skills without the support of soft skills are lame."

It seemed participants easily got the point Karen was trying to communicate except Dan. He seemed confused. "Software by themselves are useless. They need the right hardware." He protested.

"Yes, both need each other. Unfortunately, many professionals misplace their focus. They undermine the place of soft skills. They keep on working on their technical knowledge and abilities neglecting to invest in their soft skills." Karen clarified.

International Talent Management Strategist and Coach- Dorothy Dalton, used a relevant analogy to explain the complementary nature of hard and soft skills. She wrote, *"Hard skills are the foundation of a successful career. But soft skills are the cement."* In construction, it's impossible to have any enduring foundation without using cement. It's used to glue rocks and other hard materials together to build a solid foundation.

Mostly because of lack of awareness, many undermine the critical roles of soft skills. Very few understood the rightful place of soft skills at the early stage of their career. These are the ones that have avoided paying dire prices that come from failing to work on soft skills, which take a relatively long time to develop.

Upgrading both hard and soft skills

Dmitry Egor is an immigrant from Ukraine. He is the new Chief Information Technology Officer. He complemented the analogy Karen used earlier. "When we are requested to upgrade our computers for better performance, we don't go out to purchase the latest hardware just because they perform better than the existing ones. We make sure to upgrade the operating system (software), and software applications too. Otherwise, the new hardware (CPU and memory chips) may not be compatible with the existing software. Even if the two systems (both the hardware and operating system) are compatible, without the right upgrade, the applications that are running on our computers cannot deliver the performance improvements we desire."

"Thanks, Dmitry!" Karen complimented. "We need to develop and fine-tune our soft skills as we continue to improve our technical skills. We need to upgrade both proactively."

Measuring the progress of soft skills is harder

Fernandez Juan is a senior scientist from Mexico. He marveled. "You said soft skills are intangible skills so how can we measure whether we are making progress?"

Karen enjoyed the active participation of the class. Even those who weren't asking and commenting, they were participating by nodding their heads.

She underscored, "Both hard and soft skills need improvements. It's easier to evaluate the improvement we make in our hard skills. I agree. It may not be that easy in the case of soft skills." She then suggested, "Seek feedback from the people you work with to see if you're making progress on your soft skills. You may also consider having coaches and mentors to get feedback and make progress on a consistent basis."

The three parts of the program
As the orientation session approaching to end, Karen quickly explained the purpose of the overall soft skills development program and the three parts that would be covered in the coming twelve weeks:
- Part I: Mastering Self,
- Part II: Getting Along With Others, and
- Part III: Leading Others.

"Each one of you has a folder, and within each folder, there are important materials including a welcoming letter, an outline of the program, and dates and places of where each workshop will be held." Karen further clarified. Next, she walked participants through the outline, introduced some ground rules, and then gave them a chance to ask questions about the program.

Why only 12 soft skills?
Martha Michael manages the Procurement Department. She used the opportunity and asked, "Why only just twelve soft skills? Are these the only soft skills we need to work on?"

"No! These aren't the only ones. But, these are the bare minimum. These twelve soft skills make or break our success." Karen admitted and suggested, "However, while working on these crucial soft skills, it's a good idea to work on our other soft skills continually to solidify our success."

Are the soft skills only for leaders?
Even if she was out of time and visibly rushing to conclude the orientation session, some participants weren't done. Without raising his hand and waiting for Karen's permission, Kofi hurried to ask. "Are these skills needed only to those who are leaders and would like to become leaders?"

Karen quickly answered. "Our company strongly believes that everyone is a leader in the area of her/his passion. In the workplace, each employee needs to develop their leadership skills to fulfill their respective responsibilities. These twelve soft skills are essential to all who desire to attain success in what they do regardless of whether they have official leadership titles or not. Our journey toward achieving indisputable success in what we do requires mastering self, getting along with, and leading others. And, this program is designed to those who would like to succeed in what they do including those who are already leaders and those that are aspiring to become leaders."

Some participants raised a couple of more clarification questions. Karen briefly answered all of the questions. The orientation was ended successfully.

No more excuses…

Dan used the return trip to think and reflect. He looked back and remembered how he began this journey complaining and feeling cornered. The orientation session convinced him the significance of soft skills to succeed in his role as the manager of a mega project. It changed his attitude.

Now, he started to see how much the organization valued him. Rather than letting him go or immediately demoting him, he was given a second chance. Not only that, they decided to invest thousands of dollars in helping him grow. They allowed him to have a flexible schedule that permits him to succeed on both fronts (research and training) for the next three months.

As he drove back home that afternoon, Dan was a different person. No more defensiveness and complaining. He took some responsibilities and promised to have a new attitude. That was a great start. Marshall Goldsmith recognized twenty habits that pose serious challenges to successful people. One of these habits is making excuses. Goldsmith wrote, *"If we can stop excusing ourselves, we can get better at almost anything we choose."*[7] Dan got rid of this habit before even starting the program.

By the way, we all are the product of our decisions. Who we're and where we're in life is the result of our own actions. But, very few are daring enough to take responsibility. Earl Nightingale was right when he said, *"We are all self-made, but only the successful will admit it."*

Slowly but surely, Dan began embracing what had happened. He considered the experiences so far blessings in disguise. He felt that everything worked out in his favor. Dan got another chance to prove to his superiors, colleagues, and team members that he is ready to take his leadership to the next level. He is up to the task, positive, and prepared to be an active participant in this program.

Be proactive

Think about this. Dan is a very successful researcher whose unique talent and experience the company desperately needs. He was successful when he was working as a solo researcher on his thesis. He was celebrated and promoted because he had outstanding technical skills that gave him the competitive advantage as a researcher.

The challenge began when he was promoted to lead a mega project. That was when the lack of certain soft skills surfaced. Even then, they didn't push him out for fear of jeopardizing the current project, and the future fund attraction he brings to the table.

What would have happened if he were any regular John Doe? He would have been fired right away without the CEO knowing about it. And nobody would have missed him. Take a moment and think about those people your company has been letting go. How many of them got a chance like Dan? Very few or none…

We need to work on our soft skills proactive. We shouldn't wait until the lack of certain soft skills brings us in front of our superiors. By then, it could be too late. We may not have the same leverage like Dan. We may not be able to negotiate and get a second chance as he did.

Developing our soft skills is so significant in the 21st C where customers are kings. On top of getting along with people within our team, we are expected to get along and influence both internal and external customers. The stakes are high in this very competitive era. We are expected to over deliver, not just only in what we do but also in our interactions with others.

Therefore, whether you are a young professional or an entrepreneur or an aspiring leader to climb the corporate ladder or a technocrat in the field of science or politics or a community leader or a politician or a business owner, your ultimate success depends heavily highly on your soft skills than your technical abilities.

I'm glad that you're reading this book. I'm sure that the next three parts will give some great insights, tools, processes, and methods that can help you improve your soft skills that make or break your success. Good luck!

Part I: Mastering Self

"The height of a man's success is gauged by his self-mastery; the depth of his failure by his self-abandonment… He who cannot establish dominion over himself will have no dominion over others."
Leonardo da Vinci

Better people, better company…

If an organization's desire is to experience continual success, it needs to invest in the personal growth of its people. Zig Ziglar had been advising organizations by saying, *"You build a better company by building better people."* Individuals become better as they continue to grow. The more people grow, the more they attain personal mastery.

People with personal mastery get along easily and lead others better, and in turn, contribute their share for the betterment of their organizations. Unfortunately, many companies want their people to get along and lead others without investing in their personal growth first. They don't hesitate to spend millions of dollars on in-house or external programs that aim at developing the managerial and leadership skills of their supervisors, managers, and executives.

Nowadays, nonetheless, this trend seems to change. System Scientist, Peter Senge, indicated that empowering their people to have personal mastery have attracted a growing number of organizations. He acknowledged that these companies *"recognize that an organization develops along with its people."*[8]

Self-mastery is a win-win

Some companies also began to understand that workers of the 21st are not just one of the means of production like it used to be. They recognized that employees of the new century don't have the Industrial Age mentality any longer. In his book "The 8th Habit", Stephen Covey argued that in the Industrial Age workers were considered as things like capital and machines. The ultimate goal of the Industrial Age management was to be efficient with things including the individual. Covey wrote, *"When all you want is a person's body and you don't really want their mind, heart or spirit (all inhibitors to the free-flowing processes of the machine age), you have reduced a person to a thing."*[9]

Unlike *"Companies [of the nineteenth and twentieth centuries that] wanted "hire hands" who were not paid to think, who checked their brains at the factory gate"*[10], Ed Oakley and Doug Krug stated in their book 'Enlightened Leadership' that the 21st C workplace is filled with knowledge workers. Most of these workers don't come to work for the sake of paychecks alone. The majority aspires to use their job to pursue their passion, maximize their potential, and get fulfilled in life. That is why this is the responsibility of the 21st C organizations to assist their knowledge workers to increase their self-awareness and ultimately attain self-mastery, which is a win-win for both the individual and the organization.

Knowing self is true wisdom and power

Another strong reason why the 21st C organizations should give personal growth a priority is because it gives their people true wisdom and power. The ancient Chinese philosopher and writer, Lao Tzu declared, *"Knowing others is intelligence; knowing yourself is true wisdom. Mastering others is strength; mastering yourself is true power."* The journey to get along and lead others successfully should begin with knowing and mastering self. And, this part of the book is dedicated to narrate the discussion on self-mastery followed by the subsequent workshops on the four soft skills necessary to master self.

First day of the program

On the first day of the Soft Skills Development program, Dan arrived 15 minutes to 9 am. Around seven participants had already taken their seats. The room was silent. Many of the participants were sipping coffee while checking their emails on their smartphones while some were reading newspapers, and still, others working on their laptops.

The room was set up for fifteen participants. Each circle accommodates three people. There were five small circles.

Introduction...

The facilitator of this program was Joe Muller. Joe is an experienced soft skills trainer with years of experience. He was assigned to facilitate this program because he had a science background and had been a researcher before he became an instructor.

Joe began the first workshop by introducing himself (though they already knew him from their email interactions), his experience as a researcher, what he has been doing as a trainer with the current company, and his expectations from this program. Next, he gave the group a purposeful icebreaker: to meet five attendees who are not at their table and spend two minutes max with each person to introduce themselves, what they do, and share their expectations from the program. Participants walked around, greeted one another, talked, and listened.

Areas of focus to achieve self-mastery

Once the icebreaker was over, Joe displayed his slide that shows the outline of the program. He explained, "Succeeding in our career requires us to master ourselves, get along with, and lead others. And, today, we're going to cover the first topic under Part I, Increasing Self-awareness."

Joe reminded participants, "First, I'm going to give you a little background about the importance of self-mastery before we dive into the first workshop." He then continued. "Personal mastery begins by increasing our awareness of who we truly are, our strengths, and limitations. Personal mastery can be achieved not only by being aware but also by controlling what is happening inside and around us." He further indicated, "We need to start this rewarding journey by expanding on our existing self-awareness. Increasing self-awareness is the foundation of self-mastery. We then continue to develop self-mastery on this foundation by:

- Developing the skill to understand and control our emotions,
- Managing the time and energy we have at hand,
- Solving problems that we face on a daily basis by making ethical and right decisions."

100% self-mastery is unachievable right away

"Is it possible to master self hundred percent?" Joe asked a rhetoric question. The whole class murmured and said a big No. No. No.

Joe joined the class while smiling and said, "No. No. No. We're not here to attain perfection. When we designed this part of the program, we knew that attaining 100% self-mastery is impossible."

He is absolutely right- hundred percent self-mastery is unattainable. The journey of personal mastery takes one's lifetime. Even then, it may not be possible to climb and stand on the Peak of the mountain of self-mastery. Very few individuals to have been lucky enough to achieve this daunting task in their lifetime.

Self-mastery is a continuous process

After a brief pause to give participants enough time to process what he just said, Joe continued, "We also believe that this journey is a continuous one.

You all have begun that voyage and you're somewhere right now. We trust that you'll continue on this expedition and work on yourself long after this program is over. This is our hope that you will take from this program some valuable insights, techniques, and tools that would empower you to continually improving your self-mastery. Self-mastery is a continuous process and a lifetime task."

Total self-mastery in all areas of our life is impossible

"Let me see a show of hands," Joe asked, "How many of you think that mastering self in every area of one's life is possible?" No one raised their hands. "No one could master self in all areas of her/his life." Joe stressed.

Joe broke participants into small groups. Each group was told to identify areas that contribute toward personal mastery and prioritize them according to their importance. Once the discussion was over, he asked each group to report the top 2 areas of focus to the whole class.

Let me share with you the seven dimensions Ziglar identified in his book 'Born To Win': Physical, Family, Mental, Financial, Spiritual, Career, and Personal.

Once the reporting was done, together with Joe, the class narrowed down the list to five areas of focus. Joe then gave them an individual exercise. He told them to gauge their level of mastery for each category.

Next, Joe smiled broadly and encouraged participants. "Don't worry much if you find yourself not having a high rating for some of the areas. The most important thing is that wherever you may be on the scale right now keep on working on those aspects of your life on a consistent basis." Joe is right. Ziglar advised, *"You must master some degree of success in each area of life before you can experience the true satisfaction of total success."*[11]

Self-mastery is the prerequisite to influence others

"Has self-mastery direct relevance to leaders like yourselves?" Joe asked. Almost all heads nodded in agreement. "Why is that?" Joe probed seeking participation from the group.

A couple of participants shared their take on the relationship between self-mastery and leadership. They argued that everything begins with self. Before we lead others, we must lead ourselves first.

Joe consented. "You guys nailed it. Before we successfully get along with others as team members and influence others as leaders, we need to master self. Our company firmly believes that impactful leadership begins with leading oneself first. And, we cannot lead ourselves effectively unless we have some forms of personal mastery. Self-mastery is the foundation to get along and influence others. In this program, four important soft skills are selected to enable y'all attain self-mastery."

Leadership begins with self. Counterintuitive?

Usually, Dan prefers to listen and take notes when he attends workshops. He doesn't jump to share his thoughts or ask questions in large group setting. Nonetheless, Dan had determined to become proactive in this program and to push himself out of his comfort zone. And therefore, he noted, "Interesting! You're saying that leadership begins with self. It looks like counterintuitive, don't you think?"

"You're right!" Joe agreed and elaborated. "When people think of leadership, they think of others. The main reason is that there are hundreds of leadership definitions that portray leadership as if it's about others: inspiring, motivating, guiding, and influencing others. These undertakings are necessary but the starting place of impactful leadership should be self."

Joe clarified, passionately. "Many cultures nurture their inhabitants to seek dominance by conquering some 'mountains' out there before they master self first." Joe's point aligns with what Jim Whittaker said, *"You can never conquer the mountain. You can only conquer yourself."*

It seemed participants wanted to hear more, so Joe further pushed. "Many individuals come up with lists of mountains they would like to conquer, but they end up failing to subjugate none. Very few people start the journey of attaining extraordinary success off on the right foot by mastering themselves first."

Analogy- Climbing Mount Everest

Sensing that the idea he was talking about hadn't hit home yet for some participants, Joe decided to use a metaphor. He hoped that this analogy would get through to them. "Mount Everest stands tall as the world's highest mountain over 29,000 ft. Out of billions of humanity, a little more than 4000 people have stood on its top. It's a perilous mountain. Aspiring climbers prepare for years, or at least months, before setting their foot near to this giant creature. They knew what was at stake! Close to 300 people have died so far attempting to climb this massive mountain. I bet those who climbed Everest had disciplined themselves first- they did their homework before taking on Everest."

Most participants nodded their heads. They had heard or read about Everest. They already knew that Everest is no-nonsense mountain. No one could climb it without enough preparation and discipline.

We all have 'mountains' we would like to conquer

As an experienced trainer, Joe tied the analogy with the theme of the discussion. He recognized the fact that many of us don't believe that we could be able to climb the world's towering mountain. And therefore, we don't try at all. But, almost all of us have 'mountains' in life and our career that we would like to climb.

"What are your mountains?" Joe smiled and asked a rhetoric question. "Of course, your mountains are different than mine, and someone else's." The expressions on their faces said yeah.

Desiring to involve them, Joe asked another question. "What are your mountains that you aspire to climb?" Joe paused for several seconds. Surprisingly, no one ventured. It seemed they weren't yet ready to reveal their 'secrets'.

Thus, Joe continued to answer his question. "By the way, some of you may have mountains in life and profession that are grander than 'Everest.' There is nothing wrong in being ambitious as far as you are willing to match your efforts with the size of your dream. As you attend this program, some of you might have already climbed a few of your mountains, and now looking forward to conquering more. Some of you might be climbing your dream Mountain right now, and very close to the top. In any case, good for you! You've done your homework before climbing your mountains, and now you're reaping the benefits of personal mastery in those areas you have conquered. But, many of us are struggling to climb our 'Everest' one step at a time. And thus, we need to keep working on ourselves first to succeed in our adventures."

"For those of you who are still climbing, the question is: where are you in climbing your mountains in life and your career?" Joe asked playfully.

Dan with a big smile inquired, "I'm at the lower end of many of my mountains. People like myself, what should we be doing?" The whole class cracked up.

Once the laughter was subsided, while still laughing, Joe continued, "For those who haven't begun yet or at the lower end of their mountains- like Dan (pointing at Dan), it isn't too late to stop wherever they are, step down, and regroup and do their homework first if they haven't yet. It's okay to restart. It's a better choice than to reach close to the top and return to the base, or worst, 'dying' in the process of trying to climb our mountains because we haven't first disciplined to master ourselves enough."

Though Dan said that he is at the lower end of many of his mountains, when it comes to his profession, he really advanced quickly. And then, he stumbled and almost fell off. The good thing is that Dan made the right decision to return to the base to regroup. If he had rejected the offer to join this program and work on himself, he would have been like those who continued to climb their mountains and died in the process because they refused to work on themselves first.

The butterfly first conquered its own world

If we review the lives of those who succeeded, they disciplined themselves before endeavoring to climb their mountains, which were outside of their control. A butterfly that is flying high in this 'brutal' environment today wouldn't have made it thus far if it had failed, as a caterpillar, breaking through its little, safe, and comfortable world (it's shell) first. Likewise, to be successful (climb our mountains) and fly high (like the butterfly), in this highly competitive world, we need to master self first (while we're still caterpillars).

As a coach, consultant, and corporate trainer for some government agencies, technology companies, and non-profit and community organizations, one of my jobs is to empower leaders develop self-mastery. Using well developed and tested concepts, approaches, tools, and assessments, I train, counsel and advise leaders to increase their self-awareness, learn how to manage their emotions, time and energy, and solve problems creatively and make tough decisions ethically. As a result, I found out that these leaders' ability to get along and lead others increased tremendously. On the other hand, it's common to witness people who haven't spent enough time to influence self first struggling to work with and lead others. And when that happens, most of the times, the results aren't pretty!

Unfortunately, unlike the caterpillar, life allows humanity to 'fly' even if it hasn't yet fully developed and broken through its 'shell' first. Those who may think that they have broken through their 'shells', and now they're free to 'fly' as they wish without self-mastery are mistaken. Epictetus said, *"No person is free who is not master of himself."* To succeed and fly high in this world, we need to be free first. And, the ticket to that freedom is personal mastery.

The first and greatest victory is to conquer self

Great philosophers have been reminding us to make the precedence right. For instance, Plato said, *"The first and greatest victory is to conquer yourself."* Those who failed to heed this wise advice learned the truth after facing hurdle after hurdle, before they came face to face with the truth. That truth is: mastering self before attempting to master anything outside of self.

Whether you're a leader or a professional, or a business owner, or a community organizer, or a politician, or someone who is passionate about climbing a 'mountain' for fun or entertainment or just to see how far you could climb, if you overcome the unruly and undisciplined inner world first, you will definitely climb your 'mountain' in the outside world, which is more brutal, competitive, unforgiving, and deadly. When we outgrow self and the safe environment we are in right now (our shell), we could fly high and attain our dream. It's a matter of time!

Self-aware leaders are authentic

Once the class was on the same page about the importance of self-mastery, Joe briefly shared the philosophy of his company concerning self-aware leaders, "We strongly believe that self-aware leaders are authentic. They had first influenced themselves and walked the talk before they attempted to influence and lead others."

Joe's line of argument is in alignment with Steven Covey, the author of *"The 7 Habits of Highly Successful People"*, who proposed to have private victories before seeking public victories. In this classic book, he called the first three habits private victory. And the next three habits public victory. Covey rightful argued that achieving the former make it easy to achieve the latter.

Plutarch is also said it well. *"What we achieve inwardly will change outer reality [in the outside]."* Sadly, many leaders are tempted to start leading from outside in. In his #1 National Bestseller book entitled 'Leadership From The Inside Out' Kevin Cashman wrote, *"People who project themselves entirely into activity, and seek themselves entirely outside themselves, are like madmen who sleep on the sidewalk in front of their house instead of living inside where it is quit and warm."*[12]

Self-leadership is a prerequisite for lasting leadership

Joe further explained his company's leadership philosophy. "Leadership is illusive for many because they think that the places where they become better leaders are public arenas as they lead others. Unfortunately, the foundation of impactful leadership is self-leadership.

- Understanding who we're, our strengths, and limitations,
- Conquering our thoughts and regulating our emotions,

- Managing our time and energy,
- Overcoming obstacles and solving problems, and
- Making wise and right decisions and demonstrating commitment to our decisions are where we learn how to lead self first."

"Without first conquering self, the chance to prevail upon anything else outside for which we don't have control is a huge hurdle, to say the least." Joe underlined.

Self-leadership is a prerequisite for lasting and impactful leadership. The molders of great leaders are those private dens where these leaders had been shaped before they came out to take leadership initiatives to influence others. However, that doesn't mean that those who didn't get a chance to lead self first aren't qualified to lead others. What they need to do is to keep working on themselves and lead self well while leading others. Dee Hock-CEO of VISA International said, *"If you seek to lead, invest at least 50% of your time leading yourself"*.

A leader who never won himself first, cannot stand a chance to influence others. Even if he gets the chance, he cannot continue to influence for a very extended period. If one fails to lead herself for whom she has full control, how can she lead others on whom she doesn't have any control?

As the legendary painter, Leonardo da Vinci said, *"You will never have a greater or lesser dominion than that over yourself…the height of a man's success is gauged by his self-mastery; the depth of his failure by his self-abandonment."* He continued, *"And this law is the expression of eternal justice. He who cannot establish dominion over himself will have no dominion over others."*

Leading self the greatest challenge

As much as self-leadership is a prerequisite for lasting and impactful leadership, it's not easy to lead self. In one of his leadership conferences, when the leadership guru John C. Maxwell was asked what has been his greatest challenge as a leader, he surprised the audience. *"Leading me! That's always been my greatest challenge as a leader"*. In his book 'Leadership Gold', he noted. *"I think that's true for all leaders regardless of who they lead and what they accomplish. We sometimes think about accomplished leaders from history and assume that they had it all together."*[13] He gave some examples, *"But if we really examine their lives, whether we're looking at King David, George Washington, or Winston Churchill, we'll see that they struggled to lead themselves well."*

Joe glanced at his watch and realized that they stayed too long on the importance of self-mastery. Joe displayed the self-mastery process and explained the process very briefly. And then, he opened the floor to questions.

Fig. 1: The Self-Mastery Process

It was an interactive discussion. Due to space limitation, I cannot narrate everything. Nonetheless, let me quickly summarize the main points for you:

Self-Awareness
- Self-awareness is the first and critical stage of the process.
- At this juncture, almost everyone has some forms of awareness.
- The goal of passing through the initial stage of the process is to expand one's awareness at both ends- to continue elevating the already existing consciousness while also expanding beyond the current knowledge level into new territories.
- Increasing self-awareness takes time and consistent efforts.
- It also demands choosing one's battle. Choose a couple of top self-awareness areas that could bring significant enlightenments, and make them your top priority.

In his book 'The 80/20 Principle', Richard Koch wrote, "*80 percent of outputs result from 20 percent of inputs; that 80 percent of consequences flow from*

20 percent of causes; or that 80 percent of results come from 20 percent of efforts.'[14] Identify those 20% awareness areas that could bring 80% awareness improvement.

- Here are some of the questions to ask in order to choose your areas of focus. Am I:
    - Cognizant of whom I truly am?
    - Aware of my passion, talent, uniqueness, strengths, and limitations?
    - Conscious about the dominant thoughts I entertain in my mind the majority of the time?
    - Mindful of my prevailing emotions?
    - Able to manage my scarce resources such as my time and energy wisely?
    - Capable of solving problems and making the right decisions when I face with critical choices? And so on. Attempting to answer these questions helps you to know where to invest the majority of your time and energy.
- Asking the right questions is mandatory to increase our awareness.

In her book 'Change your questions change your life', Marilee Adams disclosed the power of asking the right questions. She wrote, *"Questions open our minds, our eyes, and our hearts. With them, we learn, connect, and create. And with them, we can create better futures and better results.'*[15]

- Workshop one covers increasing self-awareness.

Self-Management

- The previous stage is knowledge acquiring. The second stage uses the new awareness to manage self, to develop self-control.
- It's impossible to achieve self-control in every aspect of one's life.
- Choose a few focus areas to have control: Emotions, time, energy, and problems.
- Without the handle on one's emotions, self-control is unthinkable.
- Self cannot be managed without managing one's time and energy.

Peter Drucker said, *'Unless time is managed, nothing else [including self] is managed.'*

- Likewise, without having a good handle on the problems and decisions that one faces on a consistent basis, it is hard to have control over self.

- During the second stage of the self-mastery process, the individual may struggle to have personal mastery. When the individual no longer struggles to control self, the person has transcended to the next stage, which is, self-mastery.
- Though the heavy listing of self-mastery resides in the second stage where the person takes proactive actions to manage self, it doesn't mean that the first and the last stages aren't important.
- Self-management not only leads to self-mastery but it also contributes toward effective management beyond self.

Shad Helmstetter, who is an expert in the field of neuroplasticity and personal growth wrote, *"I believed that mastering one's future must surely start with managing one's self."*[16] He further argued, *"All of us are 'managers' of one kind or another … Effective management always begins with successful self-management … True leaders have their own selves firmly in control; they are in command of their actions, their feelings, their attitudes, and their perspectives."*[17]

Peter Drucker too underscored that self-management is the basis for effective management when he wrote, *"That one can truly manage other people is by no means adequately proven. But one can always manage oneself. Indeed, executives who do not manage themselves for effectiveness cannot possibly expect to manage their associates and subordinates."*[18]

- Workshops two – four cover the three soft skills mandatory to management self.

Self-Mastery

- Once someone manages self successfully, he/she enters into self-mastery phase.
- Unlike the first stage where knowledge is acquired, and the second stage where self-control is practiced, this stage is a state.
- Those who increased their self-awareness, and practiced self-management finally attain personal mastery.
- Self-mastery is a cycle. Once one masters those things that he/she became aware, with the new mastery comes new territories for which one doesn't have full awareness. This leads to repeat the process again and again starting from self-awareness, then to self-management, and self-mastery.
- The process of self-mastery repeats itself continuously until one reaches the point where the person will have less and less things that he/she is unaware. Passing through this process as many times as possible allows

us to unleash many of our unknown strengths and talents, and uncover many of our blind spots and vulnerabilities.

Before concluding the discussion about Part I, Joe showed the class the direct relationship between part one and the following two parts of the program. He explained that the skills developed to master self and the experiences gained as one passed through the process will empower the individual to get along with and lead others. Joe clarified, "The skills, experiences, and tools you will acquire as you work on your personal mastery are going to help you:

- **Understand the purpose, gifting, talent, needs, aspirations, strengths, and limitations** of your team members and also to know how to help them tap into their uniqueness and strengths to contribute their share for the success of the team and organization.
- **Develop emotional intelligence** to recognize the emotional state of the people you work with, demonstrate empathy, and use this competency to drive performance within your team.
- **Improve your ability to manage the time and energy** of your team effectively so as to advance the goals of your team in particular and the organization at large.
- **Acquire the necessary abilities to solving problems** facing your team, and making the right and ethical decisions to move your team forward.
- **Also empower your team to master themselves, manage their emotions, time, and the ability to solve problems, and make decisions by themselves.**"

By the way, the last quality is the mark of a true leader. Remarkable leaders don't stop at excelling and mastering self. They also empower others to excel and even become better than they have been. And, you are a candidate to become a remarkable leader. Begin that journey by mastering self, if you haven't begun this path yet. Self-mastery is the first step toward getting along with and leading others successfully. This journey begins with increasing self-awareness; developing the skills necessary to regulate your emotions; managing your time and energy; and solving problems creatively by making the right decisions.

Joe displayed the slide that showed the themes of the next four workshops:
a) Increasing Self-Awareness,
b) Regulating Emotions Wittingly,
c) Managing Time and Energy Wisely, and

d) Solving Problems and Making Right Decisions.

Finally, he wrapped up the discussion on Self-mastery by pointing out that:

- "The first topic is about increasing our knowledge concerning certain aspects of self. Knowledge is power, as the saying goes. We need to know ourselves before we attempt to manage, and master ourselves.
- The next three topics are categorized under the second stage of the self-mastery process.
- The second topic is managing our emotions. The latter dictate our behaviors and actions. Without regulating and managing our emotions, we cannot achieve self-mastery.
- The third topic is managing our time. Time is a non-renewable resource. It should be managed wisely. That is why the father of modern management, Peter Drucker noted, *'Time is the scarcest of resources'*. Before we are entrusted to other peoples' and organizations' time and energy, we must begin managing our own time and energy.
- Likewise, before we become problem solvers and decision makers on millions of dollars of other people, that journey must begin by becoming creative problem solvers of our own personal challenges, and by making the right ethical decisions for the personal choices we face on a daily basis. And, this part provides you insights, stories, tools, and methods that empower you to mastering self."

Joe concluded the introduction of part one of the program. "Once self-mastery is achieved, the rest is history. Of course, we shouldn't wait to get along with and influence others until we attain personal mastery. The latter is a very protracted journey. We should begin it as soon as we recognize its importance and invest on it while also trying our best to get along with and lead others." Next, he jumped to facilitate the workshop on the first soft skill.

Remember. Though it's an expedition worth taking, personal mastery is a very long, twisted, and protracted journey. Queen Christina of Sweden noted, *"It is necessary to try to surpass one's self always: this occupation ought to last as long as life."* Thus, don't forget to enjoy the ride.

Soft Skill 1: Increasing self-awareness

"Self-awareness is probably the most important thing towards being a champion." **Billie Jean**

Great champions have a great sense of self-awareness

In the above quote, Billie Jean King, the former World number one professional tennis player underscored that self-awareness is the most important factor to become a champion. Billie won 39 Grand Slam titles. She is a real superwoman. She won championships and stood at the top of her industry. In 2009, President Obama awarded King Medal of Freedom, US's highest civilian honor. Life Magazine also named her as one of the 100 Most Important Americans of the 20th C.

Whether you are seeking championships in sport, entertainment, business, science, politics, for that matter in any field, the right place to start a remarkable journey toward achieving unquestionable success is to have a great sense of self-awareness. Marketing expert, author, and speaker Tom Hopkins advised, *"Getting in touch with your true self must be your first priority."* When we review the lives of highly successful people who succeeded extraordinarily, we come to realize that they got in touch with their true self.

Jason Hedge observed that highly successful people throughout history share one thing in common, a great sense of self-awareness. They have profound self-awareness about who they are, their strengths and limitations. Jason explained, *"They [highly successful people] don't underestimate what they can do, they don't sell themselves short and they know their own limitations."* [19]

Highly successful people examine their life and grow continually

Highly successful people also make continual efforts to tap into their strengths and work on their limitations. Jason wrote, *"By understanding themselves [highly successful people], they are able to develop plans to overcome their shortcomings and take full advantages of their strengths."* [20] They examine their life and grow on a consistent basis. They understand that, as Socrates said, *"The unexamined life is not worth living for a human being."*

I. Key lessons

Dan arrived at Rafael's office at 1 pm. The door was already open. Knocked the door to signal that he arrived. He walked to greet Rafael warmly.

After exchanging greetings, they walked toward the sofa at the right corner of Rafael's office. Once they sat comfortably, Rafael began the discussion by reminding Dan the structure of their mentoring session, "Dan, we're

going to cover three things:
- The main lessons you have learned,
- Assessments, tools, processes, and methods that you found helpful, and
- Action (s) you're going to take because you have attended this workshop." Dan nodded.

Rafael went on. "Let's start with the first item. Let's talk about the main lessons you learned from the first workshop."

Without wasting any time, Dan jumped in. "The first workshop was packed with so many great insights. It covered the importance of self-mastery plus how to increase our self-awareness. It helped me examine myself." Rafael interjected. "Did you like it?"

"To be honest, I hadn't expected to learn anything new about self before the workshop. Boy, I was wrong. It was a very practical workshop, at least for me." Dan confessed.

"You're not the only one." Rafael was impressed by the apparent honesty of Dan, and remarked, "The overwhelming majority doesn't have holistic self-awareness."

"Here are the four things I took out of this workshop." Dan opened his notebook and read the following points:
1. The relevance of self-awareness to succeed in our personal life, career, and other endeavors
2. The four dimensions of self
3. The benefits of holistic self-awareness
4. The prices of not increasing self-awareness continually

1.1. The relevance of self-awareness
"Tell me a little bit about each lesson." Rafael sipped his coffee and leaned back against the sofa cushions. Dan moved at the edge of the couch, and with a passionate voice, shared: "The first workshop convinced me the very relevance of self-awareness to succeed in my personal life and career."

Dan further explained that before attending the seminar, he had questioned the very relevance of the topic. With a sarcastic voice, he added: "I had asked myself why this workshop should be given to grown ups like myself? I had also wondered why this topic is incorporated into the program designed for a corporate audience. However, after attending the workshop, I changed my mind and fully understood the necessary role self-awareness plays toward self-mastery, to get along with and lead others."

Rafael chimed in. "I'm glad that you found this topic relevant. Many companies ignore or, at least, undermine the importance of increasing the self-awareness of their people. Because of that, they are paying dire prices for this negligence. GHR, on the other hand, understood the critical roles self-awareness plays, and that was why it was incorporated in the Soft Skills Development program."

From skeptic to advocate

"It was a smart decision." Dan appreciated GHR's decision and declared. "By the way, I'm convinced that this workshop should be incorporated as a mandatory or, at least, an elective course in every college. Corporations should also add it into their orientation and boot camp programs." While laughing loudly, Rafael commented, "Wow, an amazing transformation! From skeptic to advocate."

With a lack of self-awareness comes confusion, conflict, and disarray

Seeking Rafael's take, Dan asked, "Why do you think many organizations neglect, or at least, reluctant to invest in the personal development of their people?"

"The reasons of this negligence may vary from organization to organization," Rafael admitted and continued. "But, there is one apparent reason that I can think of why many organizations remain unenthusiastic. Understandably, since they have so many urgent challenges and immediate needs that they may find it hard to give the personal growth of their people a priority."

Dan looked perplexed. He jumped in, but softly. "You said, understandably. Are you endorsing their priority?"

Rafael quickly cleared the misunderstanding without being defensive. "No. I'm not. They should have straightened their priorities. Unfortunately, they don't realize that if they had empowered their people to increase their self-awareness, their people would have recognized their uniqueness and strengths, and therefore, they would have given their best to address the urgent difficulties, and meet the immediate needs."

"I got you," Dan nodded and added. "More than just addressing the existing problems and responding to the needs of their team, self-aware employees would have taken their team to the next height."

"That is right." Rafael acknowledged and remarked. "The consequences are more severe when their leaders lack holistic self-awareness though."

"Tell me more?" Dan asked for extra. Rafael responded quickly. "Many of the confusions, conflicts, and disarrays that are rampant in today's organizations, communities, and nations could have been avoided if their leaders have solid self-awareness."

Concurring with Rafael, Dan shared the conclusion of a small group discussion they had along this line. "We agreed that when leaders lack self-awareness, they doubt themselves; uncertain about their abilities; unclear about the direction to take on each turn, and thus, become slow in making decisions." Rafael complemented. "These kinds of people make terrible leaders."

Characteristics of highly self-aware individuals
Based on the lively discussion they had, Rafael realized that Dan had a solid grasp about what happens when self-awareness is missing. Nonetheless, he sought to make sure that he also fully understands what it looks like when self-awareness is present. And therefore, he asked, "Now, after attending the first workshop, can you tell whether someone has a concrete self-awareness or not?"

I think so was Dan's short version answer. Rafael wasn't satisfied. He paraphrased his question. "What do you say are the main characteristics of highly self-aware individuals?" After a few seconds of silence, Dan enlisted, "We learned that highly self-aware individuals are:
- Aware of who they are and their uniqueness without a shadow of a doubt.
- Comfortable in their skins.
- Mindful of what is going on around them.
- Accommodative of other people including those who are different than them."

Knowing our uniqueness, our competitive advantage
Let me say a few words concerning the first characteristics Dan enlisted above. Individuals who are highly self-aware know who they're and their uniqueness. Remember, we all are unique! However, finding that uniqueness is the challenge.

We cannot discover our uniqueness without passing through the process of self-awareness. Knowing who we're and our uniqueness increases our chance to succeed in our personal, career, and business lives. The unhealthy competitions we witness everywhere are the result of people who aren't awareness of their uniqueness. Our uniqueness is our competitive advantage. It's our ticket to climb the corporate ladder successfully. For that matter, it is the key to unleash our greatness in the workplace and beyond.

Dan audited his self-awareness

Before moving to the next lesson, Rafael was curious to see if Dan has already conducted auditing on his self-awareness using the characteristics he just shared with him. "Have you got a chance to sit and make an audit about your self-awareness?" Dan briefly responded by acknowledging that the workshop awakened him to another level of awareness, and at the end of the workshop, he quickly conducted an audit to understand his level of self-awareness.

"I looked back in my life and realized that people around me might have known more about myself than I did. Most importantly, I was astounded how lack of self-awareness has been sabotaging my ability to get along with some of my team members, peers, and Susan. With this one workshop, I came to understand that many of the problems I was facing as a leader could have been fixed, or at least mitigated, if I had worked a little on my self-awareness."

After carefully listening, Rafael appreciated Dan's openness. However, he wasn't done. Rafael wanted Dan to be specific. "Do you mind to share some of the results of this audit?" Dan laughed loud and admitted that the result wasn't that much pretty. "I had thought I knew myself very well prior to the workshop. Now, I realized that I:
- Haven't had full knowledge concerning who I truly am,
- Didn't know my uniqueness,
- Lacked the solid understanding of all of my strengths and limitations,
- Was only aware a few of my blind spots,
- Have been inattentive of my own words, thoughts, emotions, etc."

1.2. The four dimensions of self

Rafael moved forward. "Tell me a little bit about the second lesson." Dan cleared his throat. "We learned that it's a daunting task to know everything about self. There are several dimensions of self. However, Joe encouraged us to focus on the four dimensions of self." Dan was talking about the four dimensions of self based on Stephen Covey's book 'The 8th Habit':
1. Body,
2. Mind,
3. Heart, and

4. Spirit[21].

For your information, Covey expanded on the needs of these four dimensions in his book 'First Things First.' He wrote, *"The need to live is our physical need… The need to love is our social need... The need to learn is our mental need… The need to leave a legacy is our spiritual need to have a sense of meaning."*[22]

Rafael nodded and inquired, "Among these four dimensions, which ones do you have a pretty reasonable awareness?" Dan quickly answered. "I had a good grasp when it comes to my physical body and mind before I joined the program. I firmly believe that I've met the needs of these two dimensions. Nonetheless, I need to work on the remaining two dimensions and their needs."

Many people may not have full awareness of their physical body
Among the four dimensions, knowledge about body seems obvious, isn't it? But it isn't. Let me give you a good example. I was reading the autobiography of Jack Welch, the former chairman and CEO of General Electric, "Straight from the Gut" in 2007 or 2008. I was stunned when I read one of his blind spots. Welch wrote, *"Decades later, when looking at early pictures of me on my sports teams, I was amazed to see that almost always I was the shortest and smallest kid in the picture."*[23] For decades, Welch was 'unaware' of his relative physical height and size.

Welch revealed why he had a biased view of his physical dimension. His mother pumped him with confidence as he grew up. As a result, Welch didn't have any clue about his real physical height and size when he was a kid, during his teenage years, and in the majority of his adult life. He confessed, *"Yet, I never knew it or felt it. Today, I look at those pictures and laugh at what a little shrimp I was. It's just ridiculous that I wasn't more conscious of my size".*

I've to admit that reading this part of Welch's autobiography caused a light bulb to go on in my head. I never had a clear sense of my real physical dimension before reading that passage. In the past, whenever I looked at group pictures, my preoccupation was how I looked, who was next to me, and so on. I never compared my height or size with my peers. I hadn't known that I was that 'short.'

Reading Welch's funny story led me to pay closer attention to my physical dimension. Since then, not only I found myself aware but also began making fun of my height. End of March 2016, for instance, I spoke at a conference about bridging the leadership gaps, and we had a group photo afterward with the rest of the panelists. Guess what?

I was the shortest! I posted the pic on my Facebook timeline with this caption; *"I need this kind of group picture to remind me how short I am."* Many of my Facebook friends loved the self-deprecating post. I even got so many encouraging words intended to lift up my spirit.

If there are chances that many of us might have been harboring some blind spots concerning our physical dimension, what about those dimensions that may not be easy to figure out? What are the prices we've been paying for sheltering these blind spots? What are our plans to uncover our blind spots?

Some approaches to have a holistic self-awareness
At the end of the discussion on dimensions of self, Rafael emphasized that it may be easier to elevate our physical awareness with minimal efforts. He stressed out. "However, holistic self-awareness in the four dimensions of self requires using comprehensive approaches." Dan didn't waste any time. He intervened and asked. "Do you have some suggestions?"

Rafael shared his own experience, and suggested to Dan to try the following:
- Taking assessments
- Meditating and reflecting regularly
- Using personal coaches and mentors
- Attending more personal development workshops and training

1.3. The benefits of holistic self-awareness
Upon Rafael's request, Dan began sharing the third insight he gained. "This workshop gave me a chance to appreciate the benefits of holistic self-awareness. Knowing the individual and the corporate benefits of increasing one's self-awareness motivated me, and I see that there are lots of return on investment when we enhance our self-awareness individually and collectively."

"Let's first talk about benefits at a personal level," Rafael suggested.

A) Individual level benefits
Dan gladly shared. "With self-awareness come so many personal level benefits, which we discussed in one of the small group discussions." Dan then mentioned a few benefits and briefly explained each:
- **"Understanding one's true worth.** When we become self-aware, we know our true self. Once we are self-aware, we won't settle for less. We start to say more of I can than I cannot.

- **Humility**. With self-awareness also comes humility. We realize that we have weaknesses, limitations, and vulnerabilities. We let go of our ego and pride.
- **Stop judging others**. True self-awareness causes us to cease judging others. We come to understand that we too have our struggles, and far from being perfect.
- **Productivity**. We know our priorities and where to invest our time and energy best.
- **Collaboration**. The more we know our place in our team and society, the more constructive roles we may play. We seek to contribute our best and bring out the best from others. We become cooperative with the people around us and improve our relationships both at home and in the workplace, which in turn enhance our productivity."

Indicators of increased self-awareness

Rafael wondered to know some of the mechanisms Dan uses to measure whether he is enjoying these benefits. "Dan, as you already know, unlike other hard-core science fields, there are no fixed scales to measure the progress we're making in the area of our self-awareness. How do you plan to monitor your progress and make sure that you're enjoying these great benefits you just enlisted?"

This question reminded Dan the discussion they had in the class. They talked about some of the signposts that show whether one is making progress in his/her self-awareness journey. He mentioned three of those indicators:
1. Sense of security,
2. Focus, and
3. The feeling of contentment.

a. Security

"Elaborate sense of security for me." Rafael probed. "When we become self-aware, we develop a sense of security. We accept who we're and become comfortable with it regardless of what others may think of us." Dan answered with confidence. "Give me a concrete example?" Rafael further pushed Dan, politely, to be practical. Dan paused and took enough time to come up with a good example. He decided to share his progress. "Sense of security develops with increased self-awareness. I've already started to notice that a few of my self-doubts leaving." On top of the words Dan used, his confidence was visible to Rafael. He could read Dan's confidence from his gestures, body languages, and voice pitch too. Dan wasn't done. "For the first time in my life, I embraced some of my limitations. I accepted who I'm. I decided to focus on my strengths, and to team up with others where I've limitations." Rafael was impressed. He complimented, "I like your sense of security!"

b. Focus

"What about focus?" Rafael moved to the next benefit. This time, Dan didn't wait until Rafael pushes him to be practical. "I've taken a time to get clarity about who I'm and my mission in life, and a sense of my uniqueness including my unique contributions to the project and also at GHR. This clarity has already added some focus, and kept me from being distracted." Rafael nodded in agreement and interjected to make a quick comment, "With increased self-awareness we become laser-focused. We become selective. We refrain from jumping to grab every opportunity that comes on our way." Dan concurred and added, "Absolutely. The more we increase our awareness, the more we start to say no to those things that don't increase value toward the main thing."

c. Contentment

"The third indicator that I found helpful is the feeling of contentment." Dan paused for emphasis, and continued, "I believe that I'm now contented with who I think I'm. For that matter, I vowed to stop competing with others any longer." With a big smile, Rafael complimented, "That is so awesome. When we come in contact with our true self, we stop trying to be someone else. We fall in love with it and embrace it with all its flaws. We are so much excited about who we are, what we could do with our lives, and where we are going from where we are now, we don't have time and interest to step on others toes." Dan agreed and added. "With increased self-awareness, we stop from tripping others. We don't change lanes frequently and cut off others. Rather, we complement other's with our unique contributions."

Lack of awareness leads to insecurity

Those who continually increase their self-awareness have unshakeable security. On the other hand, those who lack self-awareness not only harm themselves but also cause so many pains against others. The world has been in trouble mainly because of insecure individuals than bad ones. The damage and chaos are severe when insecure persons are at the helm of families, organizations, communities, and nations. Such people know more about who they are not, what they don't have, and their weaknesses and limitations than their uniqueness and strengths. Rather than tapping into their true self, and spend their valuable time and energy on what they can do well, they are focused on what is missing and wrong.

The consequences of insecurity

Insecure individuals are thorns inflicting constant pain against the people around them. They are always feeling inadequate, and anxious of what other people think of them. They dread to become vulnerable and ask feedback to know more about their weaknesses, limitations, and vulnerabilities. Deep inside, mostly at a subconscious level, they firmly believe that they are seriously flawed and unredeemable. That is why they lash out aggressively whenever people closer to them mention their limitations and weaknesses inadvertently (or with good intentions), and when critics point them out.

With increased self-awareness comes unshakeable security

On the other hand, individuals who are willing to enhance their self-awareness have unwavering self-assurance. It's not because they are perfect. Such people understand that we all have some strengths, and for obvious reasons, some limitations and weaknesses.

That is why we shouldn't be bothered by the so-called 'perfects.' If you find some people in your life, organization, and/or community who are acting as if they are perfect and judging others who have imperfections, these individuals must be aliens from another planet.

In the land of the living, we were purposefully wired to seek completion/perfection by seeking complement from others. We are parts of the larger body. We're unique and made perfectly to carry out our mission, and pursue our passion. Our fulfillment in life, and within our team and community meets with success when we give our best as per our unique talent, gifting, and strengths while willing to team up with others in the areas of our limitations.

Remember, as much as you need the complement of other fellow humans, you too add value to others, and make them WHOLE. It's a win-win.

Thus, no one should:
- Feel insecure about the way they are,
- Bow down his/her head because they cannot be like someone else or
- Feel inferior just because they cannot do certain tasks and jobs like others.

The truth is that if you aren't good at certain things means you're not cut out for them. You should get over it. And focus on who you are and what you can do best for both individual and collective success.

B) Corporate level benefits of increasing self-awareness

"Let's quickly chat about the enterprise level benefits." Rafael wanted Dan to move to the next level of advantages. "In my group, we identified some cool benefits but here are the top three," Dan enlisted the corporate level benefits of increased self-awareness:

- **High productivity and competitiveness.** Dan expounded, "No community, organization, or nation can rise above the collective self-awareness of its members. The more we have self-awakened individual members, the more collective awareness we'll have. The more enlightened members we have, the more corporate success and productivity we may enjoy, and the more competitive we may become." Rafael nodded to indicate that he was listening.

- **Fewer conflict.** Dan described, "When the majority of our people are self-awakened, they most probably avoid conflict." Dan continued. "We enjoy more peace and friendship among our self-awakened people. We don't spend invaluable resources, energy, and time to resolve conflicts." Rafael further supplemented. "You're right. Self-aware team members are capable of turning conflicts into opportunities."

- **Improved synergy.** Dan explained, "Once our people know who they truly are and their relative position within the team, it's easy to get along and contribute their share. They are clear of their unique contributions." Rafael commented. "No question. When the majority are self-aware, they collectively create synergy and make continual progress. The team rolls in one direction. It functions like a well-oiled machine."

1.4. The prices of failing to increase self-awareness continually

"The fourth lesson?" Rafael moved to the next discussion point. "It was about the costs of failing to increase one's self-awareness continually." Dan recapped. Rafael nodded signaling Dan to continue. "Individuals who lack self-awareness may succeed initially, but they cannot continue to thrive and keep it up. They get stuck and keep stumbling." Dan's pointed out.

"You're right, Dan!" "Without continual self-awareness, one cannot sustain the initial benefits of self-awareness. They may get where they want, but they cannot stay there for a very extended period." Rafael added.

The author of 'Derailed' Tim Irwin attributed a lack of self-awareness for the derailment of former Home Depot's CEO Nardelli. He wrote, *"He [Nardelli] may have lacked self-awareness- a common denominator of those who derailed".* Have you experienced or watched train derailments? If you have, you already know how messy and ugly it's. When we fail to increase our self-awareness continually, we too will experience derailments, if not now, in the future.

One's lack of self-awareness disturbs others

Dan added another consequence of failing to increase one's self-awareness. "By the way, the absence or failure to continually increasing one's self-awareness affects beyond self. People find it bothersome to interact and relate with someone who lacks self-awareness."

Both laughed as some people came into their mind. Once the laughter subsided, Rafael observed, "I can tell you right now half a dozen people that just came into my mind who don't have self-awareness at all, and in turn bother the people around them."

American writer, director, actor, and producer for television and film- Mike White complained: *"Yah, it's disturbing when someone has no self-awareness."* If we take time and run through the list of people around us, we will quickly recognize that the ones that disturb us the most are the people who lack self-awareness. If you witness relationships that struggle at home, work, and in the marketplaces, lack of self-awareness of one or more parties involved could be the most likely reason.

II. Assessments, Processes, and Tools
2.1. DISC

Dan shared, "Joe had emailed instructions asking us to take an assessment called DISC." He further explained. "We all took the assessment before the workshop. We had large and small group discussions about this behavioral type assessment, the results we got, and how to apply the newly acquired awareness in the workplace."

"Did you find it relevant?" Rafael probed. Dan looked at Rafael's eyes and firmly replied, "Yes, it opened my eyes and increased my self-awareness." Rafael laughed. "I can see that." He then expressed his happiness and informed Dan that they're going to take more personality tests in the future such as MBTI, TKI, EI, Strength 2.0, and so on. "And, I'm sure that you'll find these too very helpful."

Even if Dan wasn't required to share any info from his assessments, he volunteered to reveal some of the results, which allowed Rafael to offer him some tailor-made feedback. Rafael also enlisted the assessments he had taken in the past. He also disclosed on how these assessments enabled him to understand his personality type, preferences, strengths, and uncover areas for improvement.

Uncovering your weaknesses/limitations

Rafael purposefully emphasized the importance of taking as many assessments as possible to uncover as many weaknesses/limitations as possible. He became vulnerable and revealed some of his limitations and what he has been doing to mitigate their impacts. In return, Dan too opened up and disclosed his. Next, they talked about Dan's action plan to deal with his limitations.

Increasing self-awareness requires uncovering our drawbacks and doing something toward overcoming (or at least mitigating) their effects. As much as we need to keep on working on things that are already our strengths, we also need to work on our limitations and weaknesses if our desire is to attain personal mastery. Here is what Playwright August Wilson said, *"Confront the dark parts of yourself, and work to banish them with illumination and forgiveness. Your willingness to wrestle with your demons will cause your angels to sing. Use the pain as fuel, as a reminder of your strength."*

Comprehensive Self-Awareness

Before concluding the discussion on the importance of knowing more about self by taking more assessments, Rafael highlighted, "Self doesn't exist in a vacuum. Don't stop at knowing about yourself such as your uniqueness, passion, talents, gifts, purpose, goals, priorities, strengths, limitations, blind spots, and so on." He encouraged Dan to develop a comprehensive and holistic self-awareness, which demands to continue expanding his awareness by understanding others and his environment too. "By the way, this is of particular important to get along successfully." Rafael pointed out.

2.2. Johari Window

"I found Johari Window a useful tool to increase my self-awareness." Dan pulled out his exercise book and began drawing the window. Looking at the well-painted diagram, Rafael joked. "You're in a wrong profession. You should have been a painter." This comment enticed laughter out of Dan. "Joke aside, please share with me your experience with this tool."

While smiling sheepishly because of Rafael's compliment about his sketch, Dan explained, "I teamed up with one of the participants and discovered a blind spot in that one brief exercise. I can imagine the kind of self-awareness information I could gain if I use this tool with some people who know me very well."

Dan paused and glanced at Rafael. He noticed that Rafael was listening attentively and nodding for him to continue. Dan was willing to be vulnerable. "During that brief exercise, I was told that I speak fast and don't listen as I'm supposed to. Right there, I discovered a blind spot."

He was so enthusiastic about uncovering this blind spot that he spoke with animation. "I have to be honest with you. Susan had kept saying that I don't listen, but I didn't get it up to that point. I thought I was a listener. I gave my ears. Now, I learned that I need to engage with my mind and heart too to listen actively." Dan's demonstration of trust by disclosing his blind spot and his struggle to get along with his boss because of lack of active listening thrilled Rafael, "Thank you, Dan, for sharing this with me. I really appreciate your forthrightness." Dan started to trust Rafael. That was why he opened up and began revealing his intimate struggles. Trust is very vital for a mentoring relationship to flourish.

Rafael shared with Dan his own and the experience of others on how active listening is hard to master. He comforted him, "You're not the only one. Many people struggle to develop this soft skill. The good news is that you'll get a chance to get great insights and tools to improve your active listening when you guys cover Effective Communication in part two."

Background about Johari Window
For your information, the inventors of this tool- Joseph Luft and Harrington Ingham- designed it in the 1950's.[24] It is a simple grid you can use to map your (your group's) personality awareness. What you need to do is to pick those adjectives that best describe you from around 56 lists of attributes, and then ask your group (partner) to describe you by selecting those adjectives they think may represent you. Using these data, you fill the four windows:
- Open (You and everybody knows),
- Hidden (You know, others don't),
- Blind (You don't, others do), and
- Unknown (You and others don't know).

Where to focus to increase your self-awareness?
The most important window to increase our self-awareness tremendously is the Blind (Others know, but you don't) grid. To enlarge this window, we need to be vulnerable to share what we are aware but others don't (Hidden) so that others may open up and reveal to us what they know but we don't. Otherwise, we're already aware of those behaviors, motives, strengths, and weaknesses that are known to you and others (Open).

Others cannot help us that much when it comes to our Unknown (feelings, attitudes, fears, wounds, strengths, talents, gifts, and so on). We're the ones to uncover them. But, we cannot easily get access to the Unknown. They're below the surface (at a subconscious level).

Let me give you one strong reason why you should, as an incentive, invest your time and energy to unearth the unknown. Your breakthroughs come from what you haven't known. What you've known brought you this far. If you feel stuck, unhappy, and constrained, go to the next level by uncovering those things that sabotage your success; by discovering those great talents, passions, and strengths that are untapped. Your ticket toward greatness lays here- in the Unknown.

III. Action item

"This one-day workshop is the beginning of a long ride. Increasing self-awareness is a life long journey. What are your plans to keep the momentum going?" Rafael sought to know Dan's next steps.

Dan flipped the pages of his notebook. "I enjoyed the workshop. It ignited my interest to increase my self-awareness on a consistent basis. However, I realized that I've just scratched the surface. That was why I made a commitment to continue self-discover, manage, and at the end of the day, master self by keeping the momentum going long after the workshop was over. Going forward, I've come up with some actions I would like to take."

Rafael interjected to help Dan prioritize. "That is awesome Dan, just share with me one thing that you would implement right away."

"At the top of my list is increasing the self-awareness of my team." Rafael understood that unless Dan grows together with his team members, the chances are high that he may not make progress and enjoy corporate level benefits, as he would like to. But, he was concerned whether Dan should make this move at this stage.

Rafael cautioned Dan. "Dan this is an excellent idea. I completely understand the corporate level benefits of empowering your team members to increase their self-awareness. However, you have to be very careful about when you should venture out to help your team members. You should first work on your self-awareness and achieve some results before you take it to the team. It's important first building credibility."

Rafael's suggestion was on the mark. Dan should first bear some fruits before selling self-awareness to his team. Otherwise, it may backfire. Ken Kesey: *"You don't lead by pointing and telling people some place to go. You lead by going to that place and making a case."*

The case of LeBron James

Let me give you a good analogy. On June 19, 2016, America was captivated when Cleveland's Cavaliers won the NBA championship. The win was bittersweet for many fans because of their superstar player- LeBron James, who left Cleveland in 2010 in search of a championship.

If you may remember, following his decision to leave the Cavaliers, he was vehemently criticized. James was desperate to win a championship. He knew that he has limited time to make it great in this sport. And thus, James decided to make it to the top before time passes him by. He joined a team he thought that would give him a chance, and therefore, he joined Miami Heat.

Miami Heat won two championships in two consecutive years: 2012 and 2013. Once James achieved the championship; however, he didn't want to stop there. He sought to repeat the success with his hometown team. Consequently, he returned and could be able to win the championship with Cleveland's Cavaliers in 2016.

The initial intention of James might not be to go somewhere and learn how it is done to come back and repeat with his original team. However, this story serves a purpose about the importance of making a strong case. That is, be there first before you ask others to follow you where you have never been.

John C. Maxwell declared, *"A leader is one who knows the way, goes the way, and shows the way."* James first knew the way to the championship, passed through the process, and came back to show the way to the championship to his hometown team. And, he did it. Likewise, we should first increase self-awareness before becoming crusaders to elevate the self-awareness of others.

Dan agreed and decided to delay this task. The second action item on his list was seeking feedback from his wife, and other colleagues who work with him closely by using Johari Window. They talked about on how to implement this task, and the first mentoring session was concluded very successfully.

Summary

Success in what we do requires mastering self, getting along with, and leading others. However, the journey toward success begins with mastering self. Increasing self-awareness is the gateway to self-mastery. Self-mastery is the foundation of getting along with and leading others effectively. The logic behind is straightforward. We can't master what we don't know! If we don't know a lot about ourselves, the chances are high that we cannot manage ourselves very well. In whichever industry we may be, we need to develop this soft skill if our desire is to solidify our success in our personal life, business, organization, and community. Knowing our uniqueness, strengths, limitations, and blind spots increase our awareness and therefore empowers us to contribute our unique share toward the success of our team, organization, and society. However, holistic self-awareness doesn't stop at knowing about ourselves such as our uniqueness, passion, talents, gifts, purpose, goals, priorities, strengths, limitations, and so on. Rather, comprehensive self-awareness demands people to continue expanding their awareness by understanding others and their environment too. Increasing self-awareness, nonetheless, shouldn't be left to individuals alone. Organizations of the 21st C need to be proactive to increase the self-awareness of their people. The overall awareness of a given organization is dependent on the collective consciousness of its members. And, the organization cannot go any higher than the collective consciousness of its people.

Soft Skill 2: Regulating Emotions Wittingly

"If your emotional abilities aren't in hand, if you don't have self-awareness, if you are not able to manage your distressing emotions…then no matter how smart you are, you are not going to get very far." **Daniel Goleman**

Emotional awareness is a prerequisite to emotional management

- Workshop one covered the first stage of self-mastery, Increasing Self-awareness.
- The first stage is the gateway to manage and finally attain personal mastery.
- Increasing self-awareness includes elevating one's awareness about the dominant emotions that frequent the most.
- Understanding our emotions, which was covered in Workshop one, is a prerequisite to regulating our emotions effectively and in our favor.

We need to achieve increased emotional awareness before we could be able to control our emotions. The father of modern Emotional Intelligence-Daniel Goleman, in his first Coast-to-Coast #1 Bestseller book 'Emotional Intelligence' underscored, *"Self-awareness is the building block of the next fundamental of emotional intelligence.'*[25] In his other book entitled 'Working with Emotional Intelligence', he provided four competencies that are important to increase emotional awareness:

1. Know which emotions we feel and why
2. Realize the links between our feelings and what we think, do, and say
3. Recognize how our feelings affect our performance
4. Have a guiding awareness of our values and goals[26]

Without emotional mastery, no self-mastery

Self-mastery is unattainable without developing the soft skill of regulating emotions. Success is an uphill battle without a good handle on one's emotions. In the above leading quote, Goleman expressed his skepticism by saying that if one doesn't have the ability to manage his emotions, his smartness cannot help him reach very far. Without understanding and managing our emotions, our technical and intellectual competencies alone couldn't assist us to advance in life and our career - we cannot go very far.

The missing link

By the way, the critical roles managing emotions play toward continual success is relatively new. For years, experts couldn't be able to figure out why certain people with average intelligence outperformed those who had high intelligence up until recently. The authors of 'Emotional Intelligence 2.0.' unveiled, *"People with the highest levels of intelligence (IQ) outperform those with average IQs just 20% of the time, while people with average IQs outperform those with high IQs 70% of the time.'*[27] The missing link for this disparity was emotional intelligence: *"Scientists realized there must be another variable that explained success above and beyond one's IQ, and years of research and countless studies pointed to emotional intelligence (EQ) as the critical factor.'*[28]

Unfortunately, there are still individuals and organizations that fail to give emotional intelligence a proper place. Very few organizations deliberately invest in their people and assist them in developing the soft skill necessary to regulate emotions. Experts in the field revealed, *"a global deficit in understanding and managing emotions remains…two third of us are typically controlled by our emotions and are yet skilled at spotting them, and using them to our benefit."*[29]

The biggest predictor of performance

The latest data show that developing emotional intelligence increases performance and in turn income of those who possess high EQ. Travis Bradberry and Jean Greaves shared, *"EQ is so critical to success that it accounts for 58 percent of performance in all types of jobs. It's the biggest predictor of performance in the workplace and the stronger driver of leadership and personal excellence."*[30] The authors also noted, *"Naturally, people with high EQs make more money- an average of $29, 000 more per year than people with low EQs. The link between EQ and earnings is so direct that every point increase in EQ adds $1,300 to an annual salary."*[31]

Earning increase isn't the only benefit from increased EQ. The latter also contributes toward continual success in our career. The authors of 'Primal Leadership: Realizing the power of emotional intelligence' indicated, *"EI-Based competencies played an increasingly important role at higher levels of organizations, where differences in technical skills are of negligible importance."*[32]

I. Key lessons

Dan was looking very much to his second mentoring session. He arrived at Rafael's office on time. After exchanging greetings, they dove into the session. "What are some of the key lessons you learned from the second workshop?" Rafael asked. Dan opened his notebook and enlisted the four important lessons he learned:

- Expressing emotions intelligently
- Using emotions to our advantage
- Developing empathy
- The importance of auditing our emotions

1.1. Expressing emotions intelligently

"Before the second workshop, I had never thought that it's a good idea to express emotions in the workplace. I tried my best to hide, or at least, subdue my feelings." Dan admitted.

Rafael consoled and shared his own experience on how he used to struggle to avoid being emotional in the workplace until he realized that suppressing emotions is unhealthy. "Many people stifle their emotions, even for those things that matter to them the most. What they don't understand is that we all are emotional beings!" Rafael laughed loudly.

Dan joined the laughter and underscored, "You're right. We're emotional beings. Now, I'm convinced that we should express our emotions in our favor. We don't need to subdue our emotions all the time." Rafael added. "Emotionless doesn't always serve us."

Expressing emotions unintentionally creates havocs

Though Dan recognized the significance of expressing emotions in the workplace, he was wondering whether manifesting all of his emotions is a very good idea. "By the way, do we need to display all of our emotions in the workplace?" Dan wondered. "No," Rafael quickly responded, smiling. Dan felt relieved.

Rafael recounted a couple of incidents where employees let some of their explosive emotions out without filtering, and how these episodes caused havocs. He recommended, "Neither suppressing one's emotions nor unwittingly expressing them is productive. We need to:

- Understand our emotions,
- Their meanings, and
- Be skillful to express them intelligently." Dan nodded his head in agreement, and pointed out, "The key word is intelligently."

Suppressing emotions unwittingly has serious consequences. Goleman argued that every emotion has its own unique place. It shouldn't be suppressed. He elaborated, "*When emotions are too muted they create dullness and distance; when out of control, too extreme and persistent, they become pathological, as in immobilizing depression, overwhelming anxiety, raging anger, manic agitation.*"[33] His advice is to maintain the balance, and this requires developing expressing one's emotion intelligently.

Handling emotional outbursts to achieve personal mastery

Though it was covered in the class, Dan sought Rafael's take on the link between the ability to manage outbursts of emotions and how that contributes toward self-mastery. Rafael expressed his strong conviction that with increased emotional intelligence, improved personal mastery follows.

He further stressed, "Developing emotional intelligence allows us to:
- Apprehend,
- Articulate, and
- Manage our emotions wisely, which directly contributes toward managing and mastering self."

And then he concluded, "On the other hand, the inability to control unwanted emotional outbursts undermines personal mastery."

1.2. Using emotions to our advantage

Moving forward, Dan shared the second lesson with excitement. He told Rafael that unlike IQ (Intelligence Quotient), EQ (Emotional Quotient) isn't fixed. "I could develop my emotional intelligence and utilize my emotions in guiding my behaviors, and in turn influencing my actions. It never occurred to me that I have the ability to purposefully generate positive emotions when necessary and use them to my advantage, to lead myself successfully."

"I like this. Rather than waiting situations to happen for us to generate positive emotions, why not come up with clear strategies to create some positive emotions to improve our performance, and also boost our relationships," Rafael complimented Dan's point.

From his own experience, Rafael knows the importance of employing emotions to one's advantage very well. He further expounded the importance of engaging emotions to lead self effectively. "When we become emotionally blind- when we are unaware of our own emotions and when we are unable to generate the right emotions to lead our behaviors and actions proactively, we struggle to lead ourselves effectively- we become blind guides," Rafael warned.

Incidents are neutral

What Rafael just said triggered Dan's memory. By going back retrospectively, he shared some of the little things that used to set him off and affect his performance and relationships at home and in the workplace. "Now," Dan declared confidently, "I understand that incidents are neutral. I'm in charge."

With the same enthusiasm, Rafael joined Dan and acknowledged, "Yes, we have the last say. We can decide on how to respond emotionally, even to those incidents that might have seemed negative consequences. Behind every undesirable emotion, we express, there is (are) underlining reason (s). Once we know the root cause of a given emotion, we have two choices."

After a quick pause, Rafael suggested, "We can either:
- Change the very situation, if we can, that caused us to feel bad, or
- Make a choice to consider the situation as something that doesn't merit reacting negatively."

"In both cases, our mood changes from feeling bad to feeling good, or at least, to remain in a neutral mood. We shouldn't allow emotions to take charge and lead us where we don't want to go." He concluded resolutely.

After giving him a couple of examples on how he had been using emotions in his favor, Rafael gave Dan an assignment. "Until our next session, be intentional. Identify certain emotions proactively that could help you generate the right behaviors and actions you need to be in charge." Dan accepted the task, and promised to report back his progress.

1.3. Developing Empathy

The third lesson Dan decided to share with Rafael was about the importance of developing empathy. "One of the primary emotions I need to develop proactively is empathy. Lead myself in relation to others is necessary. Self doesn't exist in a vacuum."

"By the way," Rafael interjected to make an important link between emotional and social intelligence. "Developing emotional intelligence contributes toward increasing one's social intelligence- the ability to excel in social relationships. The latter cannot happen without developing empathy though."

For your information, Goleman in his book 'Social Intelligence' admitted that human social and emotional abilities are intermingled. He agreed with Richard Davidson, director of the Laboratory for Affective Neuroscience at the University of Wisconsin who said, *"All emotions are social. You cannot separate the cause of an emotion from the world of relationships- our social interactions are what drive our emotions."* [54]

"What is empathy mean to you?" Rafael inquired. "As far as I understand it, empathy is the aptitude to understand someone's feelings and emotions," Dan responded briefly.

Alvin Goldman defined empathy, *"The ability to put oneself into the mental shoes of another person to understand her emotions and feelings."* Empathy is also one's ability to put others' needs ahead of her. Here is how Goleman defined it, *"Awareness of others' feelings, needs, and concerns."* [55] Martin Hoffman also put it this way, *"An effective response more appropriate to another's situation than one's own."*

It's possible to develop empathy

Though Dan completely understood the significance of empathy as an important emotion, deep inside he knows that he doesn't have enough empathy. On the other hand, he is aware of the extraordinary empathy Rafael possesses. This same trait attracted Dan to Rafael- to trust and be his mentee. He wants to get some tips, especially about how to know the emotional states of others. "Rafael, I could see that you have got a well-developed empathy…" Rafael interrupted Dan gently.

Rafael knows that he has empathy, but he didn't brag about his innate compassion toward others. "We are diverse. Some of us have natural gifting and preferences toward certain things. We don't sweat about this stuff. They're our second nature. However, that doesn't mean we don't need to develop those traits that we don't have yet. This is especially true for individuals who are professionals, business owners, community organizers, politicians; you name it. As we work with and lead others, we need to develop certain emotions such as empathy for which we may not have home court advantage." Rafael's explanation induced hope in Dan and encouraged him to develop empathy.

Abraham Lincoln and his extraordinary empathy

Rafael is right. We may not have empathy naturally. Developing it worth the trouble since it is a win-win for us and others. When we develop empathy, not only we help others, we too develop intuition and discernment, which we need to lead ourselves and others successfully. Let me share with you a good example that may cause you to consider working on this emotion.

Abraham Lincoln has been recognized for his extraordinary empathy. In 'Teams of Rivals', his biographer wrote, *"He possessed extraordinary empathy- the gift or curse of putting himself in the place of another, to experience what they were feeling, to understand their motives and desires.'*[86]

Interestingly, empathy was one of his greatest assets. It distinguished him and significantly contributed toward his success. People who closely witnessed his political career such as Helen Nicolay, whose father would become Lincoln's private secretary, suggested that that the same attribute-putting another first, *"gave him the power to forecast with uncanny accuracy what his opponents were likely to do."* His biographer also agreed and wrote, *"Such capacity to intuit the inward feelings and intentions of others would be manifest throughout his career."*

Going beyond the surface, watching the non-verbal

Dan was in need of advice. He inquired, "Demonstrating empathy, putting oneself in someone's shoes, requires first to understand the emotions of others. However, many people in the workplace don't reveal their feelings. How can we overcome this challenge?" Rafael is familiar with what concerned Dan. After acknowledging the existence of such blackouts, he proposed, "Yes, many may hide their emotions. This barrier, thus, forces us to go beyond the surface and understand what is going on in someone's mind and emotional space."

A short silent.

Dan wasn't enthusiastic about Rafael's proposal. "How can I go beyond the surface?" Dan wondered. Rafael paused to give Dan practical suggestions. "Personally," Rafael shared, "I've been cultivating discernment to read well beyond the surface. But, I admit that sometimes it may not be possible to detect the emotions of others quickly. That is when I ask intelligent questions to probe and understand what is really going on. I also carefully watch the non-verbal cues." The latter is very helpful. Goleman stated, *"Others rarely tell us in words what they feel; instead they tell us in their tone of voice, facial expression, or other nonverbal ways."*[37]

1.4. Auditing our emotions

"As part of managing emotions," Dan began sharing the fourth insight he gained. "It was suggested that we should intelligently regulate our emotions by conducting auditing on a consistent basis." Rafael quickly interjected and pushed on. "There are hundreds of emotions we may express on a daily basis. Is it possible to regulate all of our emotions?"

After pausing to collect his thoughts, Dan admitted, "We cannot!" He further elaborated, "That's true, we may entertain hundreds of emotions on a daily basis. We cannot regulate all of them. However, we should target those emotions that visit us frequently. We should focus on regulating those dominant emotions."

The physiological impacts of emotions

"This is a smart approach!" Rafael acknowledged. By the way, Roger Fisher and Daniel Shapiro noted, *"Emotions are too important to ignore, yet too many to deal with."* Rafael then emphasized, "Recognizing all emotions but zooming in on those dominant emotions is smart and strategic."

Rafael decided to further probe. "Once you figured out your dominant emotions, how do you influence those emotions you don't want to express?"

As a scientist with an analytical mind, Dan enjoyed the discussion they had in the class concerning the process of emotion formation. He quickly understood how emotions are formed and at what level to regulate emotions. And thus, he responded, "The easiest way to influence our emotions is at thought level."

Rafael resisted himself leaving this topic too soon. He simply requested. "Tell me more."

Dan was thrilled to explain. "Let's say that a person thinks that he is an underdog in his profession. Whether the person is conscious about this thought or not, this dominant thought finds its ways to express itself in the form of certain emotions such as lack of confidence and timidity. When the brain senses these distressing feelings, it releases the corresponding hormone that manages stresses- cortisol. The latter interacts with the muscles of the body and dictates the outward expressions of the person. Accordingly, the individual sits, walks, talks, and looks intimidated, nervous, restless, and people could easily perceive that even if the person himself may not be aware."

Rafael nodded. "Are you saying that the person, if he desires to influence his outward expressions, he better target the thoughts behind, not the emotions or their manifestations?" Rafael double-checked. Dan responded quickly, "Correct. It'll be an uphill battle for the person to change his feelings and emotions, and in turn, manifest confidence and self-reliance in the outside."

Dan is right. We can only manage our thoughts, not our emotions. Every emotion that we experience on a moment-by-moment basis has an origin. The origin is a thought (s). Bernard Roth, in his classic book 'The Achievement Habit', asserted, *"To learn how to get a better handle on your perceptions, emotions, and behavior, it is useful to look at how you think."*[88]

Upon Rafael's request, Dan explained how the person could influence his thought and bring the desired change outwardly. "If that the same person changes his thoughts and starts to think the other way around, he feels differently, and his outward expressions change drastically. The moment the person thinks that he is a competent and able person, his thoughts generate the corresponding feelings and emotions such as confidence, boldness, and self-reliance."

"When the brain senses these emotions, it issues a different kind of hormone, serotonin. The latter stimulates (influences) the person's muscles, and therefore, his outward moods, and in turn, expressions change. And, people can easily read- if not consciously subconsciously, his confidence from his non-verbal cues such as the way he gestures, walks, his body languages, and so on."

Rafael was satisfied with Dan's explanation. Nodded. "I agree. We have the ability to change the emotions that we dislike at thought level. Rather than trying to control or change our distressing emotions, which is too much work; we should alter our emotions at ideas level, which is relatively easy."

To help Dan see the strong relationship between their earlier discussion about using emotions to one's advantage with their current conversation about using thoughts to influence emotions, Rafael asked. "Yes, you talked about how to regulate and influence the existing feelings. What about if you figure out from your auditing that you lack certain vital emotions. How do you plan to become proactive and generate certain emotions using thought, for example, to bring the changes that you desire in your personal life?"

Dan took a deep breath while quickly processing his answer in his mind. "It's a futile attempt to bring the change we want at emotion level. To display desirable behaviors, and ultimately actions that enable us to accomplish great things, we need to entertain the right thoughts. The latter generates the right emotions, and in turn, we could be able to manifest the proper outward expressions- the desired change." Dan responded with certainty. Rafael nodded to show his satisfaction with his answer.

II. Assessments, Processes, and Tools
2.1. EQ Assessment
Dan informed Rafael, "I had heard about emotional intelligence before, but this was the first time I attended a workshop and took an EQ assessment. The results gave me many insights and areas where I need to work on to improve my emotional intelligence."

Pulling out the results of his assessment from his bag, Dan explained. "It shows that I've high Self-Perception Composite, above average Self-Expression Composite, average Interpersonal Composite, high Decision Making Composite, and above average Stress Management Composite."

Rafael too shared some of his EQ assessment results he still remembered. He explained what he had been doing to improve those areas where he needed improvements. Next, he asked Dan's plan on how he is going to work on his. They spent some time to strategize.

2.2. The Process of Emotion Formation

Dan pulled out a piece of paper and began writing down the five stages of emotion formation:

1. Feelings,
2. Emotions,
3. Thoughts,
4. Behaviors, and
5. Actions.

Rafael asked him to explain the process. Dan described, "In the first stage, feelings are generated based on what we see, hear, touch, and taste using our sense organs. These feelings may translate into positive emotions such as excitement, joy, pride, elation, contentment, calm, hope, and so on. Or into negative emotions such as guilty, regret, embarrassment, resentment, rage, fear, depression, etc."

Dan concluded. "In a given time, the dominant emotion (s) dictates the kind of thoughts that are entertained in one's mind. These thoughts, in turn, are the ones that finally express themselves in the form of external behaviors, and ultimately into actions."

"Which part of the process intrigued you?" Rafael probed.

"I was impressed to learn that the regions in the brain that generate emotions and thoughts influence each other," Dan quickly acknowledged what intrigued him.

As a Neurologist, Rafael understood what Dan was talking about. To reinforce learning, he sketched an image of a brain and illustrated where emotions and thoughts are formed. He drew a diagram and penciled the path the sensory information takes in the brain.

Rafael further elaborated, "Researches show that we gather data using our senses, and the data first passes through the limbic part of the brain that deals with emotions. The data further passes to the frontal lobe that processes the data and generates thoughts." By the way, *"This journey ensures you experience things emotionally before your reason can kick into gear."*[59]

Emotions and thoughts influencing one another

Dan was listening intently. Rafael could see that Dan wanted to hear more. Thus, he continued, "The same sensory information might result different emotions and in turn a totally different thoughts, behaviors, and actions from person to person. That means, the initial emotions dictate the kind of thoughts one entertains. Of course, the initial thoughts can be modified as we discussed earlier and in turn alter the final emotions the individual displays. The latter express themselves outwardly in the form of behaviors, and ultimately actions."

Experts in the field agree that our emotional intelligence improves, as we understand the relationship between our thoughts and emotions. The more we develop the neural pathways between the two regions of our brain, the more we develop our emotional intelligence. For instance, Travis and Jean revealed, *"The two areas do influence each other and maintain constant communication. The communication between your emotional and rational "brains" is the physical source of emotional intelligence."*[40] Likewise, Daniel Goleman, Richard Boyatzis, and Annie McKee pointed out, *"The emotional intelligence competencies, so crucial for leadership, hinge on the smooth operation of this prefrontal-limbic circuitry."*[41]

The same data different outcomes
To reinforce learning, Rafael decided to give a practical example. "Let's say that you heard the news. At this stage, you are using one of your sensory organs- your ears. This news first passes in the form of a signal through your Limbic part of the brain and quickly generates an emotion. The signal, however, continues to the Frontal lobe part of your brain for interpretation and reasoning. The thoughts that are produced in the Frontal lobe either reinforce the initial emotions that were generated earlier in the Limbic area or override and alter them depending on the dominant thoughts you entertain. That means, two people may hear the same news and may finally display different emotions, and ultimately take different actions."

2.3. Awareness Wheel
"I really loved the Awareness Wheel we used to communicate our feelings and emotions. Communicating my emotions has been very hard for me." Dan acknowledged with a tense emotion. He is still having difficulties to express his emotions verbally.

Sherod Miller, Phyllis Miller, Elam W. Nunnally, and Daniel B. Wackman explained how the wheel works in their book entitled 'Couple Communication I: Talking and Listening Together.' They wrote, *"The Awareness Wheel is a map to help you become more aware of yourself- what you are experiencing at any given point in time."*[42]

Rafael sensed the tense emotion. To dispel it, he asked Dan to elaborate how the tool works. Dan began, "This tool facilitates effective communication between two or more people. The wheel assists us to go beyond the words and non-verbal others and ourselves use to describe a situation. It enables us to understand the feelings and emotions behind the scene. The group exercise we had in the class helped us to recognize the significance of paying closer attention to ours and the feelings and emotions of others when we communicate and listen so as to become effective communicators." It worked. Dan felt better and relaxed.

III. Action item

"This time, what is at the top of your to-do list?" Rafael asked. Dan became vulnerable, "To work on my emotional outbursts. My team members and colleagues know me as someone who struggles to calm down and composes when someone touches my nerves. At this point, I understand that I cannot just get rid of my negative emotions right away because I attended this workshop."

After appreciating Dan's openness to admit his emotional struggle, Rafael inquired, "Going forward, what is your plan to overcome this challenge?" "I've already begun auditing my feelings. So far, I know my dominant emotions. What I need to practice is to interpret them on the go and as negative emotions surface, change my thoughts behind these emotions quickly, and express positive emotions outwardly instead." Dan explained his plan.

Dan's optimism is high, but we all know that managing emotional outbursts is easier said than done. Rafael understood the magnitude of change Dan should pass through before he controls his outbursts. Accordingly, he decided to caution him the reasonable time it may take to make this transformation.

"Dan, it is great that you determined to overcome your public emotional outbursts. However, I'd like to caution you. It won't be that easy. It requires patience." Rafael forewarned. He continued, "Until you develop the competency to regulate your emotions at thought level and make changes at a deeper level on the go, you may consider using affirmative words with a positive tone, body language, and gesture. These are relatively easy until you develop the ability to regulate your thoughts and make changes promptly. These force your emotions to be positive, at least, temporarily."

Rafael could be able to tell from Dan's facial expression that he looked puzzled. Accordingly, he decided to clarify. "While you're in front of people, there're many factors involving. It may be a little overwhelming to pause and alter your emotions in a split second. Of course, once you develop this competency at a thought level, it becomes your second nature." With this, they concluded their second mentoring session.

Summary

Regulating emotions wittingly is one of the essential soft skills to develop self-mastery. This journey to manage our emotions should begin by understanding how emotions are formed and expressed. The ability to control our emotions requires developing our emotional intelligence. To use emotions to our advantages, we also need to be proactive. Rather than waiting to manage unwanted emotions when they burst out and manifest themselves, we should strategize ahead to contain those emotions that are counterproductive. We should also proactively generate those emotions that could help us express our passion, message, and boost our performance and relationships. We should also develop empathy to understand others' feelings and emotions. We don't live and work in a vacuum. To develop personal mastery and successfully lead ourselves, we need to develop our emotional intelligence to regulate our emotions and also intuit the emotions of others. The latter enables us to behave and act properly, interact appropriately, and be caring. The good thing is that the ability we develop to regulate our emotions in our private space and as we develop self-mastery is going to help us as we work with others.

Soft Skill 3: Managing Time and Energy Wisely

"Time is the scarcest of resources, and unless it is managed, nothing else can be managed." **Peter Drucker**

Managing self around time

Before we proceed, let me quickly refresh your memory.

- Workshop one covered the first stage of self-mastery: increasing self-awareness.
- Workshops two, three, and four were designed to cover the remaining three stages.
- Workshop two, regulating emotions wittingly, provided participants the opportunity to develop the soft skill necessary to manage their emotions for their advantage.
- Nonetheless, personal mastery is unattainable without the ability to manage self around time.
- Workshop three gave participants the chance to learn latest approaches, tools, and methods to manage time wisely.

Time is the scarcest of all resources

Managing time effectively is critical to manage self, and in turn, for self-mastery. As the father of modern management clearly stated in the leading quote above, time is the scarcest of all resources. Though other resources are also scant, time is exceptionally scarcest:

- Once it is gone, it's gone forever.
- It is non-renewable, perishable.
- We cannot sell, buy, borrow, store or restore it.

Once time's gone, it's gone forever

One of the wisest men whoever lived on earth Benjamin Franklin said, *"Lost time is never found again."* He is right, there are other things we could be able to recover and regain, not time. Samuel Smiles- Scottish author, cautioned, *"Lost wealth may be replaced by industry, lost knowledge by study, lost health by temperance or medicine, but lost time is gone forever."*

Time doesn't wait for no one

Time baffles humanity. It comes and goes fast. It doesn't give second chances to anyone. The deal time gives each one of us is: Either use me now or lose me forever! The ancient poet Virgil observed, *"Time is flying never to return."* The father of English literature Geoffrey Chaucer also conceded, *"Time and tide waits for no one."*

Time is a great equalizer

What is more? Time is a great equalizer in the world. We all have equal time regardless of who we are. Whether we are rich or poor, educated or unlearned, tall or short, popular or obscure, time treats all of us equally. We all have 24 hours per day. That is why C. S. Lewis, who was a lecturer at Oxford and Cambridge Universities, noted, *"The future is something which everyone reaches at the rate of 60 minutes an hour, whatever he does, whoever he is."*

Susan found a different Dan

Dan found the first three workshops very informative and educational. Susan dropped by Dan's office the other day to say hi, and found a very different person.

For starters, he smiled. He came out from his desk to shake her hand. In her part, Susan smiled broadly while shaking his hand. And asked, "How are you, Dan?"

"I'm doing great. Thanks for stopping by."

After expressing her happiness to know that he is doing well, she inquired, "How is the workshop going?" Susan asked a follow-up question. "Well, as you already know, I questioned it at first. Now, after three workshops, I love it. The workshops were eye openers, informative, and at the same time fun." More than his words, his cheerful facial expressions and animated body languages, and voice pitch revealed his excitement.

Susan in turn couldn't hide her gladness when she realized how much he liked the program. They chatted a little more about some other work stuff and planned to meet over coffee next week. Susan left Dan's office delighted.

Dan was skeptic

The themes of the past two workshops were new territories to Dan. In the contrary, Workshop three was one of his favorite topics. Dan is good in managing time so are the majority of the participants. Prior to the third workshop, Dan was a skeptic and wasn't sure whether he would learn anything new.

Sure enough, in the beginning of the workshop when Joe asked participants to share what they hoped to gain, Dan was frank about it. Indicating that he had attended similar other workshops in the past, he told Joe that he was cynic whether this one would be any different; whether he would learn anything new. But, once the workshop progressed, Dan changed his mind.

At the end of the workshop, he gained lots of insights, and tools he cannot wait to share with Rafael.

I. Key lessons

As usual, Dan showed up on time. They chatted a little bit about family and work, and began their third mentoring session. By now, Dan knows the drill, and thus, he enlisted the four key lessons he learned from the workshop:

- Time management shouldn't be left to chance
- Managing self, not time
- Having both long and short term plans
- The importance of generating and managing energy

1.1. Time management shouldn't be left to chance

Dan expanded on the first lesson he learned from Workshop three. "I had thought that time management is easy and everyone in my team should manage their time wisely. I've been, however, frustrated because some of them missed deadlines, mismanaged their time, and wasted the team's time and mine."

"Have you found out the root cause why this has been happening?" Rafael interrupted politely.

Looking relieved, Dan responded, "Yes. This workshop opened my eyes. I came to realize that many people think that time management is common sense. Now, I clearly see that how this mentality has been the stumbling block for many for not being able to manage time effectively."

"Managing time in one's private space and on those things that may not have serious consequences could be treated as common sense." Rafael pointed out. "However, I don't think that it's a good idea to manage time at the place of work the same way." And asked a rhetorical question, "What happens when we waste it in the workplace and unable to meet deadlines?"

"I concur." Dan nodded and added, "In this world, time is the most valuable resource that we cannot just play with it, especially in the workplace. Time management shouldn't be left to chance. There are many consequences for treating time carelessly."

Rafael supplement Dan's point. "There is nothing in this world that can be done without time. Time is constant in everything that we attempt to accomplish, and therefore, it should be treated delicately."

That is absolutely correct. Unlike other resources, Peter Drucker noted, *"Time is totally irreplaceable. Within limits we can substitute one resource for another... But there is no substitute for time."*[43] We shouldn't treat time casually. A great leader who accomplished great things, Abraham Lincoln, wasn't spontaneous. He said, *'Give me six hours to chop down a tree and I will spend the first four sharpening the axe.'"* Peter Drucker agreed when he said, *"Nothing else, perhaps, distinguishes effective executives as much as their tender loving care of time."*[44]

Dan concurred. "We all desperately need to make time on our side, to have enough time to accomplish our responsibilities. I finally realized, however, that managing time, though it seems easy for some of us, it's elusive for many." He is right. Time management isn't an easy task. William Penn underscored, *"Time is what we want most, but what we use worst."*

"Dan, it's great that now you came to appreciate that time management isn't as it looks easy for your team members. The question is, do you know the very reasons why your people undermine time management and fail to work on their time management skill proactively?" Rafael probed.

"I've not yet figured that out, but from the small group discussion we had, we identified some common reasons that may prevent people from developing their effective time management skill. And I'm sure that these reasons may be shared by some of my team members." "What are these reasons you heard?" Rafael wanted to know.

Time management takes away our freedom?
"One participant said that she doesn't want to lose her freedom by attempting to manage time. She argued that she has been thinking that developing such a skill may deprive her from being spontaneous and from enjoying the fun that comes when she does things haphazardly."

"Yes, time shouldn't be allowed to control us." Rafael agreed. "But, we can still be our own boss and use the time to serve our goals by becoming smarter in using time effectively, and by using it in our favor. I believe that we can still be skillful in managing our time without losing our freedom."

Deadline junkies?
"The other reason I heard was 'I perform well under pressure.' A couple of participants shared that they find themselves effective as they approach deadlines." Rafael wondered whether Dan knew the origin of the word deadline. Dan was quick to admit that he doesn't know and eagerly waited to know.

After acknowledging the fact that he used the word deadline a million times without knowing its origin, Rafael explained, "I was surprised to learn that the word was coined in the 19th C during the civil war. Prisoners of war were not allowed to cross certain established lines. The penalty for crossing the deadline was being shot."

Dan sat in stunned silence. "Thanks for sharing!" Playfully commented, "Wow, the price for failing to respect a deadline was dire back then." Both burst into laughter.

"The question is why one risks it all and come closer to the deadline and risk being shot at? I don't know why people wait until the 11th hour to meet their obligation." With a surprised look, Dan looked up and shaken his head.

"I share your concern," Rafael nodded. "I've heard this argument again and again. Such individuals proudly call themselves 'Deadline Junkies.' It is hard to counter-argue with someone's experience. If they say that they put their acts together and perform well when they are under pressure, well, I would like to trust them. They may perform outstandingly when under pressure."

"Me too," Dan concurred. "I'm skeptic about whether doing things at the 11th hour is wise even if I have the capacity to do so. Yes, I may deliver results just before the deadline. The question is: Can I produce quality results while I rush against time?"

The time invested in learning time management pays down the road
After several seconds of silence, Dan moved to the next excuse. "Many fail to be proactive in managing time effectively because of a dilemma. One participant shared his frustration. He said that he is already out of time, and struggling to meet deadlines. It didn't give sense to him to spend his limited time to learn latest time management techniques and methods with the hope to become better at managing time in the future?"

Rafael professed that he used to struggle to cope with new technologies. "I was hesitant to learn some tools to maximize the use of my time. Initially, I found learning new techniques and technologies taking me longer than I expected. Rather than saving time, I found myself spending."

Paused for a few seconds and continued, "But, I learned that the time we spend to develop latest time management skills pays back down the road. Such an initial investment is wise since it'll have high ROI at the end of the day." Dan nodded.

1.2. Managing self, not time

Rafael suggested moving to the second lesson. Dan breathed deep and stretched his legs, and shared, "One subtle insight I gained out of the third workshop was the fact that I couldn't manage time. I realized that I don't have direct control over time. I can only have control over myself and what I can do with my limited time."

"This is a huge difference maker." Rafael acknowledged. And remarked, "Personally, when I discovered this seemingly simple truth, things started to change. It was a humbling experience to understand that I don't have control over time!"

I relate to Rafael. What a relief I had when I first realized the fact that I only have control over my own resources, and myself alone. It allowed me to be in charge and manage self and my resources around time better. 'Managing time' started to be easier. Don't misread me here. I'm not yet where I want to be, but at least for now, I have a better handle on time than I used to. Alec Mackenzie and Pat Nickerson were on the mark when they wrote, "*You don't manage time at all. You only manage yourself in relation to it.*"[45]

Dan also learned that once he masters managing time effectively, managing other resources becomes easier. "I recognized that until I develop a good handle on effective time management, I'm at risk of mismanaging myself, and other scarce resources." That is accurate. Peter Drucker warned: "*Unless time is managed, nothing else can be managed.*"

Managing time effectively, not just efficiently

"You mentioned effective time management. There is a difference between managing time efficiently and effectively." Rafael used the opportunity to offer Dan a valuable insight that helped him. "Those of us who have tried the rat race to manage time efficiently by saving as many minutes as we could on a daily basis discovered the bitter truth. This race is not winnable. It's self-defeating."

Rafael laughed loud. Dan joined. Rafael shared his regret. "Attempting to manage the unmanageable led many of us to experience frustration. Our effort to manage time efficiently resulted in a stressful life filled with disappointments and burnouts."

Dan was glad that Rafael brought up this. One challenge he found tough, even after attending this workshop, was how to balance life and work. He struggles to keep the balance. He gets carried away in meeting his goals and finds himself hurting his health and relationships. After revealing how he struggles to keep the balance, Dan asked him to share his experience on this.

"I relate to that." Rafael acknowledged. "I was there once. I still sometimes find myself struggling to maintain the balance. For many years, however, it had been a serious issue. One insight that helped me initially was the importance of focusing on effective time management, not efficiently. It occurred to me that if I manage time effectively by doing the right things by strategizing, prioritizing, planning, scheduling, using technologies, and delegation, I could have enough time to keep the balance between my work, health, relationships, and to meet other social obligations. That was then I realized that I don't need to go after each second and make effort to save time here and there. The latter approach may make me efficient, but not only it doesn't help me meet my goals but also cannot empower me to maintain the balance between work and life."

Indeed, Rafael discovered a compelling insight. The guru of time management- Peter Drucker alluded, *"For manual work, we need only efficiency; that is, the ability to do things right rather than the ability to get the right things done."*[46] The latter is what the knowledge workers of the 21st C needs- managing time effectively by prioritizing and doing the right things. In his book 'First Things First' Stephen Covey also wrote, *"Doing more things faster is no substitute for doing the right things."*[47] That is why the purpose of time management workshops should be to help participants develop the right mindset, attitude, acquire some insights, tools, and approaches that would, in turn, assist them do the right things at the right time.

1.3. Having a long term plan

Dan moved to the next insight he gained, which is, the importance of having a long view as part of effective time management. He shared some of the benefits they talked about in the class that may come from developing a long-term plan. After carefully listening, Rafael acknowledged that many successful companies have fifty, even hundred-year strategic plan. He then gave some examples and emphasized the need to have a long-term strategic planning document to manage time effectively.

Rafael is right. Many companies these days have a long-term strategic plan. They use that as a reference and come up with middle and short-term plans. For instance, Toyota has a 100-year strategic plan. Many hospitals, recreation centers, universities, non-profit organizations, political parties, and businesses have up to a 50-year strategic plan.

Though Dan believes the necessity of a long-term strategic plan, he didn't hide his cynicism about having fifty-year and hundred-year strategic plans. "Although I see its importance and I'll try my best to have one, I must admit that I still wonder whether it is a good idea to plan that far. Considering how things change fast, I don't see the relevance of planning decades ahead like these organizations you mentioned."

Rafael heard this the same argument again and again. "Yes, it's true that things change fast and it's unlikely to find what we project years and decades ahead to remain the same. But, that should not stop us from having a long-term plan. Once we come up with a long-term strategic plan by thinking critically and strategically, we should break it into middle and short term plans. We should carry out frequent monitoring to keep updating our plan as we progress." Upon Dan's request, Rafael shared the approach he has been using:

- Have a long-term plan.
- Break it into phases.
- Have middle and short-term plans.
- Further break down the short-term plan.
- Carve out a yearly plan each year.
- Refer the latter as you come up with a quarterly plan.
- From the quarterly plan, craft a monthly plan.
- Continue like that- from monthly to a weekly plan.
- Use the weekly plan to schedule your major tasks that lead you to accomplish your primary goals on a daily basis.

Rafael further advised, "Don't stop there. Continue to:

- Monitor your progress carefully.
- Make changes daily or weekly, if necessary.
- Evaluate your short, middle, and long-term goals occasionally."

Dan was taking note. He found the explanation very helpful. Subsequently, he asked, "When it comes to evaluating the short, middle, and long-term goals, what is your suggestion?" "You may evaluate your yearly plan, quarterly; your mid-term plan, yearly; and your long-term plan, once in a few years," Rafael recommended.

'Plans are useless but planning is indispensable'
Rafael's suggestions are very instrumental. Particularly for leaders because they should lead their people while their eyes are wide open. Leaders need to have a long-term plan to have a clear vision of the future. However, they

should be ready to quickly make changes when their plans are no more relevant or need improvements. General Colin Powell fought many wars, and he knew what he was talking about when he said, *"Plans are useless but planning is indispensable."* His statement seems paradoxical but it's not. Plans are useless because, he wrote, *"No battle plan survives contact with the enemy."* However, passing through the process of planning is vital.

We have control only on the now

Rafael concluded his recommendation, "Though we need to have a long view to gain clarity and break it into middle and short term plans, we should make efforts to manage the time at hand by having a weekly plan and daily priorities. We have control only on the now. That is why we should enter into a sense of urgency to use our time in the present."

Bil Keane reminded us that *"Yesterday's the past, tomorrow's the future, but today is a gift. That's why it's called the present."* Peter Drucker also advised that we have to manage time effectively by doing the right thing in the present. Nelson Mandela once said, *"We must use time wisely and forever realize that the time is always ripe to do right."*

If we fail to treat our time now and today wisely and with care, it'll judge us tomorrow harshly since it came to us and we mistreated and abused it. When our time is up here on this planet will we be free of guilt that we have done our best and became who we suppose to be. This cannot happen without treating the time we have now right. Remember, as playwright Mae West once said, *"You only live once, but if you do it right, once is enough."* And developing this soft skill allows us to manage time wisely and to do it right.

Learn to say no

Speaking of a sense of urgency, Dan admitted that he has weekly and daily priorities but struggles to protect his priorities. Rafael suggested, "You need to learn to tell no to protect your priorities." Dan protested. "It's tough to say no to some people like our bosses and spouses."

This is not just a challenge that faces Dan alone. Many people find it hard to say no. Once I was facilitating a workshop at a government agency, one of the participants approached me during the break and shared with me that his boss gathered his team who were new and revealed to them what kinds of reasons may get them terminated. One of the reasons he mentioned was refusing to do a job.

Acknowledging that it's not that easy to say no to certain people, Rafael agreed that saying no is hard and many of us struggle with it. "That is why we should remind ourselves, again and again, that time is finite. We can't do everything with the same and equal intensity and dedication. We should prioritize! We should let go some tasks from our to-do list. We should also be bold enough to say no than taking additional responsibilities while our plate is already full."

The inability of saying no denies us from investing our scarce time on things that matter the most. Saying no is especially important if we experience lots of unnecessary interruptions and distractions! Remember, *"When you say no to something, you do it to say yes to something else- a more valid, pressing commitment."*[48] The former Prime Minister of UK, Tony Blair, remarked, *"The art of leadership is saying no, not saying yes. It is very easy to say yes."*

Rafael's response didn't satisfy Dan. He sighed. "It may be relatively easy to say no to people who are reporting directly to you and peers. But…" Before Dan finished the next statement, Rafael interrupted gently and conceded that it's tough to just say an emphatic no to our loved ones and superiors. "Still, we need to learn to say no to them nicely without appearing confrontational and damaging the relationships." He then gave him some examples to show him how to say no diplomatically.

If you're interested, you may consider trying Jim Temme's method, which I share to my workshop audience. In his book entitled "Productivity Power", he proposed an approach acronymically called USA[49].

Let's say that your boss came up to you and asked you to take an urgent assignment. You've been already swamped and struggling to meet the deadlines of a couple of important tasks. What would you do? If you think that you cannot add this new pressing duty without risking missing the deadlines of the other assignments, you better let your boss know your situation. Using the USA approach, state that:
- You understand that the new task is important and you're appreciative of getting the opportunity to work on this task (**U**nderstanding Statement)
- You're working on other urgent assignments with tight deadlines (**S**ituation Statement)
- Provide options such as 'Would you like me to delegate one of the already existing duties to someone and take this one instead or do you want me to defer one of the other tasks until later so that I can do this job now?' And so on. (**A**ction Statement)

The goal is to understand, paint a clear picture of your situation, and most importantly to offer some options. Thenceforth, you leave your boss to make the final decision. She either wants you to drop (delegate) one of the current assignments you're working on to take the new assignment or she may decide to find another person to take care of the new task so that you may keep working on the already existing tasks.

1.4. The importance of generating and maintaining energy

One thing that astonished Dan was the significance of energy management. He confessed, "I have an enough handle when it comes to time management. Conversely, I hadn't known the importance of energy management before attending this workshop."

"Time management without managing one's energy is unproductive." Rafael agreed and queried, "How do you plan to maintain your energy?" Dan declared that he has already determined to make a lifestyle change to benefit from this new discovery. Rafael is well aware of the challenges one faces when he tries to make a lifestyle change. And thus, he asked, "Have you begun making some of the changes yet? How did you find the result so far? Is it easy to make a way of life change?" Without realizing, Rafael bombarded Dan with questions.

Dan paused to answer these questions carefully. He rubbed his forehead and acknowledged that he had begun the journey. He elaborated. "Thus far, I've found it hard, as all lifestyle changes are hard first, but considering the long-term, multifaceted benefits of making this change, I'll stick with my decision."

Rafael admired Dan for his conviction. Still, he was wondering whether Dan has a clear plan to succeed in his energy management. He pushed on. Dan responded. "I have already come up with a quick plan that will guide me to eat right, exercise, take appropriate micro renewals on a consistent basis, and so on."

Knowing the lifestyle and effectiveness of Rafael, Dan sought to learn from his experience, "Do you mind to share with me how you manage your energy?" Glad to share his simple but straightforward approach, Rafael enlisted what he does to generate and maintain his energy:

- **Exercise regularly**. "I go to the gym and exercise when I get a chance. When I don't have time to go to the gym, I may take a walk. If the weather doesn't allow me to do so, I stretch at home using resistance bands, and also do some push ups and sit-ups."
- **Eat healthily**. "I eat healthy foods that don't have a high level of fat and sugar." "Are you a vegetarian?" Dan probed while smiling. "No. I eat lean meat, mainly fish." Rafael clarified.

- **Avoid energy drainers**. "As much as possible, I avoid drinking caffeine and other substances that drain my energy level."
- **Take regular breaks and enough rests.** "I don't wait for the whole year to take a vacation. I don't hold on the whole week or the day to take rest. The moment I feel tired or sleepy, I make sure to take a quick break. I may read a chapter from a book, or take a quick nap, or reflect briefly, or do other activities that are not mentally intensive." In the next several minutes, Dan asked some follow-up questions and solicited some pieces of advice to implement some of Rafael's approaches.

Realizing the importance of managing both time and energy at the same time was a breakthrough for me. I still remember where I heard about it the first time. That opportunity reminded me the fact that we only have 24 hours per day, which is limited. On the other hand, unlike time, our daily energy is not fixed. We can generate, and manage our daily energy. Since then, I incorporated energy management in the time management workshops that I facilitate.

In their book entitled 'The power of full engagement', the authors wrote, *"Learning to manage energy more efficiently and intelligently has a unique transformative power, both individually and organizationally."*[50] The book helps you to:

- Identify key sources of energy,
- Balance and renew your energy on a daily basis,
- Expand your capacity to generate energy continually, and
- Create energy management rituals.

II. Assessments, Processes, and Tools
2.1. SMART goal setting
"I found the SMART (Specific, Measurable, Attainable, Relevant, and Time-bound) process very helpful. I had been familiar with the SMART goal setting approach. What I didn't know was the possibility of using this process collectively to come up with SMART goals for our team." Dan shared.

Upon Rafael request, Dan further explained how he is going to use it in a group setting. After listening attentively, Rafael requested. "Tell me some of the benefits when team members are involved in setting the team's goals." Dan identified and briefly described the following benefits:

- **Smarter goals**. When key stakeholders participate in crafting project goals, the chance to come up with SMARTer goals is high.
- **Ownership**. When key stakeholders are invited to participate in setting goals at the early stage, they develop ownership and believe that the

goals are theirs. They won't say this is your goals. Rather, they would say, these are our goals.

- **Motivation**. Involving key stakeholders, especially team members, not only it creates commitment and ownership, but it also inspires them to give their best.

"Do you plan to use it soon?" Rafael asked a follow-up question. Yes was Dan's answer. "I'd like to use this approach to refine the existing goals of the project with the active participation of key stakeholders."

2.2. The 4 Ds
"One of the tools that I found very helpful was the 4Ds process." Dan didn't hide his enthusiasm.

"Explain to me briefly how you plan to use it." Rafael inquired. "Going forward, I've four options when a task comes on my way:

- If it's irrelevant or something that doesn't add value, I'll **D**isregard it.
- If it's not something that I can disregard, I'll ask if this is something I can **D**elay? If yes, I'll come back again to do it at a later time.
- If it's something that cannot be deferred, then, I ask myself can I transfer it? If the answer is yes, I'll find the right person to **D**elegate.
- If it cannot be delegated and I'm the only one who could do it, then I'll **D**o it right away."

Rafael interjected, "Make sure that those tasks that you decide to delay won't fall through the cracks." Dan nodded.

In his book entitled 'Getting Things Done' David Allen shared a workflow that simplifies making decisions based on "*what they are and what needs to be done about them*."[51] Some of the questions in the workflow include but not limited to:

- What is it?
- Is it actionable?
- What is the next action?
- And so on.

Emptying your inbox with the 4Ds
Allen also suggested applying the 4D process rule to empty our inbox. Here is how it works. When an email comes your way, you have four options:

- **D**elete it if it is irrelevant or
- **D**efer (archive) it if it's something not urgent or

- **D**elegate (forward) it if you're not the right person to take action or
- **D**o (respond) it immediately.

Skillful Delegation

Rafael understands that delegation is tough. And hence, he was wondering whether Dan had tried delegating. "Have you delegated before, and what was the result?"

Before even attending this workshop that covered the theme delegation, he took a proactive step and delegated Susan and also one of the senior researchers to take care of some urgent matters in his absence. "However, after the discussion on delegation, I recognized that I didn't do it the right way."

It's impressive. Do you remember? Dan had always appeared right and defensive before he joined this program. Now, he began accepting responsibilities and owning his mistakes.

"Why do you think it wasn't done properly?" Rafael delved. "I learned from the workshop that successful delegation should at least:
- Begin by clearly stating the goal of the delegation,
- Plainly explaining the tasks that should be done,
- Answering all questions the delegees may have."

Dan further disclosed. "Unfortunately, as a delegator, I didn't do my job well. I knew my goal and also had some expectations but I didn't spell them out clearly; I didn't follow the process as discussed in the workshop. So far, I liked the results, but the outcomes would have been better if I did my part right in the beginning." Rafael reminded Dan that it isn't too late. "You can still go back to your delegees and correct your missteps."

"By the way, there was a heated debate among participants about whether delegation is possible and appropriate at GHR." Rafael wanted to know the reason behind. Dan clarified, "Some of the participants who are researchers argued that most of the things they do require their unique expertise. The people who report to them don't have the necessary skills that they cannot delegate them during their absence."

Rafael agreed that in some organizations delegation doesn't work all the time. "However, many hesitate to delegate for some unconvincing personal reasons." Dan appeared unsure. This led Rafael to put forward some of the reasons:

- "Some may not want to appear incompetent by delegating the tasks they are paid to do.
- Others may love what they do so much that they don't want to transfer them to others.
- Still, others may feel like they don't have time and energy to train delegees. They don't appreciate the long-term benefits down the road."

Dan sought to know how one could decide which duties to delegate. Rafael suggested some pointers that help decide which tasks to delegate.

III. Action item
Putting the big rocks in first
"It's one thing to come up with SMART goals but achieving these goals is quite another," Dan professed. He enlisted what he is going to do to make sure the team achieves its goals:

- Breaking down each goal into manageable objectives,
- Identifying tasks to fulfill each objective,
- Assigning resources to each task, and
- Putting deadline for each task.

"Breaking down your goals into manageable tasks is smart. One thing I suggest is to prioritize these tasks." Rafael recommended. This reminded Dan the discussion they had about the 80/20 principle. He came to realize that 20 percent tasks are responsible for 80 percent of the results. Dan consented. "You're right. We need to isolate the 20% tasks that deliver 80%, and give them, a minimum of, 80% of our time and resources."

They spent several minutes on talking about the significance of prioritizing. One of the things that came up in the discussion was Steven Covey's Important/Urgent Matrix. Dan also recounted the activity Joe conducted to explain the power of putting top priorities first into the calendar. Dan enjoyed this exercise. It left an indelible impression on why he should first put his 'big rocks' (highest priorities) in first before filling his calendar with 'sands.'

The struggle between Urgent and Important things
By the way, Dwight Eisenhower- the 34th President of the US- was the one who first invented the matrix. He was quoted as saying, *"I have two kinds of problems, the urgent and the important. The urgent are not important, and the important are never urgent."* Using this tool enabled him to succeed leading the ally forces on the D- Day June 6, 1944. Nonetheless, Stephen Covey was the one who popularized the matrix in his classic book, 'The 7 Habits of Highly

Successful People.'

Activity log

Rafael had a concern. "Dan, you made a significant decision. I'm sure you could easily identify your priorities. How could you make the transition from where your team is now to the place where your priorities get the investment and attention they deserve?"

"The first step to make sure our priorities are given ample time is to know where our time goes." Dan recognized and continued, "This allows us to appreciate where the majority of our time is spent, and ultimately to make changes on our schedule in favor of our top priorities."

Rafael was listening intently. After a quick pause, Dan declared proudly, "By the way, I have already begun this journey." "Do you mind to share your discovery so far?" Rafael wanted to know Dan's progress. "So far, I can see that I've been spending my quality time more on those tasks that are important and urgent. I hadn't realized this up until I began logging my activities in the last couple of days."

Dan isn't alone. We all are not born with mastery of time management. We don't have the innate ability to manage time effectively. For that matter, we are predisposed to mismanage time. I concur with Peter Druker, who admitted, *"Man is ill-equipped to manage his time."* [52]

Rafael advised Dan to continue to practice logging his time and also help his team members to do so until it becomes their habit. They talked about how developing a habit may take, at least, three weeks. Dan's decision was smart because, Drucker recommended, *"The first step toward effectiveness is a procedure: recording where the time goes."* [53]

From his own experience, Rafael proposed, "Not only you should allocate adequate time to your project's top priorities, but also you should execute those highest priority tasks during those hours you operate at your best. You might have already noticed that we all have certain times where we function optimally. It is important to figure that out and adjust our schedule accordingly."

Summary

Without developing the soft skill that enables us to manage self and the resources we have around time, we are far from achieving personal mastery. However, many challenges make this journey tough. For starters, time is one of the scarcest resources in the world. Second, we don't have direct control over it. Third, managing time effectively to manage and master self demands to develop the right mindset, attitude, and some abilities like setting SMART goals, prioritizing, planning, scheduling, monitoring, evaluating, using some processes, approaches, and technologies. Most of all, it necessitates protecting our priorities from unnecessary interruptions and distractions, and making dynamic changes when necessary and on the go to make sure that our top priorities are done first. Compared to the skills we need to manage time effectively, developing the right attitude and mindset is very hard. There could be some cultural and religious beliefs and personality preferences that may deter many of us from taking effective time management seriously, which in turn may discourage us from developing this skill to manage self and ultimately achieve personal mastery. But, time management should be coupled with energy management. What is the use if we have ample time to pursue and fulfill our goals but lack the energy to execute them? That is why we should generate and manage our energy on a consistent basis as part of complementing our efforts in managing our time wittingly. Last but not least, we shouldn't forget that the best way to manage our time is to make the fixed pie bigger by delegating. We shouldn't just depend on the fixed 24 hours per day we have at hand. We could multiply our time exponentially by delegating.

Soft Skill 4: Solving Problems & Making Right Decisions

"We know there is a painful gap…between being aware of tremendous problems and challenges in the workplace and developing the internal power and moral authority to break out of those problems and become a significant force in solving them." **Stephen Covey**

Part of self-management is solving problems

- Self-mastery is a process.
- This process begins by expanding our self-awareness, which was covered in Workshop one.
- The second stage is self-management. Though there are so many areas we need to manage to achieve self-mastery, three major areas contribute the lion's share toward personal mastery. These three areas of focus include:
  a) Regulating emotions wittingly,
  b) Managing time and energy wisely, and
  c) Solving problems and making right decisions.
- If we develop these three essential soft skills, out of possibly many other soft skills, our chance to manage ourselves and achieve self-mastery is within our reach.
- Workshop two and three covered regulating emotions and managing time and energy, respectively.
- Workshop four covered solving problems and making right decisions.
- Part of self-management is developing our ability to deal with problems that we face and making the right choices, which in turn allow us to release our potential and attain our unique greatness.

Mastering problem solving to realize your greatness

Until we develop the ability to solve problems and make right decisions, we are far from achieving personal mastery. The problems we face on a daily basis stand in our way and prevent us from succeeding unless we solve them creatively and make the right decisions. If we hesitate to make tough decisions or make poor decisions, we may get stuck in one place too long, or at least, unable to advance and make progress. While in this state, attaining self-mastery is unthinkable. Without developing the mindset, attitude, and skills that are necessary to solve problems and make right decisions, one cannot be in charge and free. There exists a huge gap.

In his book 'The 8th Habit: From Effectiveness to Greatness', Stephen Covey talked about the existence of a gap. He wrote, *"between possessing great potential and actually realizing a life of greatness and contribution."* Covey suggested for us to fill the gap by developing the ability to break out of problems if our desire is to realize our personal greatness.

Decision-making is a part of problem solving

There is a clear link between problem-solving and decision-making. Problem-solving goes hand in hand with decision-making. Robert Schuller declared, *"Again and again, the impossible decision is solved when we see that the problem is only a tough decision waiting to be made."* He further reasoned, *"Unless problem solving leads to making decisions, then, what you're dealing with is not a problem."*

Helen Reynolds and Mary Tramel put it in clear terms. They explained, *"Decision making is actually a part of problem solving. There would be no decision to make if there were no problem to solve. Problem solving consists of three operations: Problem analysis, decision making, and action.'*[54]

When we lose this sight, we are unable to solve problems that are in front of us the whole time just waiting for our decision. Henry Ford noticed, *"Most people spend more time and energy going around problems than in trying to solve them."* Jim Citrin identified what happens when we fail to make decisions to solve problems, *"Uncertainty can lead to paralysis. And if you become indecisive you're dead."*

Paul felt happy that he gave Dan a second chance

Surprise! Dan got a call from Paul. He asked, "How are you, Dan?" Dan was astonished to get the CEO's call, and wondering why he called. "Thanks for asking. I'm doing well, Sir!"

There was a brief silence. Paul proceeded, "How is the soft skills development program treating you?" "I love it," Dan responded with excitement. Paul asked a follow-up question, "Did you find it helpful?" Dan assured Paul that so far he liked the program very much and revealed, "As you may recall, I was doubtful initially. After passing through the first four workshops, I've been wondering why I didn't attend it a long time ago."

Both smiled and laughed loudly.

Paul was so happy to learn that Dan found the program very helpful. He asked a specific question, "What was your last workshop about?" Dan quickly responded, "It was about solving problems and making right decisions." "Wow! Do you mind to share with me a thing or two from what learned from the workshop?" Paul asked politely.

Dan said "Sure, why not?" while thinking what to share. Though there were so many ideas popped into his mind, Dan decided to share the one thing that he thought might resonate to Paul.

Dan cleared his throat. "I've learned so many things, but one thing that I'd like to share with you is the insight I got about how there is no one problem big enough we cannot solve. I realized that it's possible to break down big problems into small manageable problems, and solve them one problem at a time."

Paul agreed. "Knowing that we can resolve any issue that may come on our way takes away the stress, especially when we are faced with daunting problems. Thanks for sharing, Dan!"

No big problems that cannot be handled

There is no problem that we cannot handle. The industrialist Henry Ford said; *"Nothing is particularly hard if you divide it into small jobs."* As a pioneer who made automobiles affordable to the mass, he overcame insurmountable challenges by breaking them into pieces. That is why he said, *"There are no big problems; there are just a lot of little problems."* Similarly, Richard Sloma counseled, *"Never try to solve all the problems at once — make them line up for you one-by-one."*

After chatting for a couple of more minutes about other project stuff, they concluded their phone conversation. Once Paul hanged up his phone, he took a brief moment to reflect on the progress Dan has shown, and he felt so happy that they gave him a second chance.

I. Key lessons
1.1. Embracing problems

Dan began. "The most important lesson I learned from this workshop was the significance of having the right mindset to be successful in resolving problems and making right decisions." Rafael chimed in to compliment. "This is a great foundation." Dan continued, "Without this foundation, we won't take positive steps to work on and enjoy the process while resolving problems and making decisions. We came to realize that many people view problems as:

- Bad things,
- Misfortunes, and
- Things to dread, hate, avoid at all costs."

Rafael remained silent for Dan to continue.

"I've had these views for an extended period. These outlooks prevented me from consciously developing the soft skill necessary to turn problems into opportunities. I've been defensive and reactive, in most cases. My preoccupation had always been to get rid of problems as quickly as possible without taking ample time to understand and finally solve them properly."

Rafael reassured Dan. "Facing problems isn't a bad thing all the time. As far as we set big goals and attempt to advance in life and our profession, we are bound to face problems and tough choices to make. As we march forward to live up to our potential, problems come on our way 'to test' whether we are up to the task and worthy of achieving our individual and collective goals."

Dan nodded and remarked, "You're right. It's in our nature to set big goals. We should anticipate facing big problems as we pursue our goals." "They're two sides of the same coin!" Rafael added.

To turn problems into assets, we need the right attitude toward problems. Theodore Rubin affirmed, *The problem is not that there are problems. The problem is expecting otherwise and thinking that having problems is a problem.* Viktor Frankl, who faced extraordinary problems while he was in Nazi's concentration camp said, *What man actually needs is not a tensionless state but rather the striving and struggling for some goal worthy of him.* He declared, *What he needs is not the discharge of tension at any cost, but the call of a potential meaning waiting to be fulfilled by him.*

"Maybe it is better not to set big goals to avoid attracting big problems." Dan joked.

Both laughed.

Rafael disclaimed. "Well, even if goals attract problems, we shouldn't refrain from setting huge goals just because they tend to attract massive problems. The alternative is not pretty. If we just fold our hands and sit on the sidelines as life goes on; well, we don't need to worry about problems. They are not interested in people on that side of the fence."

Dan chose a side. With a broad smile and playful manner, he said, "I prefer to be on the side of the fence where problems frequent."

1.2. Problems are blessings in disguise

Dan moved on. "The second lesson I learned from Workshop four was embracing problems as blessings in disguise. The more we have problems means, the more we're going to have opportunities to grow and become better individually and collectively."

Rafael liked Dan's perspective. He then shared his own experience. "I've witnessed in my journey that my significant growth came each time I outgrew a problem. I firmly believe that each problem that we face collectively is also meant to take us to the next level of growth as a team. Either we have arrived or lost if our life is devoid of problems and challenges."

Problems are opportunities for growth

There was a time when I used to pray on a daily basis in order not to have any more problem. I felt tired, stuck, and frustrated beyond measure because of the challenges I was facing. I had a big goal and desperate to make a major career shift. Back then; I didn't know that it was normal to experience continual setbacks following a big decision like that.

Well, finally, I realized that, as the saying goes, for every action, there is an equal or even greater opposite force (problem). Not long after that, it occurred to me that in the absence of challenges and problems, my life actually would have been boring. Since then, I read a lot and finally learned that problems are indications of you are alive, and making progress.

At this stage of my life, when I find myself having a free ride without challenges and problems a couple of weeks in a row, I immediately know that either I lowered my expectations (standards), or stayed too long within my comfort zone without even knowing it. Nowadays, when I experience red carpet walk in life, it doesn't take me long to figure out that I stopped growing and advancing.

That is why I strongly believe that problems are opportunities. We need to change our attitude toward problems. If our desire is to realize our individual and collective greatness, we need the right mindset that can enable us to transform problems into opportunities. Henri Kaiser said it very well, *"Problems are only opportunities in work clothes."*

The future is for problem solvers

The more problems we face, the more we develop our problem-solving ability. This soft skill is in high demand now and in the future. World Economic Forum, in its Future of Jobs Report, revealed that Complex Problem Solving is the top skill necessary to succeed in 2020.[55] In the report, currently, this same skill is at the top. Thus, to succeed now and in the future, we need to develop and continually hone this soft skill.

Taking problem-solving to the next level

Rafael paused, looked at Dan, further pointed out that we all have already solved tough problems. He stressed that attaining self-mastery, however, requires taking our problem-solving ability to the next level. As a person who knows the dedication and commitment it takes to develop this soft skill, Rafael emphasized, "Further developing this skill takes our prime attention, investment, and most importantly practicing problem-solving using latest tools, processes, and approaches."

For the next several minutes, Rafael shared his personal experience on how he developed and continued to improve his problem solving ability. When it was his turn to share his personal experience, Dan admitted that he hadn't proactively invested on this soft skill. He acknowledged that this is the first time he appreciated the critical roles this soft skill play toward achieving personal mastery. "Now, I earnestly believe that this soft skill is going to be my ticket to deal with my own and the team's problems, and to be in charge and lead my project successfully."

1.3. Bypassing some steps of the creative problem solving process

Though Dan had been solving problems before he attended this workshop, he realized that he bypassed many of the steps of the creative problem-solving process. He confessed, "I still remember how I quickly make my mind and propose solutions without understanding the problem fully, gathering ample data, and involving other key stakeholders."

Our brain is wired to offer quick solutions

Admitting that he relates with Dan, Rafael explained why we all are tempted to quickly solve problems. "Our brain is very powerful and at the same time quick. It attempts to make our lives easier. It analyzes the problems that we face using the available data in its own database and its powerful computation abilities. Our brain is wired to assist us to make quick decisions. This promptness is very helpful in some instances, not always. That is why this is our responsibility to make the call and decide when to disregard the quick problem analysis and solution suggestion of our brain."

Begin by asking what is and what isn't a problem

Dan understood that the brain is trying to be efficient when it suggests quick solutions. However, he wondered. "To overcome the temptation of following the quick route our mind suggests, what should we be doing?" Rafael stressed that restraining our brain and following the proper steps of problem-solving isn't only important to find the right solutions but also to protect our scarce resources. "We need to define each problem we face before we invest our limited time and scarce resources to try to fix it. We need to define an issue and make sure that it is actually a real problem before we spend any of our resources to analyze and then fix it."

Dan felt guilty. He had been doing that all the time. He remembered how many issues that weren't problems at all consumed his time and resources for many years. He regretted that he wasted his time and energy on those issues that didn't qualify as problems.

"What do you mean by we need to define each problem?" Dan solicited.

Situations, problems, and realities
Rafael responded immediately. "A given issue could be a:
- Situation to be disregarded or
- Problem to be solved or
- Reality to be accepted."

Dan didn't appear satisfied. Rafael further explained, "A situation, as time passes, goes away without us doing anything about it. It doesn't need to be resolved right away. It's not a problem that hinders us. Thus, we just need to sit it out. We shouldn't make it a priority. We don't need to invest our time and energy on it."

To make sure he got Rafael's point, Dan double-checked. "Are you saying that if an issue doesn't affect our project goals, if it doesn't come between us and our goals, we don't need to worry about it and invest our resources in addressing it?" Rafael nodded in agreement.

In 'Executive Time Management', the authors noted, "*Procrastination is a time-consuming habit; but calculated procrastination can save time. Some problems, if left alone, will resolve themselves. Why not keep a desk drawer for such problem?*"[56]

Rafael moved to the second scenario. "If it's an actual problem, we need to resolve it creatively. Unlike a situation, if we don't do something about it immediately, we are going to be stuck. Our progress is going to be hampered." He added, "There are also realities that are neither situations nor problems. These cannot be solved, and hence, we just need to accept them and find alternatives to deal with realities."

"What you're saying is that we should be careful not to treat everything as a real problem. Some issues may not need solving. They should either be ignored or accepted." Dan verified. "That is correct!" Rafael confirmed and jokingly quoted Abraham Maslow '*If the only tool you have is a hammer, it's tempting to treat everything as if it were a nail.*' The quote induced a smile out of

Dan.

But, one thing bothered Dan. He is a doer and believes that he can tackle any issue if he is determined to do so. Thus, he challenged, "Should we really need to give up on some issues and accept them as realities? Don't you think that this may lead some to accept tough problems as realities and refrain from doing something about it?"

Rafael recognized Dan's question as legitimate. Thus, he elaborated, "I understand your concern. Yes, it's possible that some people may use this as an excuse. The point I was making is that we should know the difference between a tough problem that must be tackled and a reality that cannot be fixed even if we give it our best. By the way, we shouldn't only avoid those that are deemed realities, but also, sometimes, we may need to avoid tackling some real problems. If the efforts, time, and resources we need to invest on them outweigh the gain from solving them, rather than trying to fix them, it's better to find affordable alternative ways to deal with them."

- If you're sick and tired of losing to problems easily;
- If you're burned out in cleaning the messes problems cause frequently;
- If you are stranded more than you should because of unsolved (poorly solved) problems;
- If your team gets stuck whenever, small or big, problems surface;
- You need to work on your and your team's problem solving soft skill.

1.4. We cannot manage ourselves if we don't manage our choices

"I learned that self-management couldn't be achieved without developing the ability to make the right choices. Our ability to manage self is highly dependent on whether we have the capacity to handle our choices, the ability to make ethical and socially responsible decisions." The lesson Dan learned aligns with what Shad Helmstetter said, *"You cannot manage your life if you don't manage yourself. You cannot manage yourself if you don't manage your choices. Manage your choices, and you will manage your life."*

The dilemma of deciding between two Right choices

"Tell me about what fascinated you the most about making the right decisions as part of managing self?" Rafael inquired.

"I found the discussion on making decisions between two rights very tough," Dan revealed. "I learned that it is relatively easy to make decisions when confronted with two choices where one is wrong while the other is right." Rafael interjected, "That is understandable because it's not hard to choose right over wrong if someone is an ethical person. No struggle to make these kinds of choices."

Peter Shaffer lamented, *"Tragedy, for me, is not a conflict between right and wrong, but between two different kinds of right."* Rushworth Kidder, who talked about this extensively in his book entitled 'How Good People make Tough Choices' wrote, *"Tough choices, typically, are those pit one "right" value against another. That's true in every walk of life- corporate, professional, personal, civic, international, educational, religious, and the rest."*[57]

"What should be considered to choose one right choice from another right?" Rafael probed. "We talked about how having clarity of our values and their precedence makes choosing between two rights a little easier." Dan quickly replied.

Dan is on the mark. The only compass that could help us choose between two rights is our value-system. Otherwise, *"Tough choices don't always involve professional codes or criminal laws. Nor do they always involve big, headline-size issues. They often operate in areas that laws and regulations don't reach."*[58]

II. Assessments, Processes, and Tools
2.1. The three phases of the problem-solving process
As a manager of a huge project, Dan faces so many challenges on a consistent basis. This workshop gave him a straightforward and practical process he can use to solve problems creatively. "I found the six-step problem-solving process very helpful. I now understand how the process works, and the main actions necessary under each stage of the process."

"By the way, there are other problem-solving processes suggested by many experts," Rafael underscored and indicated, "Most of them are six or seven steps including monitoring and celebration. However, these six or seven steps can be categorized into three core stages:

    a) Understanding the problem,
    b) Deciding the right solution, and
    c) Implementing the solution." Rafael simplified the process. This agrees with Reynolds' and Tramel's viewpoint, *"Problem solving consists of three operations: Problem analysis, decision making, and action.'*[59]

"So far, which step or steps have you been considering and which ones have you neglected as you solve problems?" Rafael investigated. Dan acknowledged that he had been bypassing the steps within the first phase. "I always assumed that I knew my problems, and thus, rushed to fix them without full understanding and analyzing them. Now, I fully understand that the first couple of stages are where I should decide whether the challenge I'm facing is just a situation or a problem or a reality. I also need to gather as much data as my team, and I could find to understand and analyze the problem thoroughly before proceeding any further."

They spent several minutes on talking about the significant role critical thinking plays. Dan finally resolved. "Okay, I'll give myself and the team enough time to think relentlessly." Great decision. Voltaire proclaimed, *"No problem can withstand the assault of sustained thinking."*

Rafael further proposed, "During the brainstorming session, on top of giving enough time for critical and strategic thinking, it is paramount to encourage your team to think outside the box." Rafael advice aligns with what Albert Einstein said, *"We cannot solve our problems with the same thinking we used when we created them."*

For a couple of more minutes, they briefly talked about the need to come up with multiple options before choosing the best choice. Rafael added, "Prioritizing the alternative options is also critical." "Why is that?" Dan probed. "This enables you to quickly go to the second choice if in case the first line of solution fails to deliver," was Rafael's quick reply.

Before they concluded their discussion on the current theme, Rafael warned, "Don't take implementing the solution lightly." Dan reacted, "Why?" Rafael elaborated, "This is the stage where the going may get tougher. As we all know, when the rubber meets the road, things may not go the way we anticipated. That is why we should be flexible and make changes if necessary. During implementation, we may also come face-to-face with new problems that may require us to start all over again to address these newly found problems."

2.2. Ladder of Inference

The tool called 'The Ladder of Inference' intrigued Dan. He couldn't wait to share it with Rafael. With great excitement, Dan proclaimed, "This is one of the most impactful tools I got from the program thus far."

This tool wasn't new to Rafael. "When I was introduced to this tool for the first time, I was shocked. I went back to review some of the biased actions I took because I had selected those data that aligned with my belief-system. Speaking of belief-system, our existing beliefs play a great role in determining which data we look for. The data may not be accurate nor adequate. Regardless, we add meaning to it, assume things, reach a conclusion, and then take actions."

"What about you?" Rafael inquired. Dan came up with some scenarios to illustrate how he used to quickly climb his imaginary ladder in his brain to make quick assumptions, conclusions, decisions, and finally actions without considering sufficient data at the bottom of the ladder.

Admitting that we all may climb this imaginary ladder quickly more than we would like to admit, Rafael emphasized that there is always a risk to make wrong decisions based on misguided beliefs. Dan agreed and remarked, "As far as our ladder controls us to make incorrect decisions that are not based on adequate data, we learned that we cannot manage self. We are slaves of our brain, and thus, we fail to achieve personal mastery."

Dan's remark is in line with what Bernard Both said, "*We don't realize how many of our fixed views of the world are based on limited samples of reality.*"[60]

Once they talked about the proper way of climbing the imaginary ladder, they deliberated on how to climb down the ladder when necessary, and also help others to do the same. However, Rafael, cautioned, "We should be very careful not to tell people in their face that they are climbing 'a ladder', let alone to ask them to come down and get more data and facts. Rather, we should ask probing questions to help them come down willingly without feeling judged, and 'dragged down by force.'"

Rafael's warning triggered Dan to laugh. He then jumped in and asked. "Can you give me a couple of examples?" Rafael used the opportunity to role play with Dan and demonstrated on how to bring people down from the top of the ladder systematically by asking the right questions.

By the way, organizational psychologist Chris Argyris was the one who first put forward this common mental pathway known as 'The Ladder of Inference.' However, Peter Senge popularized it in 'The Fifth Discipline: The Art and Practice of the Learning Organization' book.

III. Action item
On the top of Dan's to-do list is strictly following the six-step problem-solving process to address a couple of issues he has already identified. "Solving problems successfully requires understanding this process, and I'd like to use it in every opportunity I'll get starting from a couple of lingering problems that we currently have." Upon Rafael's request, Dan enlisted the existing problems his team faces. They brainstormed together on how to tackle them using the problem-solving process.

Rafael has been using some tools to supplement the problem-solving process. He decided to share these tools thinking that Dan might try some of them. "I've been using problem-solving tools such as decision tree, cause-effect analysis, mind mapping, and so on." Afterward, Rafael briefly explained how he had been using these tools.

Dan found some of these tools very helpful. He decided to try some of them right away. Rafael encouraged Dan to reach out if he needs help.

"Do you have any immediate action you would like to take concerning decision making?" Rafael asked. Dan admitted that he over depended on his intuition as he made decisions. "Because of my busy schedule, I didn't take enough time and effort when I made so many decisions in the past. From now on, nonetheless, I plan to make informed decisions based on the lessons I gained from Workshop four."

"Who blames you for making quick decisions on the fly?" Rafael sympathized. "It happens to all of us as we find ourselves under pressure at multiple fronts. But, we should discipline ourselves to avoid making hasty decisions without doing our homework."

The authors of 'Outsmart Your Own Biases' stressed that we are too far from making quality decisions when we are pressured, stressed, and fatigued. They argued, *"We're mentally, emotionally, and physically spent. We cope by relying even more heavily on intuition and less on careful reasoning. Decision making becomes faster and simpler, but quality often suffers.'*[61]

Before concluding this session, Rafael decided to share with Dan a very vital point. "By the way, decision-making is not always about making a decision on what we must do. It's also what we must not do."

After giving some personal examples where he decided to stop doing certain things, Rafael challenged Dan to take the time to identify some of the things he should stop doing.

In this regard, Peter Drucker was quoted as saying, *"We spend a lot of time teaching leaders what to do. We don't spend enough time teaching leaders what to stop. Half the leaders I have met don't need to learn what to do. They need to learn what to stop."*

Summary

As we advance in life, we face problems that stand in our way preventing us from moving forward. Self-mastery is unthinkable without the soft skill to turn problems into opportunities on a consistent basis. When we become skillful in resolving problems, we become in charge. We have control over what is going on around us. However, this soft skill is necessary beyond personal mastery. To tap into our collective potential, pursue our corporate goals, and realize our collective dreams, we need this life skill. It is going to be one of our competitive advantages as we work with and lead others. People (employers, clients, voters, etc.) desperately look all the time and everywhere, for individuals who swim with 'sharks' (tough problems) without being eaten alive by 'the sharks.' They search for leaders and team members who have the ability to solve problems and overcome challenges with confidence, grace, and those who deliver results based on sound, wise, and farsighted decisions without violating laws, rules, and without compromising their core values. One of the most important steps to pay closer attention to solve problems creatively is making sure to make sound and ethical decisions. The latter is critical to manage and master self. However, it's not that hard to choose right over wrong if someone is a decent person. What is challenging is choosing between two or more rights. The good news is that if we have clarity about our values, we could be able to make tough choices such as between two rights. Remember one thing! Before you're allowed to solve other people's and organizations' problems and make decisions on their behalves, you should first solve your own problems and make sound decisions within your private space. The problem solving and decision making soft skill you develop as you work on your personal mastery is going to enable you become successful as you get along with, and lead others.

Recapping Part I

In part one of the Soft Skills Development program, participants were introduced to new concepts, approaches, tools, and took a couple of assessments that aimed at empowering them to master self.

From the evaluation forms, Joe and his team learned that many of the participants had assumed, before joining the program, that they had a good grasp of who they really are and thought that they had some forms of personal mastery. Some of the participants admitted that they hadn't prepared for what they found out from the results of the assessments they had taken so far. A couple of them commented that the assessments revealed so many important blind spots. Dan was one of such participants.

Overall, however, participants are glad that they joined this program. They are pleased that they attended the last four workshops that equipped them to increase their self-awareness, the ability to manage self, and attain self-mastery.

Dan found the four workshops very revealing and informative. For the first time in his life, he could be able to appreciate the importance of personal mastery to succeed in his career and become an effective leader. Moreover, as an introvert, Dan found the past four topics relatively easy.

Nevertheless, he anticipated that the second part of the program is going to be a little challenging for him. Understandably, part two requires him to come out of his comfort zone. Developing personal mastery is just one of the most essential ingredients to succeed. In and of itself, self-mastery is nothing until it's used to get along with and influence others successfully.

The good news is that Dan decided to read and learn more about the next four soft skills. He wanted to give himself a head start. That was a smart decision since the lacks of these soft skills were the main reasons why he was required to participate in this program.

Part II: Getting Along with Others

"Coming together is a beginning; keeping together is progress; working together is success." **Henry Ford**

Holistic self-awareness is a significant input to getting along

- Success in any endeavor is a protracted but a rewarding journey.
- Self-mastery is the beginning of this important expedition.
- It's the foundation of the knowledge and the mastery one develops in his/her private world would be used to get along with others in the workplace.
- Besides, holistic self-awareness, as discussed in part one, entails awareness about others and the environment. This awareness is a great input to get along with others.
- Thus, the second part of the program gave participants another opportunity to apply the knowledge they acquired from the previous part of the program as they work on their soft skills that are aimed at enabling them to get along with others.

Getting along to advance our shared goals

In the leading quote above, Henry Ford- the man who transformed the way humanity lives on earth, clearly showed the continuum of getting along with others. Coming to form a team is the beginning of a very long voyage. The ultimate goal of coming together is whether the group works together and gets along to advance the common goals.

The second part of this book summarizes the four workshops that were incorporated in the second part of the Soft Skills Development program. Joe began this part by quickly summarizing the main points from the previous part. Next, he continued to use the same analogy he used at the beginning of Part I.

Trying solo has dire prices to pay

Joe recounted, "We talked about how self-discipline is critical to climbing Mount Everest. We acknowledged that aspirant climbers must exercise, and equip themselves before attempting to climb and stand on the peak of the most brutal and unforgiving mountain in the world. We created an analogy between the self-discipline one needs to develop to climb Mount Everest with Self-mastery to achieve substantial results."

He continued, "Self-discipline, however, is the beginning of a successful venture to conquer the world's tallest mountain. This task requires getting along with others. No one dared to climb Everest alone. Climbers either teamed up with other climbers or hired enough guides. Likewise, achieving top results in any field and industry demands to get along with others."

Whoever violates this principle pays dire prices. A good example is a British mountaineer- Maurice Wilson. He had an indomitable willpower. His toughness was demonstrated when he was a soldier during World War I where he was wounded and recognized as a war hero. Wilson also flew alone from Britain to India, which made him a legend. This achievement was extraordinary for a novice pilot who got 19 hours flying experience[62].

Building a small plane, for the sole purpose of flying it to Mount Everest, he crash-landed it on the upper slopes of Everest. Initially, Wilson endeavored to climb Everest solo but failed. He returned and took two guides for his second attempt. Unfortunately, he didn't listen when they recommended him to abort his second expedition because of bad weather. He stubbornly continued solo and paid the ultimate price. He died alone. [63]

Attaining a meaningful success is too big for a single person

On the other hand, recently, I watched an amazing video where ants teamed up to drag a huge millipede to their dwelling place. What would have happened if an ant attempted to move this giant creature by herself? That was what Maurice tried to attain- bold and courageous but reckless endeavor. Several of the tasks we try to tackle to achieve success are too big for a single person. We need to team-up and get along with others.

When we develop the soft skills necessary to work with others, we could be able to accomplish great things, which we couldn't even if we have attained personal mastery. With self-mastery plus the ability to get along with others, we could meet many seemingly impossible and daunting goals in the neighborhood, at work, and in the marketplace.

Getting along is easier said than done?

Joe further pointed out, "The growth you have achieved to attain personal mastery continues to help you as you work with others, and also you gain more self-mastery as you collaborate with others." And he paused to see if there was any question or comment from the group.

Dan had been relatively comfortable so far since part one was about self-mastery. This part was an unfamiliar territory for him. If you may remember the discussion between Susan and Paul, she acknowledged that Dan had a relatively good handle when it comes to managing himself. Dan's struggle was the inability to get along with and lead his team. He firmly believed that as far as everyone is doing his/her part well, there wouldn't be any problem in a team.

He is a loner who performs wonders in his private space and as he works alone. But, where does that get him? What Dan missed was that what so ever extraordinary talent and dedication he may have, he couldn't take his career to the next level without getting along with others. Dan tried to ride alone, like Wilson, and he got stuck. The good thing about Dan was that he got down on the 'mountain', and decided to regroup.

Of course, Dan was not yet hundred percent convinced why he should make lots of efforts from his side to get along at GHR. That was why he remarked, "I understand what you're saying. Getting along is vital. But, there is nothing you could do unless others are willing to play their share."

Downsides of working with other

Joe wasn't aware of Dan's story and why he was there. He was, however, cognizant of the attitude of many managers who use this the same reason as an excuse, which in turn prevents them from taking responsibilities and making proactive efforts. Regardless, Joe didn't want to be dismissive. "True, it's not easy. Not only that, getting along with others, has downsides." Joe showed sympathy.

"What are some of the disadvantages you guys have discovered as you work in a team?" Joe asked the class. Joe decided to take the team somewhere before answering Dan's question.

Edgar smiled and commented. "The least, it slows you down. It takes you more time to communicate, collaborate, and work with others. If you do it alone, it may take you a fraction of that time."

Kofi remembered that they had already covered the very reason in the previous part. And thus, he reminded the class, "It is challenging to work with others since we all have, as we found out during our discussions so far, varying interest, priority, and personality types."

Kelley added one more challenge to the list. "We also experience conflict as we work with others. Dealing with conflicts requires investing additional time and energy, which could have been used to advance our shared goals."

Complimenting those who shared their thoughts, Joe continued. "These and many other reasons make getting along and working with others challenging. However, it is one of those things you cannot live without." Then, he reminded the class that in the coming four workshops they are going to cover those critical soft skills necessary to improve their ability to get along with others.

Joe stressed. "Developing these skills empowers you to overcome the challenges you have already mentioned. It enables you to create a harmonious, safe, conducive, and inclusive environment where diverse team members come together to accomplish great things."

Should we need to get along with everyone?

Dan wasn't ready to let his question shoved aside. He raised his hand. Without waiting for Joe's permission, he moved on and rephrased his question. "I understand that we need to work with others but do we really need to get along with all people, especially with those who fail to fulfill their obligations and with whom you don't share the same values?" Dan was wondering why he should get along with everybody. Until that point in his life, he had been picky. He selected his friends and people he would like to work with very carefully.

James quickly responded saying that he doesn't need to get along with someone he just met on the road as he walks or rides a train. He continued. "I'll be nice and respect everyone that I meet on my way, but here we are talking about people who matter to us- people with whom we spend more than 8 hours per day for five days a week."

"Though we treat people with whom we work with better than others, still should we compromise who we are and what we believe in for the sake of getting along in the workplace? I don't think so." Kelley disagreed with James and shared Dan's sentiment.

Many hands went up. Two to three participants were talking at the same time. Murmurs filled the room.

Joe calmed the class and shared his perspective, "Getting along as much as we could with anyone and everywhere, when possible, is appropriate. In the workplace, however, getting along with others may require us to give and take. These don't necessarily include those things that matter to us the most such as denying who we truly are as a person, or compromising ours and the values of our organization."

Joe was on the mark. In her forward to the book 'Get Along', Sharon Fountain noted, *"Getting along is not about giving in or giving up. It's about claiming our personal power while we build positive connections with others.'*[64]

After a brief pause to give the class a chance to process what he just said, Joe indicated the key reason why we should get along with others regardless of so many things that we might not share and agree with others. He explained, "We aren't choosing to get along because it's easy nor feels good all the time.

- We cannot master everything.
- We cannot be self-sufficient alone.
- We need other people to complement us, and that is why we need to develop the soft skills necessary to get along so that we could achieve success."

While displaying a friendly smile and laughter, Martha interjected. "Hey, people! Getting along doesn't mean we should appease others, and also giving in all the time. We should create a win-win situation where everyone plays its part to get along, to give and take. We should maintain our uniqueness while still respecting the unique nature of others. As for me, getting along is a two-way street."

"That is a smart approach," Joe admired Martha's point of view and continued, "With increased holistic self-awareness, not only we know our uniqueness, but also recognize the uniqueness of others and their unique contributions toward achieving our common goals. This awareness should make getting along with others easier. With the soft skills we're going to cover, we will learn how to get along by playing teamwork, communicating effectively, resolving conflicts, and working with diverse people in the workplace."

"I don't need to get along with everyone all the time, do I?" Edgar asked, and answered his own question. "I only see some of my team members during staff meetings or some department level events. However, there're a few I meet every day including my boss, a couple of team members, and peers with whom I closely work with on a daily basis. Getting along with these individuals is a must for me, and therefore, I go the extra mile to make sure that I'm a pleasant person to work with."

Edgar nailed it. We must go the extra mile to get along with others. Of course, if our desire is to succeed in what we do. As H.E. Luccock declared, *"No one can whistle a symphony. It takes a whole orchestra."*

Time ran out. Joe must move to the content of Workshop five. Therefore, he appreciated the participation so far and went forward concluded the introduction part of Part II of the program. He then explained the four soft skills that were designed to help participants excel in getting along with others.

Getting along model:
Displaying the graphics below, Joe began describing each stage of the process of getting along very briefly. And, he opened the floor to questions. It was a very interactive discussion. Because of space, I cannot narrate everything. However, let me quickly summarize the main points for you:

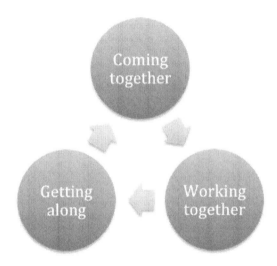

Fig. 2: The Getting Along Process

Coming Together:
- Nothing significant can be done alone in isolation. We need to come together with others.

    Mother Teresa, who mastered getting along, said it very well: *"You can do what I cannot do. I can do what you cannot do. Together we can do great."*
- Getting along with others begins with coming together.
- A team is formed when two or more people come together.

- The questions someone should ask in the coming together stage include but not limited to:

    1. What team should I join or establish?
    2. If the team is already formed, ask these questions: In which stage of the team formation is this team? And what should we do to take it to the next level?
    3. In both cases, whether the team is new or existing, what is the goal of the team?
    4. What are the roles of all team members including my self?
    5. And more.

- Workshop five- Playing Teamwork provides the necessary insights, processes, tools, and techniques to become a great team player ready to come together with others to attain common goals.

Knowing the diverse background of participants, Joe further clarified, "Some of you may be leaders of your team while some of you may be members of a team. Either way, the discussion we are going to have today is going to help you become a great team player regardless of your role."

Working Together:
- Once we come together, the challenge is staying there and working together. The latter requires developing some soft skills.
- The will to come together, seeking partnership, and forming team is the beginning of a great ride. Working together is where we harvest the results of coming together.

In his book "Winning With People", John C. Maxwell argued, *"Working together increases the odds of winning together."*

- Whether you are the team's leader or not, as you work with others, you need to be an effective communicator in order to succeed working with others. And Workshop six, Communicating Effectively, provides some important insights and tools that aim at empowering participants to become impactful communicators.
- As we work with others, we also need to promote diversity within our team and embrace inclusiveness. This requires creating a safe atmosphere where people from diverse races, ethnicities, genders, choices, cultures, and priorities work together to advance the mission of the team and its goals. Workshop seven covers Promoting Diversity and Embracing Inclusiveness.

- As we work together in a team, there are always conflicts. We need to develop the ability to manage conflicts properly to get along with others. And Workshop eight covers Turning Conflicts into Opportunities.

Getting along:
- Achieving personal mastery is the foundation to master getting along.
- Self-mastery is half victory. It should be complemented with getting along if our desire is to succeed in what we do.
- Getting along, like self-mastery, is a state.
- Getting along requires coming, and working together with others as prerequisites.
- This state is a by-product of developing the four soft skills included in part two of the program.
- Getting along has many benefits. There are also dire prices when it is absent.

In their book "Get Along," Arnold Sanow and Sandra Strauss talked about one of the benefits of getting along, *"Getting along is energizing. We thrive in climates that cultivate the connecting spirit and the excellence it inspires. On the flip side, disharmony disrupts and destroys, creating chaos that crushes cooperation, creativity, and our spirits."*[65]

- The getting along process is a cycle. As new team members join the team, the team passes through the process, again and again, starting from coming together, then to working together, and getting along.

Joe also showed participants the link between getting along, and leading others- the next part of the program: "Mastering getting along not only empowers you to succeed as you work with others but also equips you to lead others successfully because the soft skills that you develop at this stage will help you to:
- Form great teams, understand your role as a leader, identify your team members' roles, and needs. The latter is vital to inspire your team and achieve extraordinary success.
- Communicate your messages, and also skillfully listen your people.
- Lead team members from diverse backgrounds.
- Skillfully resolve conflicts that may arise within and/or outside of your team.
- Empower your team to understand their roles as team members, train them to communicate effectively, understand the importance of

diversity and inclusion in the workplace, and equip them to turn conflict into opportunities."

Finally, Joe displayed the four soft skills on a slide and moved on to cover the first topic:
1. Playing Teamwork,
2. Communicating Effectively,
3. Promoting Diversity and Embracing Inclusiveness, and
4. Turning Conflicts into Opportunities.

Soft Skill 5: Playing Teamwork

"Teamwork is the ability to work together toward a common vision. The ability to direct individual accomplishment toward organizational objectives. It is the fuel that allows common people to attain uncommon results."
Andrew Carnegie

We all are part of a team somewhere

For most of us, teamwork is a part of everyday life. Whether it's at home, in our community, or at work, or in the marketplace, we are often expected to be a functional part of a performing team. Teamwork is a household name.

Andrew Carnegie was one of the greatest industrialists of the late 19th C. In the above statement, he explained the meaning of teamwork very articulately. He showed that playing teamwork is an important soft skill to achieve common goals, and attain extraordinary success.

Teamwork isn't an easy task

Almost all organizations understand the significance of having effective teams to accomplish their mission. But, building a winning team is not an easy task. There are so many factors, which complicate building and sustaining a winning team that works like a well-oiled machine. Factors such as team members' diverse:

- Personality traits,
- Preferences,
- Styles,
- Upbringing, and
- Cultural background.

Another factor that further complicates building winning teams is when all team members are not physically located in one location. These days, almost all organizations including GHR have virtual teams. Thanks to globalization, the Internet, and other latest communication technologies, as far as we have common causes, today, we can create movements, form our own tribes, and bring changes, which weren't possible a couple of decades ago.

However, building and leading a virtual team is very challenging. The challenge becomes severe when the team over depends on technologies, platforms, and neglect the most important human factors. Seth Godin warned, *"The Internet is just a tool, an easy way to enable some tactics. The real power of tribes has nothing to do with the Internet and everything to do with people."*[66]

What does it take to play teamwork?

I never met anyone who argued against the need to have strong teams to attain extraordinary things. Most people all over the world understand the critical roles effective teams play for collective success. Regardless, very few take proactive steps to develop the necessary attributes and continually demonstrate the commitment for the well-being and proper functioning of their teams.

The starting place for getting along is to develop the soft skill ability that enables us to play teamwork. Playing teamwork requires developing the right:

- Attitude,
- Emotion, and
- Continuous enthusiasm, which demands to generate lots of energy on a consistent basis.

Dysfunctions of a team

If you observe an organization that is thriving, it's because of the success of the team behind it. Likewise, if you witness an organization that struggles, it's due to the team that runs it. That is why the author of "The Five Dysfunctions of a Team", Patrick Lencioni contended that teamwork is the ultimate competitive advantage. Quoting his friend- the founder of a billion dollars company, he wrote, *"If you could get all the people in an organization rowing in the same direction, you could dominate any industry, in any market, against any competition, at any time."*[67]

I. Key lessons
1.1. Working with others isn't easy but mandatory

With a frown face, Dan began. "Before the start of the program, I found working with others too much work, especially with those who aren't scientists."

Rafael chimed in. "It's true that working with others, especially with people with whom you don't have so many things in common, isn't easy."

"Don't get me wrong," Dan interjected very quickly to avoid any misunderstanding. "I understood that people should come together to accomplish great things." Rafael nodded his head and asked a follow-up question, "What did you dislike?" a brief pause. Dan recollected his thoughts and shared. "I used to complain why I should be responsible for other people's responsibilities? Why don't they take care of themselves? Aren't they grown ups and should know better?"

"What made you now to make a shift," Rafael wondered. Dan confessed, "In this workshop- credit to Joe, there was a discussion at the beginning that answered many of my doubts and gave me some strong reasons why the benefits of coming together as a team outweigh its drawbacks. This justification, in turn, convinced me to put some extra efforts to become a better team player."

Dan made a huge change of attitude. If you may remember, Dan had complained to Susan and Paul about how hard it is to work with others. He even said, "I don't have time and the mood to cuddle my staff and those with whom I interact."

"That is true," Rafael asserted. He further noted, "From my own experience, playing your parts to create and sustain an effective team where each member plays its unique role isn't an easy task. The efforts, however, worthwhile since having such a team has so many great advantages at many levels."

"By the way, I had attended similar workshops on the same theme previously." Rafael was eager to hear what made this workshop special compared to the other workshops Dan attended.

Dan pondered. "I found those seminars in the past unrealistic and even manipulative. I felt that they painted as if teamwork is easy, and what is required from each member is to drop their uniqueness and be like everybody else to get along. In this workshop, I learned that working with others isn't easy but mandatory to succeed in getting along. Besides, now, I understand that I don't need to drop who I'm to team up with others and achieve extraordinary success."

1.2. Insignificant-Incomplete-Insufficient
Moving to the next lesson, Dan began. "I learned that I'm too insignificant without teaming up with others. Before attending this workshop, somehow I had a very inflated opinion of myself. I thought that I could realize my potential and succeed by myself with minimal help from others."

"What made you change your mind?" Rafael asked. "In one of the small group discussions, we spent some time to talk about the insignificance of a single person. At the end of the discussion, we came up with the acronym 3Is to justify the need to work with others."

Rafael inquired, "What are these 3Is?" Dan enlisted, "We concluded that one person is:

1. **Insignificant**. Too small in size to matter.
2. **Incomplete.** Too inadequate to complete significant undertakings by itself alone.
3. **Insufficient.** Too deficient to be all things necessary to accomplish extraordinary things.

He liked the 3Is so much that Rafael took note and repeatedly read them loudly. Since he found this lesson very critical, he stayed on it a little more. Accordingly, he shared some examples in his own life how he has become better, achieved more, and advanced faster because of accepting this principle at the early stage of his career.

Helen Keller was right when she said, *"Alone we can do little, together, we can do so much."* John Maxwell too decided to put, in his book 'The 17 Indisputable Laws of Teamwork', *'One is too small a number to achieve greatness'* as number one indisputable laws of teamwork.

1.3. Characteristics of successful teams

"There are hundreds of characteristics of successful teams. This workshop enabled me to zoom in and focus on the most important factors that determine the success of my team," said Dan. He then looked at Rafael and noticed that he was listening attentively. Hence, Dan enlisted the five common characteristics of successful teams shared by most participants:

- Well-defined goals.
- Clarity of roles.
- Participation and involvement.
- Effective communication between the leader and members, and among team members.
- Trust.

Rafael acknowledged the vital roles these five elements play to create a winning team. He used his high school football team to illustrate their importance further. "I still remember this team whenever I think of successful teams." Detailing what made his team successful, he showed Dan how the five features he mentioned earlier contributed toward the success of his high school team. Rafael then wanted Dan to pick a team that he was a part of that succeeded, and what made it successful.

Once they exchanged their takes on Dan's favorite team, Rafael inquired which factors are present, and which are missing from Dan's current team. "I think, the first three are present, but the last two seem missing," Dan spoke with a quiet voice.

Though both factors are crucial, knowing very well the vital place of trust in teams, Rafael pointed out that the lack of trust should concern Dan the most. "If you see a team succeeding and advancing, there is a high level of trust among team members. If you witness any team that struggles, it is most likely that there is no trust at all or trust has been eroded."

Jim Temme enumerated in his book 'Team Power: How to build and grow successful teams' the key traits of successful teams. Three out of the thirteen key traits are similar to the four elements identified in the class:

- *Trust,*
- *Basic Communication Skills,*
- *Authentic participation, and*
- *Goals and Objectives.*[68]

1.4. Without trust, one cannot get along

"I'm glad that you have already emphasized the significance of trust." Dan jumped to share the last lesson he learned from the workshop. "I quickly recognized the vital role trust plays to have a well-functioning team more than other factors."

Wondering to know, Rafael asked, "What made you reach this conclusion?" Dan quickly responded. "It became clear to me that with increased trust, it's going to be easier to work on the other elements and bring quick improvements. However, if trust lacks, it doesn't matter having the other factors in place. It's going to be hard to function as a cohesive and successful team without the presence of trust."

Dan pinned it. In 'The Five Dysfunctions of a Team', the author declared, *"Trust lies at the heart of a functioning, cohesive team. Without it, teamwork is all but impossible."*

To double check whether Dan is aware of the sources of mistrust that exist in his team, Rafael probed, "What is the level of trust your team has on you?" Dan had never thought about it. "I'm not sure," Dan responded with a broad smile, and continued, "But, I believe that I'm a trustworthy person."

Rafael was straightforward. "Even if you think you are trustworthy, you have to earn their trust." Dan interjected and asked. "How do I know whether they believe in me or not?" Rafael jumped in quickly. "If they aren't vulnerable, take risks, and open with you, they may not trust you yet. It doesn't matter whether we are trustworthy or not. It's all about whether others perceive us dependable."

Lencioni wrote, *"Trust is the confidence among team members that their peers' intentions are good, and that there is no reason to be protective or careful around the group. In essence, teammates must get comfortable being vulnerable with one another."*[69]

To figure out whether Dan has been proactive or not, Rafael investigated, "What have you done to earn their trust so far?" Dan conceded that he hadn't done that much in this regard.

In the next few minutes, Rafael shared his experience on how he had been building trust proactively, and the results he has achieved. He finally emphasized the importance of trust not only to get along but also to influence others successfully.

Almost all leadership experts agree that trust is a prerequisite to succeed in one's leadership. For instance, John C. Maxwell in his book 'The 21 Irrefutable Laws of Leadership' recognized that Trust is the foundation of leadership and one of the laws- The Law of Solid Ground. He wrote, *"If you boil relationships down to the most important element, it's always going to be trust- not leadership, value, partnership, or anything else. If you don't have trust, your relationship is in trouble."*[70]

Likewise, the authors of 'The Leadership Challenge' James Kouzes and Barry Posner emphasized, *"Without trust you cannot lead. Without trust you cannot get people to believe in you or in each other. Without trust you cannot accomplish extraordinary things."*[71]

By the way, long ago, I stopped buying- let alone reading, books that talk about organizational success but failed to emphasize the importance of trust. Books that leave out, neglect, or undermine the significance of trust for team success, are either outdated or irrelevant. Trust is the glue that holds a winning team.

II. Assessments, Processes, and Tools
2.1. The 360-degree assessment
"At the start of the program, we were asked to take the 360-degree assessment. This assessment takes time since it requires soliciting feedback from superiors, peers, self, and subordinates. I'm still sending reminders," Dan shared.

As Rafael had sent and also responded to several 360-degree assessments, he was familiar with this assessment. He assured Dan that he is going to get comprehensive information once it's completed. Rafael encouraged him to share with him when he gets the results since it helps him to tailor his mentoring. Dan agreed gladly.

2.2. The four personality types

"The people that I interact and communicate with may fall into one of the four personality types," Dan shared one of the tools they talked about in class. "What are these types and their preferences?" Rafael asked. Dan then enlisted and briefly described each type:

1. "Directors (They want to get things done)
2. Thinkers (They want to get things right)
3. Relators (They want things to have human touch)
4. Socializers (They want to get noticed)" Dan is referring to the work of Tony Alessandra[72].

"How about your personality type?" Rafael was eager to know Dan's type. "I'm a Director." Rafael cautioned. "Of course, some people may oscillate between personalities and border with more than one personality types."

He then asked, "How do you plan to apply this knowledge?" "Understanding the personality types of the people I interact with allows me to understand their preferences better, communicate accordingly, and ultimately get along successfully." Dan responded confidently.

I frequently mention this tool as I train project managers. I remind them that project management is people management. You cannot lead people without knowing their personality types. The latter reveals their preferences and interests- Their sweet spots. Your interaction should be tailored according to their individual personality type and preference.

2.3. Team formation process

"This workshop equipped me with so many great ideas on how to get along and play my share for the success of my team. The team formation lifecycle was one of the tools I found very helpful. It gave me a clear picture on how a team evolves." By the way, Dan was talking about Bruce Tuckman's team formation process.

Rafael asked, "In which stage is your team?" "Storming," Dan didn't take any time to think. He knew it very well. To make sure Dan fully understood the process, Rafael asked him to explain each stage briefly:

- **Forming**. "This is the stage where the right team members are recruited; the team's goal, objectives, and priorities are set; team members are clear about their responsibilities, and so on." Rafael inquired, "Looking back retrospectively, do you think that your team passed this stage properly?" Dan's response was brief. "I now admit that the problems that are bogging down my team right now are the results of not passing this stage appropriately…"

- **Storming**. "Once a team is formed and begins working together, issues may crop up, and the team may find itself in trouble and experience storing." "By the way," Rafael underscored, "This stage is the most challenging one. Many teams get stuck or get disbanded at this stage. They couldn't make it pass this stage. Even those who got a chance to unstuck may continue to struggle for a while if they failed to handle this stage appropriately." Dan marveled and asked, "What makes this stage so challenging?" Rafael explained. "Many team members and leaders don't realize that experiencing storms is natural until team members understand one another and begin to get along. It's normal to face resistances when the rubber meets the road. Since many think that it is abnormal, they don't take proactive measures to weather the storm and take their team to the next level." Dan didn't hide that he was too the victim of this mentality. "Up until now, I had been asking why my team has been experiencing storming right after I thought we had formed a great team…"

- **Norming**. "Once teams weather the storm, they enter into normalcy. Reality sets in. They begin to embrace their differences that surfaced due to the fact that they are diverse with different backgrounds, preferences, priorities, personality types, and so on. They reach consensus or, at least, develop a common understanding to tolerate one another, rally behind the common goal, regroup, and reenergize themselves to move forward as one coherent team…"

- **Performing**. "This is the most envies stage. The goal of every team is to arrive at this place where the team begins delivering outstanding results." Rafael recommended, "Dan, your goal should be to quickly move your team from the current storming stage to the performing stage. But, bringing the team to this stage may not be enough to perform like a well-oiled machine. It takes also sustaining the team and remaining in this stage until the project is completed successfully…"

- **Adjourning**. "Once the team accomplishes its goal, it disbands or commences a new cycle with a different goal (s)…"

2.4. Giving and receiving feedback

"I found giving and receiving feedback as a powerful tool to get along and succeed in playing teamwork." Dan acknowledged. Rafael solicited, "What are some of the lessons you learned about feedback giving?" Dan shared some of the lessons he learned:

- **Finding the right time and place**. "When and where we offer our feedback determines its outcome," Dan pointed out. Rafael nodded and added, "Choosing the right atmosphere and timing is vital for your feedback to work."

- **Creating a positive environment**. "It's a very good idea to always begin with a positive tone. Everyone has some strengths and things that are going very well," said Dan. "I concur with you," Rafael agreed and continued, "Acknowledging the strengths of the person and what has been working well before you talk about what went wrong, weaknesses, and limitations of the individual are very essential."

- **Stating the issue very clearly**. Dan indicated, "Clearly stating what isn't working and what must change is also very important."

- **Being specific**. "We shouldn't just use generic terms and beat around the bush." Rafael commented, "That is right. Giving effective feedback requires being specific and giving some examples and certain cases when appropriate." Dan wanted Rafael to expand on this, "Do you mind to give me an example?" Rafael was glad to provide a simple illustration, "For instance, if you would like to tell someone a feedback about his listening ability, give some instances where he listened well: You listen well. I know that because, for instance, in our team meeting last week you asked thoughtful questions, nodded your head, and maintained eye contact."

- **Providing some options.** "If the feedback requires making changes," Dan stated, "We should give the person the opportunity to suggest some ways to improve the situation. If the individual doesn't have anything to suggest or if we have better options, we should provide some options." Rafael nodded.

- **Offering support**. Dan concluded. "Once we reach agreement on how to resolve the issue or improve it, we should ask the person any help he/she may need from us. If the issue requires monitoring and arranging subsequent meetings, work out the details with the person."

"The ultimate goal of feedback giving is a performance improvement." Rafael reminded Dan and cautioned, "We shouldn't give feedback to flatter or belittle someone. We should master giving tailor-made feedback that empowers others to improve their performance."

The power of self-criticism and begging for feedback

Before concluding this section, Rafael encouraged Dan to conduct self-criticism, and also solicit feedback from others proactively. "To be a successful team player, we need to perform self-criticism to evaluate our performance, and also beg others to give us honest feedback," Dan admitted that he hadn't developed the habit of self-criticism. Wanting to know how Rafael conducts self-criticism, he asked him to demonstrate for him. Rafael gave a couple of scenarios to show how it is done.

Once they covered self-criticism, they moved on to talk about begging for feedback. Rafael emphasized that seeking feedback from others helps us to uncover our blind spots. Dan appreciated the value of proactively soliciting feedback from others. He remarked, "You're right. Who knows, there may be one or two blind spots that might have prevented me from excelling in life and my career. I should be intentional about seeking others' feedback."

"Yes, you got it!" Rafael almost jumped out of his seat. He knows how this habit has benefited him tremendously. He reinforced what Dan said, "We may be uncovering a blind spot or two away to take our career to the next height, and beseeching people to give us feedback is the gateway to go to the next level."

III. Action item
Generating trust

"The immediate action I'd like to take is to start generating trust," Dan decided. "But, I'm not sure whether it works yet." He was tentative. Assuring Dan that he isn't the only one, Rafael informed him that many leaders think that trust is something that happens, and therefore, they don't play proactive roles to generate it intentionally. He encouraged him to be proactive and take some measures. He also suggested some of the steps he should take based on his own experience.

Stephen R. Covey in his book 'The Speed of Trust' wrote, *"There is a lot we can do about it [creating trust]. We can increase trust."*[73] Covey proposed 13 behaviors that enhance trust. Let me just pick one of the behaviors Covey suggested, which is very different than the rest of the twelve behaviors- Extend Trust. According to Covey, extending trust creates reciprocity. He noted, *"When you trust people, other people tend to trust you in return. Additionally (and ironically), extending trust is one of the best ways to create trust when it's not there."*[74]

Colin Powell, in his book 'It Worked For Me: In life and leadership', wrote, *"If you trust them [your people], they will trust you, and those bonds will strengthen over time. They will work hard to make sure you do well. They will protect you and cover you. They will take care of you."*[75] Trust is a two-way street. Temme wrote, *"Trust begets trust. If you want others to trust you, then trust them unless they give you good reason not to."*[76]

Summary

Playing teamwork is one of the essential soft skills we all need if our desire is to get along with others and succeed in what we do. What so ever great our talent and experience are, we are too insignificant to make any meaningful impact and achieve extraordinary success without working with others and playing our share in the success of the team. To play our share, we need to be aware of the process of team formation. We should know where our team is in the team formation lifecycle and our contribution to take it to the next stage. We should also recognize the key characteristics of successful teams and the steps we should take to create and sustain a winning team. Understanding the vital role trust plays is also critical for us to play teamwork. Most importantly, we need to be proactive in generating trust. Without being perceived as a trustworthy member of a team, we cannot play teamwork and contribute our share to the success of our team. Giving feedback artfully, and constantly begging for feedback also contribute toward playing teamwork, and in turn, getting along with others successfully.

Soft Skill 6: Communicating Effectively

"Effective communication is the number one tool to succeed in any endeavor. Effective communication determines whether people vote for you, write you a check, invest in what you do, buy your services and products." **Les Brown**

A team that doesn't communicate well perishes

Let me quickly refresh your memory:

- One of the soft skills necessary during the second stage of the getting along process (Working Together), is communicating effectively.
- The first stage (Coming Together) and believing in the importance of teamwork is the beginning of a long but rewarding journey.
- Team members should communicate well as they work together for the team to function properly and meet its goals.

We communicate more than we would like to admit

Unfortunately, communication has been given less emphasis. Many of us don't think that it needs some extra work. Though we all communicate more than we would like to admit, we don't invest enough time, energy, and resources to work on our communication abilities.

Speaking of communicating more than we would like to admit, one of MIT surveys I mentioned earlier showed that even Scientists and Engineers who are in technical fields spend the majority of their time communicating. If my memory serves me correctly, closer to 70 percent of their time is spent talking, around 10 percent on actual scientific and engineering works, and the rest of writing. That means 90 percent of the time is used to communicate verbally and in writing. You can imagine how much time other professionals who interact with their clients on a daily basis may spend on communication. The question then is, are these communications effective? If they are not, there are messes and lost opportunities as a result of miscommunication.

Regardless of the profession we belong, effective communication is critical. We need to communicate with internal and external clients well. Effective communication is mandatory to meet our organizational goals, and achieve our teams' bottom lines. That is why in the above quote, Les Brown said, *"Effective communication is the number one tool to succeed in any endeavor."*

Poor communication could get in the way

Dan found workshop six very helpful. Communication was one of the challenges he had already identified. He realized that some of the problems he had with his team, boss, and peers were as a result of poor communication.

This workshop showed him the areas where he needs to work to improve his communication skills. Dan recognized that communication could enhance or deter him from succeeding in getting along with others. It could come in the way and prevent him from working with others unless he identifies those communication barriers and gets rid of them by regularly working on his communication skills.

I. Key lessons
1.1. Characteristics of highly effective communicators
"One of the key insights," Dan began sharing, "I gained from this workshop was understanding the characteristics of highly effective communicators. At the start of the workshop, we were divided into small groups to identify those individuals we consider extraordinary communicators. Next, we talked about what made them successful. This opportunity gave me a chance to understand the most important characteristics of effective communicators." For a couple of minutes, both Rafael and Dan exchanged names of those persons they considered exceptional communicators and what made these individuals communicate effectively.

Below are some of the characteristics they identified. Great communicators are:
1. Confident.
2. Passionate.
3. Illustrate their points by sharing stories, statistics, and facts.
4. To the point, specific, and focused.
5. Engaging.

Rafael asked Dan how he plans to develop these characteristics. After listening to Dan's approaches, Rafael shared his own strategies and the steps he had taken to improve his communication abilities.

Why is communication is harder for technical professionals?
There was one question that bothered Dan. He would like to hear Rafael's take on this. "Why communication is more difficult for technical professionals?"

Rafael laughed, and Dan joined.

"We're guilty!" Rafael conceded and further elaborated, "I worked with so many great colleagues who were superb in their technical skills. Because of that they were rewarded, promoted, and admired a lot. Some of these professionals, however, stopped there. They thought that the most critical things for their career success were their hard skills, and therefore, they neglected their soft skills. And, they paid dire prices." Then, Rafael complimented Dan for taking this important step to develop his soft skills at the early stage of his career.

I agree with Rafael. I'd been a technical professional since the turn of the new century up until I decided to become a trainer in 2007. Between 2000 - 2005, I worked as a researcher for an international research organization. I also worked as a production operator and then a software engineer for a multinational corporation between 2005 - 2007.

These great opportunities gave me chances to work with so many outstanding technical professionals. The majority of these technically competent professionals, though experienced in their field of studies, they struggled to continually advance in their career and climb the corporate ladder due to lack of certain soft skills such as the inability to communicate with diverse stakeholders.

Many technical professionals in accounting, medicine, engineering, math, science, IT, and so on over depend on their technical abilities, and thus, give minimal attention toward improving their soft skills on a consistent basis. They assume that the technical expertise that brought them thus far would take them to the next height. Marshall Goldsmith disagreed. He declared, *"What got you here won't get you there."*

Rafael recognized that the majority scientists have great written communication ability than other technical professionals. "However," he emphasized, "In the 21st C, we need to communicate using various methods beyond writing." It didn't take long for Dan to confess. "Though I communicate in writing very well, I struggle to communicate verbally effectively. I still experience stage fright whenever I stand in front of people to present my papers and project reports. Not only that, I stumble a lot as I communicate during team meetings."

Communication styles
"We all experience stage fright during the first couple of seconds. That is normal." Rafael comforted Dan. Then, Rafael shared with him some of the techniques he used to overcome stage fright and said, "Through practice, I learned to channel my nervousness through purposeful gestures, eye

contacts, and body movements."

Another communication challenge Dan revealed to Rafael was the unpleasant one-on-ones he has had with some team members. "I sometimes find myself being aggressive with some disagreeable team members."

This disclosure gave Rafael a chance to talk about the different types of communication styles: Assertive, Passive, Aggressive, Passive-Aggressive, Submissive, and Manipulative. "The best style for getting along is assertive communication." Upon Dan's request, Rafael gave him some insights to help him communicate assertively and also demonstrated to show him on how to communicate assertively without being rude and aggressive.

In her 'Assertive Communication Skills' DVD, Debra Fox explains the:
1. Critical roles emotions play,
2. Most important features of various communication styles,
3. Proven assertive communication techniques that empower us to communicate assertively while still:
   - Calm,
   - Nice,
   - Positive, and
   - Getting our points across.

1.2. Active Listening

Dan began. "The vital role active listening plays is another insight I gained from this workshop." He continued, "I used to think that I had been a pretty good listener because I gave my ears. After attending this workshop, I came to realize that there are three levels of listening and I had been listening at level 1 most of the time."

Rafael inquired Dan to explain the three levels of listening. Dan briefly illustrated each level and role-played with Rafael. Here are the three levels of listening based on the listening model of the authors of Co-Active Coaching:[77]
- **Level 1**- Listening is focused on self- Internal Listening.
- **Level 2**- Listening is focused on the other person- Focused Listening.
- **Level 3**- Listening is focused on us- Global Listening.

It's imperative to understand that all of these levels are important depending on the circumstance we may find ourselves. For instance, if you're visiting your mechanic, you should better listen at level one to fully understand everything the good mechanic is telling you about your car. Listen for you! Of course, for your vehicle.

On the other hand, if your friend or coworker is sharing with you his/her happy moment or concern or pain, you should focus on him/her and adapt empathetic listening. Listen for him/her!

When you find yourself having a conversation with someone on an issue that matters for both of you, you should adapt global listening. The latter entails paying attention to the non-verbal cues as well. I like what Peter Drucker said, *"The most important thing in communication is hearing what isn't said."* Global listening requires taking into account the environment and investing ourselves emotionally too.

Referring the discussion they had during the previous session about generating trust, Rafael created a connection between active listening and trust building. "When we fail to listen, it becomes a barrier beyond affecting our communication ability. It denies us the opportunity to create a trust-filled communication atmosphere."

Many relationships and partnerships have been ruined due to the lack of listening. When we have an active listening skill, on the contrary, not only we succeed in communicating in a given instance but also enable the relationship to continue. Once people see that we listen, they are encouraged to further relate to us. They consider us respectful and trustworthy individuals. They trust us for their time. They also know that we care and love them. This is because listening is an expression of love. Paul Tillich said: *"The first duty of love is listening."*

1.3. Non-verbal communication

The third key lesson Dan learned from this workshop was the major role non-verbal communication plays. "I had neglected this form of communication. I was shocked when I realized how verbal communication, which I used heavily, was unimportant in terms of impact."

Rafael interjected. "What so ever golden words we may use as we communicate in person, people may not connect with us because of our outstanding contents and mere wordsmith skills." Dan nodded.

With a big smile, Rafael continued. "We are humans. Our brain is wired to gather, analyze, add meanings, and reach a conclusion at the speed of light, so to speak. Our brain takes in data both verbal and non-verbal cues through our eyes and ears (intuition too) to reach quick conclusion about the messenger (his/her credibility, authenticity, trustworthiness, etc.)"

If we only depend on our verbal communication alone, we can only transmit a fraction of our message. Don't get me wrong. Our words (contents, statistics, facts) are still important. Yet, we should also be aware that our voice's tone, bitch; and most importantly, the way we dress, gesture our hands, move our body, and so on play the lion's share in transmitting our message to the intended audience and in turn to meet our goals from a given communication.

Albert Mehrabian, in his book "Silent Messages", revealed that liking is a total of:

- 7% spoken words,
- 38% voice, and
- 55 % body language.[78]

This data shows that the non-verbal takes precedence over spoken words and vocal tones. Mehrabian shared, *"For instance, if a person's facial expression and posture are domineering, no matter how submissive his words imply him to be, the message will be interpreted in a manner consistent with the dominance revealed by his facial expression and posture."*

In our presentation skills workshops, we advise participants to understand that they could be perceived as credible worthy of their audience's time or counted out as untrustworthy who doesn't worth listening. When our audience considers us incredible, they won't take action and make the change we want them to make as a result of our message.

What is the use of standing in front of people unless we meet our goals? Therefore, to win people's heart, influence, and inspire them to take the action you want them to take, you need more than just uttering powerful words. You need to display passion, exude energy, and use your voice and body in your favor to communicate effectively.

After showing the vital role non-verbal communication plays, Rafael suggested two areas to work on to improve this competency. "First, we need to be aware of our body languages. We should not send wrong signals that contradict our words and voice tone. Second, we need to decipher the non-verbal signals of others as we communicate."

After carefully listening, Dan decided to be proactive, use every opportunity he may get at home and in social gatherings to work on his non-verbal communication proficiency. "This is smart." Rafael admired Dan's strategy. "You don't need to wait until you get formal opportunities to develop your non-verbal communication abilities. You can practice anywhere." Rafael teased, "Of course, without telling people that you are practicing on them." The joke cracked Dan up.

"I found Joe's demonstrations of different gestures and body postures, and their meanings very helpful." Dan took upon himself to stand and demonstrate the proper ways of gesturing and making proper body movements that increase one's credibility. After observing Dan carefully, Rafael cautioned, "It's great that you have this awareness but don't forget that some gestures and body languages may not be the right fit depending on the occasion and your audience. Besides, the meaning of these gestures may vary from culture to culture."

Rafael's warning is very critical in organizations like GHR where people from various cultures work together. William B. Gudykunst and Young Yun Kim wrote, *"Gestures used by people in one culture often do not mean the same thing in another culture. Trying to communicate through nonverbal means, therefore, may lead to misunderstandings."*[79]

Communicating via phone and email
Dan conducts lots of virtual communications with some of his team members in other states and continents. He was concerned that he cannot tap into the power of non-verbal communication. He solicited Rafael's advice on this.

Though Rafael acknowledged that virtual communication doesn't allow using non-verbal communication to have maximum impact, he shared with Dan those approaches he found very helpful as he communicates virtually using various communication technologies. "I cannot use my body languages, movements, and gestures for maximum impact if I use email and phone communications. That is why I use video conferencing whenever possible. Whenever I cannot, I tap into the tone and pitch of my voice. I'm intentional about the media I use and adjust my communication approaches accordingly for maximum impact."

1.4. Cross-cultural communication
Dan had limited exposure to cultures outside of the US. Though he traveled a couple of times, he didn't have a chance to interact with natives of those cultures he visited. His trips were brief. Even then, he stayed in hotels and immediately returned to the US once his business was done. The only real exposure he had was with some team members and peers who are from other cultures. After giving Rafael this background, Dan shared some insights he had gained from the workshop in this regard.

After listening carefully, Rafael stressed, "Developing cross-cultural communication competency is important at GHR. As a research organization, we've staff and visiting researchers from diverse cultures. Many of our scientists closely work with scientists around the world. We also have many stakeholders including donors from different cultures. This diversity requires our staff and researchers to develop their cross-cultural communication skills so that they may avoid committing deadly cultural sins as they cross cultures."

Cross-cultural communication is very critical not just at GHR. The world has changed. We interact, work, and do business with people from diverse cultures. Thomas Zweifel wrote, "*Never before in history have humans dealt with humans of so many different cultures. Most of us meet people from other cultures every day.*"[80] This new reality calls for working hard to improve our cross-cultural communication abilities.

Nonetheless, Rafael didn't push this theme any further. He reminded Dan, "The next workshop's theme is diversity and inclusion. You're going to get more insights, tools, and techniques that will help you improve your cross-cultural communication competency. Let's talk more about it then." Dan agreed, and they moved to speak about the next item on their agenda.

II. Assessments, Processes, and Tools
2.1. Myers-Briggs Type Indicator (MBTI)

"Taking MBTI and learning my personality type increased my awareness concerning my preferences and perceptions." Dan expressed his delight. Rafael has his assumption about Dan's personality type. Rather than directly asking him, "Me too. I took the MBTI assessment, and my type code is ESFP." Dan was encouraged to share his; INTJ- the opposite of Rafael's.

Rafael asked Dan to share what he felt when he knew his personality type the first time. He also inquired whether Dan was okay with the results. Next, Rafael asked, "Tell me briefly about your personality type?" Dan disclosed that he prefers to:

- Focus on his inner-world (**Introversion**). Generates energy when he spends the time to think, reflect, read, and spend time alone.
- Interpret and add meaning to the information he takes in (**iNtuition**).
- Look at logic and consistency when he makes decisions (**Thinking**).
- Get things decided as he deals with the outside world (**Judgment**).

Rafael took the turn and expanded on his personality type. They further chatted about how their personality types may impact their interaction with others from differing personality types. Afterward, they deliberated on the need to be mindful of their preferences while also understanding the choices of others to succeed in communicating and in turn getting along successfully.

Isabel Briggs Myers advised, *"It is up to each person to recognize his or her true preferences."* Yes, we need to know about our preferences to get along. It also makes communication and getting along easier when we are aware of the preferences of others. Most importantly, we need to adjust our communication based on the personality type of the person (s) we communicate.

2.2. The STAR communication model

"I found the STAR model very helpful to sharpen my communication," Dan shared and continued, "I even got a chance during the workshop to write a message following the format of the process, and stood in front of our small group to present it."

Rafael asked Dan to expand on the acronym. Dan was delighted. He expounded, "The STAR model is beneficial as we prepare for interviews, one-on-one conversations, reports, or speeches. The format works this way:

- **Situation**. What was (is) the situation? Give background and context.
- **Task**. What was the task? Explain what needed to be done.
- **Action**. What measures did you take? Talk about the action and how you did it.
- **Results**. What were the results? Specify the achievements."[81]

They further talked about the feedback Dan got from his presentation and some of the things he could do to make his presentation ability superb. Rafael recommended him to find opportunities outside of GHR to work on his presentation skills. "Practicing regularly is vital to communicate effectively. You need to find in-house and outside chances to practice and continually improve your communication abilities."

Dale Carnegie in his classic book 'The Quick & Easy Way to Effective Speaking' advised, *"Join organizations and volunteer for offices that will require you to speak. Stand up and assert yourself at public meetings, if only to second a motion. Don't take back seat at departmental meetings. Speak up!"*[82] Jim Rohn too recommended, *"Take advantage of every opportunity to practice your communication skills so that when important occasions arise, you will have the gift, the style, the sharpness, the clarity, and the emotions to affect other people."*

2.2. Triads of communication- Relating, Connecting, and Listening

Dan recognized that communication isn't all about talking. The workshop equipped him to become an effective communicator. "I found the triads of communication a very empowering tool. I realized that becoming an effective communicator requires having these three elements in place: relating, connecting, and listening." Dan acknowledged.

In response to Rafael's request, Dan briefly explained the importance of the three factors. Since Rafael knows the relative significance of connecting, he further pushed the discussion. "Tell me, how do you connect with others to succeed in your communication?" Dan came up with a couple of suggestions. "I need to:

- Relate at a human level.
- Find common grounds.
- Figure out those things that we share in common."

Rafael nodded, and showed the interconnectedness of the three factors. "A proper relationship opens the door for us to create connection. The relationship cannot last, and we cannot remain connected unless we listen attentively."

"Which stage is the most critical for you?" Rafael asked a follow-up question. Dan recognized that all of the three steps are important. "However," he stressed, "Connecting has been very critical and challenging at the same time for me. Because of lack of connecting at a deeper level with the people that I work with, I'm struggling in my relationships. It has also prevented me to listen actively."

This is not just a challenge for Dan alone. John C. Maxwell declared that everyone communicates, but few connect. He wrote, *"Connecting is the ability to identify with people and relate to them in a way that increases your influence with them."*[83] He further emphasized, *"Talent isn't enough. Experience isn't enough. To lead others, you must be able to communicate well, and connecting is key."*[84]

III. Action item

"I need to work on my presentation skills. Since I don't have frequent opportunities to stand in front of people here at GHR, as you suggested, I need to look for outside opportunities to practice." Dan put forward his immediate action item.

To help Dan get focused, Rafael inquired, "What are some of the areas you want to concentrate first? You cannot master everything at once. You need to select a couple of priority areas first. Once you see improvements in these areas, you next target the second focus areas and the third…"

Dan was honest about it. He hasn't prioritized. "I've not thought about it yet, but I see your point. I'll make sure to select one or two areas."

"Have you identified places where you could practice yet?" Rafael was wondering. "I've not yet," was Dan's quick response.

Since Rafael has been a member of some organizations that offered him platforms to improve his communication skills, he encouraged Dan to try some of them. Dan agreed to pay visits and check them out.

Summary

It's impossible to get along with others and succeed in what we do without becoming effective communicators. Especially in the 21ˢᵗ C where using multiple forms of communication is mandatory, excelling in one form of communication isn't enough. Unlike what many assume, communication isn't just talking. It also entails relating deliberately, connecting, and also listening attentively. In the latter case, just lending our ears isn't enough. Active listening requires hearing at multiple levels. Non-verbal communication is also at the center of effective communication since we humans are wired to validate what we hear with what we see. Besides, unlike in the past, effective communication has become more challenging as many of us work with people from diverse cultures. The 21ˢᵗ C workplace is filled with employees from culturally different backgrounds, which requires developing cross-cultural communication skills to get along and achieve extraordinary success.

Soft Skill 7: Promoting Diversity & Embracing Inclusiveness

"Companies with more diverse workforce perform better financially by 35%." **McKinsey & Company**

- The first stage of the getting along process- Coming together- compels teaming up with others and 'Playing Teamwork', which was covered in Workshop five.
- But, Coming together is the beginning of a protracted journey.
- Getting along also entails Working together, the second stage of the process.
- Succeeding in the second stage requires developing three soft skills: Communicating Effectively, Promoting Diversity and Embracing Inclusiveness, and Turning Conflicts into Opportunities
- Those who came together need to communicate well in order the team to function properly, and Workshop six adequately covered the soft skill Communicating Effectively.
- Workshop seven covered Promoting Diversity and Embrace Inclusiveness.

Participants of the Soft Skills Development program were diverse. They were consisted of:
- Men and women,
- Black and whites,
- Immigrants from Africa, Asia, and South America.

Age wise, the majority of the participants were baby boomers while a few Y and X genres, and a couple of millennials.

Diversity is the norm
GHR isn't exceptional. In the 21st C, most workplaces are filled with diverse individuals from:
- Different cultures,
- Age groups,
- Professions,
- Races,
- Ethnicities,
- Genders,
- Religions, and political affiliations with different preferences, interests, priorities, and so on.

These days, thanks to globalization and the Internet, the chance to work with diverse people in person or virtually using latest communication technologies is high. For that matter, every one of us interacts with various people on social media such as Face-book, LinkedIn, Twitter, Instagram, Pinterest, and so on.

IQ, EQ, and Social intelligence aren't enough

With the opportunity to meet, interact, and work with diverse people comes the challenge to get along and succeed in what we do individually and collectively. This challenge is understandable. One may have extraordinary social intelligence when it comes to interacting and working with people who are within his/her native culture. The individual knows the customs, beliefs, and anathemas very well. Thus, getting along is relatively easy since he/she communicates, interacts, behaves, and acts according to the cultural codes without offending and entering into any misunderstanding and conflict with others.

However, to get along and succeed in the 21st C, it takes more than having superb IQ and social intelligence. The author of 'The Cultural Intelligence Difference' David Livermore wrote, *"The number one predictor of your success in today's borderless world is not your IQ, not your resume, and not even your expertise."* He continued, *"It's your CQ (Cultural Intelligence), a powerful capability that is proven to enhance your effectiveness working in culturally diverse situations."*[85]

Sadly, many organizations still depend on IQ and social intelligence when they select supervisors and managers. The author of 'Cultural Intelligence: CQ: The competitive edge for leaders crossing borders', Julia Middleton said, *"Organizations often appoint leaders for their IQ. Then, years later, sack them for their lack of EQ (Emotional Intelligence)."* She predicted, *"Common Purpose argues that in the future they will promote for CQ - Cultural Intelligence."*

Experiencing Culture shock

What do we all experience when we interact and work with people who are unlike us? We experience culture shock though the degree may vary from person to person. The reason is simple. We aren't familiar with the cultural norms and taboos of cultures for which we're strangers. We get frustrated and also easily frustrate others because of the lack of understanding their expectations. These in turn sure affect our relationship, and the ability to get along and work together harmoniously.

'All the threads of the tapestry are equal'

Of course, diversity isn't all about cultural differences alone. Diversity in individuals' preferences, interests, genders, ethnicities, races, and so on should also be considered. The 21st C organizations should become intentional about promoting diversity. Maya Angelou highlighted the importance of fostering diversity when she said, *"We all should know that diversity makes for a rich tapestry, and we must understand that all the threads of the tapestry are equal in value no matter what their color."* Organizations that understood this fact are proactive. They take measures to promote diversity and embrace inclusiveness to tap into the potential of all of their employees.

'Diversity is about all of us'

Jacqueline Woodson believes that fostering diversity is a win-win. *"Diversity is about all of us, and about us having to figure out how to walk through this world together."* This scenario where each member of a given organization and community is embraced and allowed to contribute its share for the greater good is a win-win for all parties involved.

Diversity isn't a liability

Louis van der Merwe is an organizational development expert and former executive of South African based Ekom- the nation's primary electric power utility. He noted, *"South Africans are discovering that our diversity can be a strength, not a problem."*[86] South Africans figured out that diversity is not a liability, rather it's a competitive advantage.

Promoting diversity and embracing inclusiveness has so many great rewards. Nonetheless, harvesting these prizes entails some upfront investments- creating a space to grow together. Mark de Pree, the former CEO of Herman Miller advised, *"We need to give each other the space to grow, to be ourselves, to exercise our diversity. We need to give each other space so that we may both give and receive such beautiful things as ideas, openness, dignity…inclusion."*

I. Key lessons
1.1. Avoiding committing deadly cultural sins

Workshop seven helped Dan to understand what diversity is all about fully, and how he could contribute his share to promote a diverse workplace that embraces inclusiveness. "The workshop showed me why various people from different cultures:
- Communicate,
- Behave,
- Interact, and
- Do things in certain ways." Dan summarized the first lesson he learned.

He continued, "It also enabled me to develop the skills necessary to communicate, relate, connect, and work with individuals from diverse backgrounds, upbringings, and people with varying priorities and interests successfully. Most importantly, it provided me strategies on how to avoid committing deadly cultural sins."

"Why is that important to you?" Rafael inquired. "First and foremost, I desperately need to develop the ability to mitigate culture shock and avoid committing cultural sins as I work with diverse people from cultures for which I'm a stranger," Dan responded with conviction. "Developing this soft skill takes time. Till then, prepare to accept that you may not even know when you commit some cultural sins." Rafael quickly interjected and cautioned. Dan laughed and remarked, "I want to make sure, at this point, to avoid committing the ones that are deadly." Rafael joined the laughter.

Next, Rafael shared a couple of instances from his past where he didn't even know he had committed some cultural sins. Dan found these incidents informative and at the same time funny. Rafael then remarked, "After faltering so many times as I crossed cultures, I'm still on the learning curve. But, now, it may not take me long to recognize and quickly correct my stumbling immediately."

In his book 'Culture Clash', Thomas Zweifel shared an instance from his initial stay in Japan. Not long after he arrived, he found himself treated harshly by his host without even knowing why. He wrote, "*Had I done anything to deserve such brusque treatment? I will never know...You never know if you just made a mistake or even committed a capital sin, because you may not find out for 10 years, if ever.*"[87]

1.2. Benefits of diversity

"The second lesson that I learned from this workshop was the tremendous benefits organizations might enjoy if they create an environment that promotes diversity and embraces inclusiveness," Dan shared delightedly. Rafael nodded and further probed, "Do you mind to share with me some of the benefits?"

"One of the advantages is enhancing the ability to tackle problems when diverse people are involved in resolving severe and complex challenges that would have been impossible to crack without the collective contribution of various individuals." Without waiting to hear additional benefits, Rafael quickly interjected, "Why is that?" Dan paused to articulate his answer. "This is because diverse people bring multitudes of options and approaches to solve complex problems."

Rafael recounted, "GHR understood the importance of promoting diversity some years back, and took proactive measures since then. We have diverse stakeholders, and we figured out that the best way to serve these different stakeholders is by tapping into the:

- Talent,
- Passion,
- Skillsets, and
- Experiences of our diverse people."

Dan was curious to know. "What has been done so far to promote diversity and embrace inclusiveness within GHR?" Rafael enumerated some of the changes that were made on GHR's policies, procedures, and processes to foster diversity. "What kinds of results have been achieved due to these changes?" Dan wondered. "The changes brought significant results such as improved:

- Productivity,
- Harmony,
- Synergy, and
- Innovation," Rafael proudly listed.

McKinsey's Diversity Matter report stated, *"We know intuitively that diversity matters. It's also increasingly clear that it makes sense in purely business terms."* The report revealed, *"Companies in the top quartile for racial and ethnic diversity are 35 percent more likely to have financial returns above their respective national industry medians."*[88] The returns are greater when companies invest to increase their diverse people's cultural intelligence.

Employees with high cultural intelligence *"play an important role in bridging divides and knowledge gaps in an organization:*
- *Educating their peers about different cultures;*
- *Transferring knowledge between otherwise disparate groups;*
- *Helping to build interpersonal connections and smooth the interpersonal processes in a multicultural workforce."*[89]

Such employees also *"posses the potential to drive up innovation and creativity, due to their ability to integrate diverse resources and help the business make best use of the multiple perspectives that a multicultural workforce brings to the workplace."*[90] The author of 'The Way of the Innovation Master' pointed out, *"Diversity is the mother of creativity. Diverse teams produce more creative results than teams in which all members are from a similar background."*

1.3. Conscious stereotyping and unconscious biases

"This workshop alarmed me to know that we all may have some conscious stereotyping and unconscious biases we may not be aware of or for which we may not have conscious control," Dan stated. They talked about some of the obvious conscious stereotyping, unconscious biases, and how these things may work subtly and compromise GHR's efforts to promote diversity and embrace inclusiveness.

Rafael further noted, "As leaders, we should be vigilant to spot ours and our team members' behaviors that may undermine diversity." Though Dan agreed, he felt helpless about those biases he's not aware at all. Rafael too shared Dan's concern. "Yes, there may be some biases we have developed since childhood. These might have become part of our belief-system, and thus, never been challenged or questioned. These can come to light with increased self-awareness. Only then, we could expel and substitute those unproductive unconscious biases. The increasing self-awareness soft skill is so vital to uncover such unwanted biases."

"I concur. I've already identified a few of my thoughts, feelings, perspectives, and beliefs that might not contribute toward promoting diversity. I've also taken the time to recognize some of my team members' beliefs and biases that need to be changed." Dan's voice and body languages expressed guilty.

He promised to Rafael that he'd keep on working on these in the coming weeks and months ahead. Rafael appreciated his honesty and reintroduced the Ladder of Inference into this discussion. He explained how it's easy for us to climb the ladder quickly and form unconscious biases that may undermine diversity.

They further talked about on how to reverse those stereotypes and biases they identified by helping some of his team members to climb down from the top of the ladder to:
- Reexamine the existing outdated data, gather fresh facts,
- Give new meanings accordingly,
- Apply different assumptions,
- Reach empowering new conclusions,
- Manifest new behaviors and take actions that promote diversity and embrace inclusion.

Rafael admitted that this takes time. He reminded Dan, however, that the companywide policies support what he is trying to accomplish that he'll surely succeed at the end of the day. He offered some pieces of advice:

- "Be proactive.
- Make a thorough assessment to understand the biases and stereotyping that may undermine diversity within your team.
- You may set up a process to oust these and implement other pro-diversity measures.
- You may even arrange a mini-workshop to empower your team members to promote diversity and embrace inclusiveness in the workplace.
- You may also come up with guidelines that provide direction.
- You may explicitly state the incentives for those who uphold and consequences for violating the guidelines, respectively. If you need my help in this regard, let me know."

1.4. The severe consequences of stereotyping and unconscious biases

"I learned the serious consequences of conscious stereotyping and unconscious biases," Dan shared the fourth lesson. Rafael nodded for Dan to continue. Dan began. "Joe defined some terms, briefly shared the history of diversity and the chronology of some acts that were instituted to combat discriminations in the US."

Dan continued. "I found myself illiterate about the history and legal measures that had been taken to promote diversity. Now, I have the full context. I understand the very reason why it's important to develop this soft skill to get along with diverse people, and also avoid paying exorbitant prices."

"Tell me one of the prices," Rafael interjected and asked. "Legal consequences including litigations," Dan answered quickly. "What do you plan to do to avoid these costs?" Rafael probed. Dan said, "I determined to help my team to understand the importance of complying with these laws." Rafael complimented and stated. "You made the right decision because many organizations entangled with litigation for failing to do so."

The price of spillages

Next, Rafael narrated stories of some great personalities who were caught ranting stereotype insults toward certain sections of our society. "Think about the owner of Clippers- Donald Sterling, and the wrestling all time great- Hulk Hogan. These individuals have been regarded honorable, and even heroes, up until their spillages." He declared, "These and many other successful people could have avoided the embarrassment, the dire prices they paid, and many intangible consequences they have paid if they were aware of their own biases and stereotypes."

"I got it!" Dan complemented Rafael's point by saying, "It is understandable why GHR should take this issue seriously. It shouldn't wait till one of its leaders spill words that may cost its brand, finance, and opportunities." "That is correct," Rafael added; "That is why we recognized the magnitude of this issue and determined to give it our prime attention. That is why we empower our people to develop this soft skill."

In response to Arianna Huffington, a Uber Board member, who commented on how *"one woman on a board often leads to more women joining a board"*, David Bonderman- a fellow Board member- made a disparaging comment about women. *"Actually, what it shows is that it's much more likely to be more talking."* Because of this spillage, The New York Times reported, Bonderman was forced to resign.[91] The report further revealed that his bias toward women was unsubstantiated. The article quoted a recent study that showed *"Men talked far more than women did at meetings."*

II. Assessments, Processes, and Tools
2.1. Edward Hall's model
In the coming days, weeks, months, years ahead, Dan should overcome many challenges since this theme is new to him. But, he found some valuable stuff. Dan looked animated and shared. "We recognized that there are thousands of cultures around the world and it is tough to understand all of them. However, Edward Hall's model gave us three parameters:
1. Time,
2. Context, and
3. Space to make this challenge a little easier."

"These factors could help us divide the world's cultures into two broad categories, and understand the similarities and differences between these two," Dan said with confidence.

"Tell me the two main cultures with some examples," Rafael asked. Dan drew a table that looked like below on a piece of paper, and divided it into two columns and populated the following info:

Communal Cultures	Individual Cultures
Africa	North America: USA and Canada
Asia	Europe
South America	Australia

Without waiting, Dan compared the two main cultures briefly using the three indicators, "Time is treated casually in communal cultures while it's well organized in individual based cultures. Context is high in collective cultures where people express themselves implicitly while individuals in the individual based cultures communicate explicitly and use verbal communication predominantly. People from communal cultures are less territorial while people from individual based cultures have high tendency to mark their territories."

"As a person who lived in these two major cultures," Rafael acknowledged, "You explained it very well. I've witnessed first hand how people from the two principal cultures treat time, communicate, and handle space differently." By quoting some personal encounters, he illustrated his points. Dan found these examples very funny and at the same time informative.

Like Rafael, I lived in two major cultures. I was born and raised in Ethiopia, a communal culture. Of course, don't forget that there are subcultures and individual exceptions within each national culture. I then came to the US- an individual based culture, in 2005.

At the early stage of my stay in the US, I experienced culture shock. To succeed in my new home, I have made so many changes including the way I treat time, communicate, and relate. I'm still on the learning curve- stumbling here and there once in a while, which makes me humble and open to learning continually. Let me share with you some stories.

Time
Back home, coming late is tolerable. It doesn't matter who comes first. Since the relationship is valued more than time, none of us make coming late a big deal. We smile and hug each other affectionately and continue our business.

Here in the US, coming late for work is considered as a sign of unprofessionalism and has severe consequences. Outside of work, coming late damages relationships since being late is perceived as disrespectful.

What is interesting is that many of my friends from Ethiopia and Africa compartmentalize their time here in the US. They arrive on time when it comes to their job and formal business affairs but treat time casually in social gatherings. You may get an invitation stating at what time the meeting starts. Unless you have lots of spare time to spend, you don't come on time as stated on the letter or flyer. The event may start two hours late.

I had a Nigerian classmate when I was doing my doctoral degree (2009 – 2013). Whenever we wanted to meet, we used to ask one another, is this African time or American? If it's African time, we don't fix the time. One of us may be in the library or coffee shop working on schoolwork, and the other person just stops by within the time range we agreed. If it's American time, we fix the start and end time. We come and leave on time.

Context

In Ethiopia, we use non-verbal communications heavily. On the other hand, here in the US (and other individual based cultures), people dominantly use explicit verbal communication. In communal cultures, if you explicitly talk about yourself, your accomplishments, qualifications, experiences, and needs, you may be labeled as egotistical and selfish. On the contrary, if you don't communicate verbally, explicitly, and express your needs, aspirations, and experiences in an individual based culture, you may be regarded as shy who lacks confidence.

Space

I used to share bed, clothes, and shoes with my relatives and friends all the time. It was common to find yourself going to one of your friend's home, and if it rains by the time you leave, you just pick the umbrella of your friend on your way out without asking permission. If you ask, it offends your host. He/she may feel that you distanced yourself. It doesn't show intimacy and brotherhood/sisterhood. In the US, people are mindful of their spaces. You're expected to respect other people's boundaries. You cannot just grab and take someone's stuff without risking being viewed as rude, or worst, thief.

Nonetheless, understanding the difference between the two primary cultural divides is the beginning of a long journey. We need to increase our cultural intelligence. With increased cultural intelligence comes understanding from where people come, and refraining from judging others based on the way they treat time, communicate, and handle space.

To get along with people from diverse cultures, we should stop treating our native culture as the standard bearer. We shouldn't expect everyone to behave and act the way we do. We all should increase our cultural intelligence to live and work with people from different cultures successfully. We should also make some efforts to help each other to understand one another's cultures.

2.2. Diversity Wheel

"Diversity Wheel helped us to understand the dimensions of diversity." He sketched the wheel and quickly described the four layers, which ones are permanent and unchangeable, and which ones may change through time:

- **Layer 1**- Identity/Personal dimensions (likes, dislikes, preferences),
- **Layer 2**- Internal dimensions (age, race, gender),
- **Layer 3**- External dimensions (religion, income, marital status), and
- **Layer 4**- Organizational dimensions (seniority, department, position).[92]

Rafael asked some follow up questions to reinforce Dan's understanding about the tool. They also talked about how to apply it to make sure that each and every individual within his team is treated according to their uniqueness.

III. Action items

"One of the immediate actions I plan to take is attending some cultural events; and in the long run, to take vacation and travel to one of the communal cultures and stay there for a week or two." Rafael found this plan very practical to increase Dan's cultural intelligence.

They brainstormed for a couple of more minutes on how he could capitalize these encounters. Subsequently, Rafael gave Dan some tips from his personal experience. He advised:

- Read some books to increase your knowledge about some of the dominant cultures represented here at GHR
- Join some clubs that have diverse members
- Talk to the people who lived in those cultures you are interested

Summary

Getting along with people from diverse cultures is challenging. It requires developing the soft skill necessary to promote diversity and embrace inclusiveness. Developing this skill should start by increasing one's awareness of some conscious stereotyping and unconscious biases. Scoring high in one's IQ, Emotional Intelligence, and Social Intelligence isn't enough in an environment filled with diverse members. To succeed in such environment, one needs to develop cultural intelligence. Of course, diversity isn't all about culture alone. We need to welcome diversity of preferences, interests, age groups, genders, races, ethnicities, and more. Many benefits come when you empower your team members to promote diversity and embrace inclusiveness. On the other hand, failing to increase your people's ability to promote diversity and embrace inclusiveness has dire financial, and possibly legal consequences.

Soft Skill 8: Turning Conflicts into Opportunities

"There is an immutable conflict at work in life and in business, a constant battle between peace and chaos. Neither can be mastered, but both can be influenced. How you go about that is the key to success." **Phil Knight**

Turning conflicts into opportunities is mandatory to get along

- Getting along is a process.
- Coming together is the first stage.
- The necessary soft skill in this stage is the ability to play teamwork, which was covered in Workshop five.
- The second stage is working together.
- Although there are so many soft skills essential to get along, there are three key soft skills mandatory as we work together:

  1. Communicating effectively,
  2. Promoting diversity and embracing inclusiveness, and
  3. Turning conflicts into opportunities.

- Out of possibly dozens of other soft skills, if we develop the above three key soft skills, our chance to get along with others as we work together is within our grasp.
- Communicating effectively and promoting diversity and embracing inclusiveness were covered in Workshops six and seven, respectively.
- Turning conflicts into opportunity was covered in Workshop eight.

No place is free of conflict except the graveyard

Conflict has been with us since the beginning of our history. It will continue to exist. Conflict happens everywhere. It occurs at home, in the neighborhood, the boardroom, manufacturing floor, marketplace, and workplace.

Everyone experiences conflict on a consistent basis. Wherever two or more people come together, there is bound to be conflict. The only place conflict doesn't occur is in the graveyard.

Furthermore, as much as conflict is ubiquitous and everyone is familiar with it, many people struggle to resolve conflicts and get along with others. This, in turn, is costing organizations fortunes. When team members unable to deal with conflicts, it leads to lack of cooperation, mistrust, low morale, and high turnover. These problems result in a dysfunctional team that struggles to meet its goals.

Impossible to master conflict

Conflict is part of life and common in the workplace. Our success to work together and get along with others is highly dependent on our ability to turn conflicts into opportunities. However, as Phil Knight- the co-founder and chairman of Nike, stated in the leading quote above, the goal is not to master conflict per se.

Mastering conflict isn't possible since conflict varies from situation to situation. By the time you handle one type of conflict with one individual or group, another conflict type with a different person or group awaits giving you no chance to master conflicts of all kinds. Nevertheless, successful organizations don't just train their people to resolve conflicts. Rather, they empower them to turn conflicts into opportunities.

Personalities clash is unavoidable

Dan found this workshop very interesting. One thing that he quickly realized was that even if individuals come together to achieve common goals, communicate superbly, and embrace diversity and become inclusive, they might still experience conflict on a consistent basis. Dan understood that each person has his/her own preferences, personality type, priorities, and approaches. And, as they work together, personalities clash and conflict becomes unavoidable.

Dan had come a long way. Looking back retrospectively, he would have handled the conflicts he had entered with some of his team members, peers, and boss differently. He had wished he attended this workshop a long time ago.

I. Key lessons
1.1. Conflict isn't always a bad thing

"Instinctively, I used to dread conflict like a plague. This fear is justifiable when I think of the consequences of most of the conflicts I have been involved." Dan professed. Rafael quickly asked, "Why is that?" Dan manifested visible emotions as he explained, "Conflict is powerful and triggers emotions- mostly negative ones. In its wake, it leaves relationships destroyed, trust eroded, and prevents future cooperation."

"By the way, conflict isn't always a bad thing," Rafael interjected to change the mood. Dan nodded. They had a discussion in class about how the innovations, creativities, and progresses we have experienced since the beginning of our civilization were possible because of the manifestation of conflicts of ideas, approaches, and ways of thinking. "You're right. We wouldn't have enjoyed the advancements in our organizations, communities, and nations without conflicts." Dan agreed and stated firmly.

Rafael further explained, "What we need isn't the absence of conflict. If conflicts handled well, they would result in healthy competition. Competition leads to quality, lower price, convenience, etc. When two companies enter into 'conflict' to win the local market, the customers benefit in the form of improved and affordable products and services. When team members' ideas clash, the team gets exposed to multiple and innovative ideas, and the chance to choose the best one."

Conflicts handled well, have so many merits. Margaret Heffernan announced, *"For good ideas and true innovation, you need human interaction, conflict, argument, debate."* For that matter, Thomas Paine, one of the Founding Fathers of the US declared, *"The harder the conflict, the more glorious the triumph."* We humans grow stronger as we deal with conflicts. William Ellery Channing underscored, *"Difficulties are meant to rouse, not discourage. The human spirit is to grow strong by conflict."*

1.2. Mismanaged or left unmanaged
"I realized that if conflicts are mismanaged or left unmanaged, they lead to dysfunctional teams." Dan acknowledged. Rafael inquired, "What are some of the consequences you identified?"

Dan doesn't need to go somewhere to witness the results of mismanaged conflicts. Many signs of team dysfunctions already existed within his team. Dan enumerated:
- "Broken down communication,
- Lack of cooperation,
- Mistrust,
- Poor performance and productivity are just some of the consequences of mismanaged or left unmanaged conflicts."

"Many organizations suffer due to their people's inability to turn conflicts into opportunities. Numerous teams, as we speak, are stranded due to internal and external conflicts." Rafael pointed out and added, "On top of what you mentioned, many organizations are paying dire prices due to mismanaged conflicts such as drained resources as they attempt to mitigate the impacts of conflicts, a stressful work environment that discourages creativity and innovation, lost opportunities, and more."

For several minutes, they talked about how to empower team members to improve their ability in handling conflicts. Rafael further stressed, "No one is born with conflict management skills. Now, you're well equipped to turn conflicts into opportunities. You can now help your team to develop, refine, and improve their conflict resolution skills."

The authors of 'Getting to Yes' said, *"The goal cannot and should not be to eliminate conflict. Conflict is an inevitable- and useful- part of life."*[93] They further noted, *"Strange as it may seem, the world needs more conflict, not less."* They also suggested, *"The challenge is not to eliminate conflict but to transform it. It is to change the way we deal with our differences- from destructive, adversarial battling to hard-headed, side-by-side problem-solving."*

1.3. Conflict is a blessing in disguise

"Before attending the workshop, I had a negative outlook about conflict. But, I found out that I wasn't alone. When Joe asked the class to use one word to describe conflict, they uttered words like trouble, stress, fight, pain, frustration, anger, and so on. However, we finally appreciated that conflict is a blessing in disguise." Dan shared the third lesson he learned.

Viewing conflict negatively isn't unique to participants of this workshop. As I facilitate similar workshops on the theme conflict management, many used unpleasant words to describe conflict. We all have experienced conflict of one form or another. Most of them led up to bad breakups and experiencing feelings mentioned above. Like Dan, in the end, my audiences too recognized that conflict is a blessing in disguise.

Conflict is neutral

"Dan, conflict is neutral," Rafael remarked. "Conflict isn't bad or negative of itself. The way we handle it makes the difference. One person may turn a conflict into opportunities to:
- Deepen her relationship,
- Build trust,
- Find a better way of doing things, and so on while another person may mishandle that the same conflict and:
  - Ruin his relationship,
  - Complicate things,
  - Stuck,
  - Disengaged,
  - Uncooperative, and unable to move forward."

Dan agreed. "I've already recognized that we are diverse in our cultural backgrounds, age, gender, interest, religion, priorities, interests, and goals that we shouldn't be surprised when we enter into conflict as we work together with others. Rather than avoiding or having a negative attitude about conflict, we should use every conflict instance to turn it into opportunity to fulfill our duties and meet our personal and organizational goals."

Rafael jokingly pointed out, "Witnessing conflict in the workplace shouldn't be considered as an anomaly. We should rather question if there are no signs of conflict in our organization and team."

Having the right attitude toward conflict is a game changer. William James noted, "*Whenever you're in conflict with someone, there is one factor that can make the difference between damaging your relationship and deepening it. That factor is attitude.*" The right place to bring this attitudinal change at individual and collective levels in turning conflicts into opportunities is our mind. Amos Oz- the famed writer in Israel was right when he said, "*A conflict begins and ends in the hearts and minds of people, not in the hilltops.*"

1.4. Using one conflict mode to deal with all forms of conflicts

Dan was frank about using one style of conflict resolution in all cases of conflicts, "Until I participated in this workshop, I was unaware of using one conflict resolution mode predominantly." "Why do you think you prefer this style over others?" Rafael probed.

Dan revealed, "My most preferred conflict mode is 'Avoiding.'" He further detailed, "I've been thinking deeply to figure out the possible reasons why I've preferred this style. So far, it looks like my being introvert plays the lion's share. I always avoid conflicts as much as possible. I need time to reflect before I react to a conflict situation. That is why my default reaction has been withdrawal."

Rafael appreciated Dan for sharing his most preferred mode. After sharing his own most favored and least used modes, he expanded, "Very few people are conscious about their preferred style of conflict resolution. Many handle conflicts using their default conflict mode, which in turn hinders their ability to turn conflicts into opportunities. They don't take ample time to investigate and understand their most and least preferred conflict modes. Because of that, they handle all conflicts using the same mode most of the time."

"Now, I understand that effective conflict resolution demands choosing the right conflict resolution mode to turn a particular conflict situation into an opportunity." Dan proclaimed.

Switching among conflict resolution modes
"You're right. Understanding our own modes of conflict is the beginning," Rafael admitted. And he continued, "We should treat each conflict uniquely, and choose the right mode that matches the conflict situation even if it is our least preferred mode. Before we decide which approach to pursue in dealing with a particular conflict, we need to study the situation, evaluate the relationship and decide with which mode to engage. We should not always depend on our most preferred mode. Sometimes, it may be necessary for us to totally ignore it and use another mode, which is the best bet for that particular conflict circumstance."

Dan solicited, "You mentioned evaluating the relationship on top of considering the conflict situation before deciding which mode to use. Why is that? Do you mind to elaborate?" "I don't," Rafael responded and gave Dan a simple example. "Let's say that someone you don't know at all is bothering you on the highway, cutting you in, blowing his horn, and showing you some finger signs. Is it worthy to return in kind? Do you really need to compete and confront this person whom you may not meet again for the rest of your life? You most probably avoid, and drive away from him."

This case reminded Dan some awkward moments on the highway, and laughed loud and commented, "I've had similar experiences with that kind of jerks once in a while. I always avoid such encounters with strangers. Anyway, I'm good at avoiding." Rafael too recounted a recent similar experience. He then continued, "On the other hand, if one of your team members behave rudely, compete harshly, and bother other team members, do you avoid this forever? Probably not; avoiding isn't the right choice and a sustainable way of addressing these kinds of conflicts with the people you work with on a consistent basis. At one point, you need to confront it. You need to find a solution to turn that unpleasant conflict situation into a growth opportunity to the person and also improved relationships with all parties involved."

My top preferred mode used to be avoiding while accommodating was my second favorite conflict resolution style. My least preferred mode was competing. For some years now, I have been using different modes successfully depending on the situation and the relationship involved. I now find myself competing, collaborating, or compromising depending on the situation that I face. There were some instances in the past couple of years where I used my least preferred style deliberately. Initially, it was hard. I wasn't built for it. I mastered avoiding and accommodating. But, once I started using my least preferred mode and got some results, I was encouraged to use it again and again. And through the process, I've become better and better.

II. Assessments, Processes, and Tools
2.1. Thomas Killmann Instrument (TKI)

"All of us took the TKI assessment before attending the workshop. Joe discussed the instrument, and we had large and small group discussions based on the results." Dan shared. At Rafael's request, he explained that when two basic dimensions of behaviors (Assertiveness and Cooperativeness) intersected, they create five conflict resolution modes:

1. Avoiding,
2. Accommodating,
3. Compromising,
4. Competing, and
5. Collaborating.

Rafael came up with a couple of scenarios and asked Dan which mode he would prefer for each case. This exercise deepened Dan's knowledge about each mode, and how to choose the right style for each conflict situation he faces.

2.2. Process
The process of conflict resolution

Dan found the five steps conflict resolution process empowering. "This process has five steps. It shows the stages that should be passed through to resolve conflicts smartly." Rafael asked him to briefly described the process, "The process begins by identifying the cause of the conflict, and ends with finding a resolution." And, Dan briefly explained the whole process.

"Do you plan to use it soon?" Rafael inquired. "Yes! I decided to use this tool to resolve the conflicts that already exist in my team. And, also whatever conflict I may face in the future." Dan was convinced that the process would help him to quickly turn conflicts into opportunities and mitigate their impacts before they cause severe damages.

III. Action items

Even if Dan knew his conflict modes, he thought that it wasn't enough, "My self-awareness about my conflict modes doesn't help me much unless I've some clues about the most preferred conflict resolution modes of my team members and the people with whom I closely interact and work with."

Rafael solicited, "How do you plan to do so?" Dan didn't have a clear plan except he intended to observe carefully and learn their preferred modes.

Rafael shared some of his approaches he used to understand the conflict styles of his team, and how he tailored his approaches with each accordingly. "When I got my TKI results, I immediately shared them with some of my family members and close friends. That gave me a chance to talk about the importance of refraining from using one response for all conflict situations. Most of them showed interest, asked questions, and openly talked about their preferences openly, which gave me some ideas about their preferred modes.

Concerning my team, once I had my TKI results, the next day I shared my results and talked about the importance of all of us having the same awareness about ourselves and other team members. They agreed and took TKI assessment online. Afterward, I invited a facilitator, and we had a half-day workshop."

After thanking Rafael for sharing his approaches, Dan shared what he would do. Rafael gave him some feedback, and they concluded their mentoring session.

Summary

Conflict happens as far as two or more people live, work, and do business together. To get along with others and succeed in what we do, we need to develop the soft skill that enables us to handle conflicts properly. Understanding the very nature and commonalities of conflicts is the first step in turning conflicts into opportunities in the workplace. This soft skill also requires identifying the common sources of conflict, cultivating the right mindset, and developing a set of skills to create win-win solutions whenever we find ourselves in conflict situations. Besides, it entails finding common grounds, establishing ground rules, recognizing the five commonly known conflict response styles, our own most preferred and least preferred conflict resolution modes, and the conflict modes of others.

Recapping Part II

Part two of the program introduced participants to new insights, methods, instruments, and approaches that aimed at equipping them to succeed in getting along with others. They took three assessments:

- The 360-degree feedback enabled them to know their blind spots and areas of growth.
- MBTI increased their awareness about their preferences and perceptions.
- TKI opened another world allowing them to identify their most and least preferred conflict modes.

The four soft skills covered in this part were designed to equip participants to play their fair share in the process of coming together, working together, and getting along with others. The evaluation forms showed that participants loved these workshops. They appreciated the format of the workshops. They found them informative, dynamic, and engaging. Many of the participants acknowledged that the lessons they learned and the assessments they took equipped them well to succeed in a team environment.

Dan found the four topics covered in this part of the program a little challenging compared to part one topics. The former pushed him out of his comfort zone. Looking back retrospectively, the lack of these four soft skills were the ones that got in the way and caused him to fail in getting along with his team members, peers, and his immediate boss.

The workshops gave Dan lots of great insights, processes, and tools. He couldn't wait to apply them. Dan was optimistic that if he keeps practicing what he learned in the last four weeks, he could achieve tremendous results within a short period.

John Hancock- the 1st and 3rd governor of Massachusetts and a great businessman, noted: *"The greatest ability in business is to get along with others and influence their actions."* In this part, Dan developed the soft skills that equipped him to get along with others. What is remaining is half of the equation- influencing others' action. Dan cannot wait to dive into the next part of the program, which is designed to empower him to influence others.

Part III: Leading Others

"You don't lead by pointing and telling people some place to go. You lead by going to that place and making a case." **Ken Kesey**

Self-mastery and Getting along are foundations

The soft skills that enable us to master self and get along with others are still relevant when we are promoted to take leadership. The two are essential foundations that made so many leaders great. Extraordinary leaders have personal mastery and work with others very well. They also have additional soft skills that empower them to lead and influence others successfully. Whether you are a novice or seasoned leader, you need these soft skills, which will be discussed in this part, to influence others.

Influencing others requires some key soft skills

The common practice in many of today's organizations is that when employees demonstrate self-mastery and excellent abilities to work with others, they get promoted to lead others without developing the proper soft skills that are mandatory to succeed in their new role as leaders. Most of the time, the gap is recognized once it's too late to amend it. The skill sets that enabled them to excel in their private space, and as they get along with diverse co-workers weren't enough in the space where they were required to inspire, empower, negotiate, and lead their teams through continuous change.

That was the situation in Dan's case. Fortunately, he got a second chance.

Dan came a long way

As you have been closely following his progress, Dan took the program seriously. As a very strong willed person, he came a long way since the program had started. His superiors had noticed his improvements before he completed the program. During a companywide meeting, Susan and Dan met and got a chance to talk again. From that brief discussion, Susan observed Dan's progress.

Influencing others by being exemplary

Joe opened the 9th workshop by recapping the main points from the last part of the program. He continued to use the climbing Everest analogy. "During stage one, aspirant climbers self-discipline and work on themselves. They exercise and prepare themselves for the daunting task ahead. During stage two, they team up with other climbers, guides, and begin climbing Everest." Joe refreshed their memory.

He further explained that the first two phases of climbing Everest are different than the next phase, "Some of those who successfully conquered Everest for the first time may want to motivate, transform, and influence others who would like to triumph over Everest. Remember, even in this new role; they need to discipline themselves and get along with others. However, this new position compels them to influence others and lead the expedition successfully. It demands them to:

- Motivate,
- Mentor and coach others individually,
- Negotiate when necessary, and
- Influence others through the changing situations on the ground including the:
  - Weather,
  - Supplies,
  - Climbing equipment, and
  - Other continuously changing factors."

"I got it; leaders influence others successfully if they develop self-mastery and get along with others. However, it looks like you are saying that leaders should first climb at the top of the corporate ladder to influence others successfully? Am I correct?" Edgar wondered.

The majority participants nodded.

Edgar took the analogy literally as if someone has first to reach certain heights, and then should come down to lead others. Joe reasoned, "Influential leaders are those who lead by example, not necessarily because they have titles and positions." Joe paused for emphasis.

The kinds of leaders Joe is talking about have done their homework. They first led themselves and had stories to share. They have the authenticity, not necessary titles. Brian Tracy noted, *"Become the kind of leader that people would follow voluntarily; even if you had no title or position."*

Joe continued. "Such leaders don't need to climb the corporate leader first and be at the top to influence others successfully. Impactful leaders are those who have taken the time and put efforts to take away the guesswork. While they were leading self, and getting along with others, they scouted the route and also identified where the quicksand and wild animals are. When they got a chance to lead, they had been already there and knew the way."

The point of view of Joe aligns with what Ken Kesey said in the above leading quote. *"You don't lead by pointing and telling people some place to go. You lead by going to that place and making a case."* Similarly, John Maxwell declared, *"A leader is one who knows the way, goes the way, and shows the way."*

Influencing without a title
James interjected, "Are you saying that title doesn't matter at all?" Without giving Joe the opportunity to respond, he answered his question. "I agree. Title does not matter that much here at GHR. However, in some other organizations, it is paramount to lead, for example, in the military."

James is a veteran. He knows the importance of title in the army. Joe didn't disagree but gave James a context, "Title is important for any organization to make sure that things run well and orderly. But, as you said, in some organizations, title matters a lot more than in other organizational settings. Regardless, those successful leaders who reached great heights are those who influenced others without heavily depending on their designation."

Other participants joined the debate. They shared their perspectives about the place of title in influencing others. Finally, there was a kind of informal consensus: Great leaders command influence without highly depending on their title and authority.

Successful leaders develop the soft skills that allow them to influence others without twisting arms. Robin Sharma said, *"Leadership is not about a title or a designation. It's about impact, influence and inspiration.* Likewise, John Maxwell defined leadership as influence- nothing more, nothing less. The 6th President of the US John Quincy Adams also affirmed, *'If your actions inspire others to dream more, learn more, do more and become more, you are a leader.'"*

Leading self is a precursor to lead others
Wanting to know more about the connection between self-leadership they covered in part one to the current discussion- leading others, Martha asked Joe to expand on this. Joe asked the class to share their viewpoints. Kelley ventured, "As far as I can understand it, we cannot lead others effectively

until we know how to lead ourselves. People should see from our words, behaviors, and actions that we are worthy of leading. When they see that we run ourselves very well, they trust their lives, resources, time, and energy to our leadership." Kelly nailed it! Robin Sharma said, *"If you can't lead yourself, you can't lead others. "*

Joe complimented Kelley's point, "Yes, leading self successfully is the precursor to lead others effectively." He then reminded the class that leading self of itself isn't the end goal. "It's the foundation." He emphasized. "The ultimate goal is leading others to achieve collective success- the purpose of this program. Our success as leaders is measured based on how much we multiply ourselves in others. And the last part of this program is designed to help you develop the soft skills that are necessary to become a person of influence."

Characteristics of successful influencers

Once everybody is on the same page, Joe gave them an individual exercise: To select a person they consider most influential and share the name of their choice to the class. Some selected leaders from history while others recognized their parents, teachers, and coaches from high school and college years, and so on. Subsequently, Joe broke the class into small groups and asked them to identify the common characteristics of those influencers they recognized.

Styles of leadership to influence others

Following the small group discussion, Joe facilitated a large group discussion to gather some of the characteristics of successful influencers. Afterward, he opened the floor for question and answer. Kofi asked, "Joe, in our group, we recognized that those individuals we selected as influencers have had different styles of leadership. Do you mind to shed some light on this? Which leadership styles are essential to influence others?"

Joe acknowledged that there are many leadership styles to choose from. "But, there is no one style fits all as we go out to influence others." He briefly mentioned and compared the most common leadership styles. He gave a couple of quick scenarios to demonstrate where these styles are appropriate.

Among the leadership styles they talked about, Joe asked them to recognize which style (s) they use predominantly to influence others, and why. The most mentioned style by the group was Transformational leadership style. Let me share with you what Peter Northouse said about this style. He wrote, "[transformational leadership] *involves an exceptional form of influence that moves followers to accomplish more than what is usually expected of them.*"[94]

Model for Leading Others

Joe displayed the graphics below and pointed out, "Leading others entails doing so many things at once. However, in this program, we came up with a process that has three key stages: Motivating, transforming, and influencing." He explained each stage of the process of leading others very quickly. Though the question and answer session was interactive, let me briefly summarize the main discussion points for you:

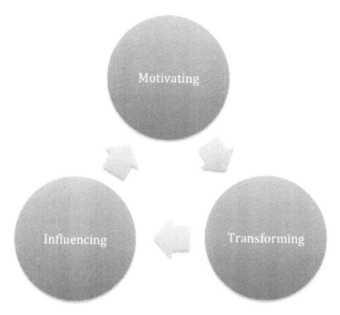

Fig. 3: The Leading Others Process

Motivating

- As part of self-mastery, we have been motivating ourselves to lead self.
- Our team leaders have been inspiring us as we work with others.
- When we become leaders ourselves, this is our turn to go beyond stirring ourselves and waiting for someone to stimulate us.
- The Leading Others process begins with motivating others to aim high and see the vision.
- Motivating, of course, continues throughout the process as leaders are required to inspire their people continually to overcome daunting challenges that prevent them from moving forward and realize the

vision.

- Motivating others is especially critical in the 21st C where fierce competition and continual change that frustrate many are the norms.
- Giving once in a while pep talks to motivate others to do great things and achieve success in what we do doesn't cut it any longer.

In his book Born To Win, Zig Ziglar wrote, *"I've frequently said that motivation is not permanent, but neither is bathing or eating! If you eat and bathe every day, you'll live longer and smell better in the process."*[95] He further reasoned, *"Staying motivated enough to win is the only way I've found to achieve long-term winning results."*[96]

- The challenge is that different people need diverse sources of motivation in order them to aim high and achieve extraordinary results.
- That is why we cannot just use those things that drive us to motivate everyone in our team. These may not motivate everyone to aim high.
- Leading diverse team members necessitates developing a soft skill that enables us continually inspire our people.

Joe displayed a slide. "Some of the questions we should ask in the motivating stage include but not limited to:

- What motivates each and everyone in my team?
- What kinds of recognitions and rewards can I offer to keep my team members motivated?
- How can I create an environment that promotes and sustains continual motivation?
- And other similar questions like these. Workshop nine- Motivating others to aim high provides you the insights, approaches, and theories that will help you keep motivating your team members on a consistent basis."
- Workshop nine coverers Motivating Others to Aim High.

Transforming:
- Motivating alone is not enough to lead others successfully.
- Once stakeholders are motivated to aim high and visualize the vision (how far they can go), they need empowerment, engagement, and leading them through constant changes to transform the team/organization from where it is to where it can actualize the vision.
- Individually and collectively, your people need to reach the height you inspired them to see in the first stage. This demands transformation.

- Transforming others requires developing additional soft skills such as coaching and mentoring to empower each member; the ability to engage with all stakeholders to create coalition through win-win negotiations, and to lead them throughout the changing terrain until the team meets its goals.
- Creating a culture that focuses on empowering your people is vital.

  Bill Gates declared, *"As we look ahead into the next century, leaders will be those who empower others."*

- Workshop ten is going to provide you insights, tools, and approaches you could use to coach and mentor your people, and in turn, transform them to do great things.
- However, leaders need to go beyond coaching and mentoring to empower their team members so as to achieve extraordinary results.
- Leading others also involves engaging other stakeholders (including distractors and rivals) to transform (convert) them from being opponents to being allies by becoming a skillful negotiator.
- Unlike in the past, these days, leaders cannot accomplish their duty by commanding alone.
- Leaders cannot just give orders, and expect things to be done.
- More and more, leaders in the workplace are expected to engage with their team members, peers, and other stakeholders including external customers in building coalitions and meeting their goals.
- They are required to negotiate on a consistent basis to influence others. This involves developing the ability to transform disagreements into win-win deals.
- Workshop eleven provides you the insights, approaches, and processes that you need to become a skillful negotiator.
- The ultimate goal of leaders should be to transform their people and the organization through continuous change.
- Leaders motivate, empower, and engage with stakeholders for what? These are a means to an end- to transform the team and the organization from where they're to where they should be through constant change until they actualize the vision.
- A team or department or organization cannot survive- let alone to thrive, without leaders at all levels leading others through change smoothly, which will be covered in Workshop twelve.
- The last workshop is designed to provide you what you need to transform your team and organization through continual change.

Influencing

- The ability to get along is necessary to lead others.
- However, leading others takes going beyond getting along.
- Leading others entails motivating, coaching and mentoring, negotiating and leading others through continuous change as requisites.
- Influencing, like self-mastery and getting along, is a state.
- This state is a by-product of developing the four soft skills included in part three of the program.
- Leading others is a cycle. A leader needs to inspire, coach and mentor, negotiate and lead change to have a dynamic and ever growing team that accomplishes great things. Besides, as new members join the group, the leader continually repeats the process starting from motivating, then to transforming, and influencing.

"At the end of the day, leaders are required to deliver. Whether a leader is assigned to lead a team that builds a bridge or a car or a team that goes out to battle, the leader needs to depend on her ability to motivate the team to believe that it can be done. The leader also needs to empower the team to handle the job; engage with all stakeholders; lead the team in the changing terrain till the job is done well. That is leadership." Joe concluded.

Yes, the success of a leader is measured based on the success the team attains. That is why Warren Bennis defined leadership as *"The capacity to translate vision into reality."* And, delivering results by transforming vision into reality demands influencing others by developing the four soft skills included in the last part of the program.

Joe finally displayed the four soft skills that would be covered in part three of the program:
- Motivating Others to Aim High,
- Coaching and Mentoring to Empower Others,
- Negotiating With Others for Win-Win Deals, and
- Leading Others Through Change Smoothly.

Soft Skill 9: Motivating Others to Aim High

"Motivation is the art of getting people to do what you want them to do because they want to do it." **Dwight D. Eisenhower**

Motivation others begins by learning how to motivate self

As indicated by Karen at the beginning of the program:

- Positive attitude,
- Optimistic outlook, and
- Hopefulness are critical for job success.

For those who have these in place, self-motivation is easier. They have intrinsic motivation. True motivation is within. This is of particular importance for leaders. They should know how to motivate themselves first on a consistent basis before they attempt to inspire others.

The task of motivating others becomes easier if the leader has learned how to inspire self. It's very hard to continually motivate others without being exemplary. It is impossible to fake motivation. A leader motivates from what is already full within her. If she doesn't have self-motivation and unless it is visible to others, it is hard to create motivation in others.

What is more? Occasional motivation isn't enough. Achieving extraordinary success is possible by generating consistent motivation from within. That is why Arsene Wenger said, *"When you look at people who are successful, you will find that they aren't the people who are motivated, but have consistency in their motivation."* Great leaders can reach deep to motivate themselves constantly and achieve extraordinary results continually.

However, though lasting motivation comes from within, leaders have the responsibility to create an environment that motivates their people persistently including those who aren't self-motivated for whatever reason. We have seen throughout history how some successful leaders ignited the motivation of millions. Of course, unless leaders are careful, with wrong moves, they could demoralize those who are inherently motivated.

Going beyond charisma and enthusiasm

People are attracted to leaders who are skillful in motivating them to become more, do more, and achieve more. Belittling leaders who are limiting easily repel people. These kinds of leaders cannot tap into the unlimited potential of their people. They cannot take them to the next level.

Unfortunately, many think that the ability to motivate others is a gift than a soft skill that can be developed. And therefore, they don't proactively invest their time and resources to learn how to motivate others. Even those who believe that this soft skill can be developed, they think that motivating others is all about giving pep talks, being charismatic, and exuding passion and energy to inspire others to do extraordinary things. Though being charismatic and speaking with enthusiasm motivates some. It's not enough to motivate all people and consistently.

Different things motivate different people

Dwight D. Eisenhower, who motivated and led hundreds of thousands of ally forces during the June 6, 1946 (The D-Day) war, believed that *"Motivation is the art of getting people to do what you want them to do because they want to do it."* Throughout his military career as a General and political career that culminated as the 34th President of the US, Eisenhower clearly understood that people are diverse with differing passions, desires, needs, and personality types. Accordingly, he tailored his motivation approaches that inspired his people to do what he wanted them to do gladly and with enthusiasm on a consistent basis.

Hollywood's highest paid star in 2012- Leonardo DiCaprio, revealed what really motivates him. For many people's disbelief, he dismissed that winning Oscar isn't his motivation. He acknowledged, *"I don't think anyone would say that they wouldn't want one [Oscar]. I think they would be lying."*[97]

You may then ask, "What drives DiCaprio to perform extraordinarily in those roles he has been playing for decades?" He admitted that he never expected winning Oscar and that is not his motivation when he plays these roles. He shared what motivates him, *"I really am motivated by being able to work with great people and create a body of work that I can look back and be proud of."*

Like DiCaprio, each member of your team has things that motivate him or her. If you discover what motivates them, you'll inspire them to do extraordinary things well beyond what they have already believed they can achieve. Henry Kissinger- the 56th Secretary of State of the US, said: *"The task of the leader is to get his people from where they are to where they have not been."*

Remember this. Your organization has a vision of where it would like to reach. In most cases, at any given time, there is an apparent gap between where the organization is and where it would like to arrive. You're hired to take the lead and contribute your share to fill this gap by continually motivating your team. However, taking your team to unfamiliar places requires developing extraordinary motivational ability by understanding their sweet spots, things that inspire them.

Dan was skeptic about motivating others. Before attending the workshop, he firmly believed that motivation comes from within. That was why he aired his cynicism at the beginning of the workshop. He shared in one of the small group discussions that he had attended many motivational speeches, and none of them motivated him the way he expected.

His real motivational moments came from inside. He didn't believe that it was possible to motive others consistently. For Dan, motivation isn't out there to be found. Rather, something people bring inside out.

He has a point. As indicated earlier, yes, lasting motivation comes from within. Though motivation necessitates the active participation of the individual, leaders should play proactive roles to create an environment that motivates others. And, that is why leaders should develop this soft skill to invoke and sustain motivation within their team.

I. Key lessons
1.1. Fear and manipulation cannot motivate people

"Honestly speaking, I thought that this is the responsibility of each team member to motivate herself or himself. When I find some of them lacking motivation, I had used all kinds of tricks including some maneuverings, and even fear." Dan was vulnerable to admit that he lacked this soft skill badly. "It didn't take long before my long-held beliefs about what motivates others was challenged. From Joe's explanation and the follow-up group discussions, I was convinced that I must change my outdated motivation approaches."

Rafael was kind. "Dan, you're not alone. Countless leaders around the world use manipulation and fear to motivate their people. Of course, such approaches won't deliver the intended results. Leaders need to be truly motivational to succeed."

Motivation without intimidation

"By the way," Rafael continued, "In the industrial era, the carrot and stick approach worked successfully, and leaders forced their people to do what they wanted either through rewards or the threat of penance. In the 21st C, however, successful leaders in today's workplace are those who gain the compliance of others without using any trick and dishonest approaches."

Bob Burg argued that leaders should justify convincingly the kinds of benefits their people may gain if they do what they don't have to do[98]. When we influence people without intimidation and manipulation, they should consider themselves beneficiaries by doing those things *"for us than they would feel by not doing"* them.

1.2. Creating discontentment to ignite motivation

"Rather than using fear or any form of manipulation, by creating discontentment, I could motivate my team continually." Dan shared the second lesson he learned from the workshop. He added, "We learned that today's organizations are jam packed with many team members who settled for less than whom they are. They operate below their potential. Such individuals are settled at where they are currently. They may fail to motivate themselves any further thinking that where they are is their best."

Rafael inquired, "How do you plan to challenge such team members?" Dan intended to create discontentment within the team by showing them their unlimited potential they failed to notice or undermine. He continued, "I should stretch and challenge my team to aim high beyond what they unusually think they can achieve."

"That sounds a great plan," Rafael complimented. He further pointed out, "Showing their people what they might have ignored or undermined, and pointing them to see their many other untapped talents is the prime responsibility of leaders. Most importantly, motivational leaders are those who provide opportunities that allow their people to push their limit and achieve extraordinary results by tapping into their hidden talents. Once their people see that they can push themselves beyond the limits they put in place, they keep on pushing to achieve more."

If leaders don't create discontentment and motivate their people to aim high, the chances are high that they may settle for less. One of my favorite motivational speakers, Les Brown famously remarked, *"Most people fail in life not because they aim too high and miss, but because they aim too low and hit."* Andrew Carnegie, a self-motivated steel tycoon who was considered as one of the richest people of 19th century lamented, *"People who are unable to motivate themselves must be content with mediocrity, no matter how impressive their other talents."*

Steve Jobs created discontentment successfully and stretched his first team to aim high. In the 1980s, a self-inspired co-founder of Apple used to motivate his team by constantly reminding them why they were there. He was quoted as saying, *"We're here to put a dent in the universe. Otherwise, why even be here."* Accordingly, rather than thinking that they were there to just come up with another kind of computer, they felt that they were there to change the world for good. And surely, they put a huge dent in the universe and left a legacy.

Using diverse approaches to motivate your people

"You said you would show them their unlimited potential to stretch them. What are some of the avenues you are going to use?" Rafael asked a follow-up question. "Some of the approaches that I'm thinking right now include sending inspirational emails, arranging one-on-ones, and group moments to share inspirational stories," Dan responded with confidence. Rafael added, "You may also consider bringing outsiders to share their inspiring stories to inspire your team."

1.3. Creating and sustaining a motivating environment

"The most sustainable way to keep motivating my team is to create and maintain a motivating environment." Dan identified the third insight he got from the workshop. Rafael sensed hesitation. He kept silent to allow Dan spell out his reservation. "But, I don't feel confident whether I could create such an environment or not yet. Besides, I don't know where to start. I need your advice on this." Dan sought Rafael's guidance.

"Why don't you start, first, by getting rid of those things that might demotivate your team?" Rafael proposed. Dan remembered the discussion they had in the class about Herzberg's Two-Factor theory. For the next several minutes, they talked about this theory and how to apply it.

They acknowledged, however, that getting rid of things that demotivate his team members are lower level needs that may not generate a high level of motivation to most of his team members. They agreed that continual motivation that leads to real success entails meeting the high-end needs of his people such as:
- Giving meaning to the work they do,
- Recognizing individual contributions,
- Providing self-realization opportunities, and so on.

Rafael suggested, "Yes, removing workplace hygiene factors such as demoralizing policies, procedures, work conditions, and supervisions you have already identified may not generate continual motivation. But, tackling these is a necessary starting place." Dan concurred and decided, "You're right! I should address the environmental factors first while working on creating and sustaining a highly motivating culture within my team."

Motivating when things aren't going your way

Rafael foresees the challenge Dan may face in creating and sustaining a motivating atmosphere especially when things don't go well. He underscored, "Motivating your people may be easier if you are succeeding and things are going the team's way. Motivating when your team faces continual setbacks and defeat, that is when your actual ability to inspire your team is going to be tested."

"What should you be doing on such occasions?" Rafael asked. Dan ventured, "Yes, it is tough to motivate my team while things are falling apart and when we cannot keep things together. It's very challenging to motivate people when we are in crisis mood. However, I firmly believe that by consciously demonstrating resilience and determination in the face of such disasters, I could be able to inspire my team."

"Inspirational leaders remove themselves from the crisis and quickly display courage and remain motivated in the midst of a disappointing situation. Leaders cannot be faint hearted. Even if they feel discouraged inwardly, they appear courageous outwardly and help the team to pass through the challenging season by investing more time and energy to motivate the team continually. Motivational leaders are skillful in showing the light at the end of the tunnel so that their people withstand downtimes." Rafael inspired Dan. Rafael's line of thought agrees with what John C. Maxwell said, *"Leaders must be close enough to relate to others, but far enough ahead to motivate them."*

Compartmentalized motivation

Dan was intrigued. "You said, 'even if they feel discouraged inwardly, they appear courageous outwardly.' How do they do this without coming across as faking it?" Dan was unable to see himself doing that. Rafael elaborated, "Consistency is vital to remain authentic. As far as they demonstrate consistency, they should be okay. It doesn't come out as if they're faking it. However, some leaders compartmentalize their lives. Their motivation end at the door. They appear motivated in the workplace, but the moment they leave, they go back to their demotivated mood. The moment they step out of office, as they walk toward the parking lot, they walk while their shoulder is down with a beaten up posture. In their neighborhood and the marketplace, they are out of energy and appear tired. What would happen if one of their people sees them in this mood? What happens when their people notice that inconsistency?" Dan answered, "People talk. They lose authenticity and the credibility to motivate their people with authority."

1.4. Wrong rewards don't motivate people

"I loved the discussion on tailor made recognitions. We learned that many companies fail to customize their recognitions and in turn unable to motivate their super achievers."

Rafael recognized, "Many organizations, genuinely and unintentionally, make mistakes in their approaches to motivate their people. And, GHR isn't exceptional. I know some flawed recognitions the management used in the past. Though the intentions were good, the recognitions failed to achieve the intended results- unable to motivate."

"Do you mind to give me an example?" "No, I don't. A colleague of mine was disappointed when she was given a round trip plane ticket to go to the Bahamas for her hard work. She was on a work visa, and going out and back into the US wasn't an easy task- the paperwork would have been a hustle. Besides, taking a vacation in the Caribbean wasn't on her priority list, hasn't prepared for it." If you were this lady, what would you feel? Would you be motivated?" Dan's response was an emphatic no.

The need to tailor recognitions for maximum impact

Let me share with you a well-customized recognition. A multinational corporation, I worked for, had been suffering a lot because of high turnover. Since a large number of immigrant students like myself joined the company in 2005, they began seeing reduced employee turnover and increased productivity.

The manager decided to recognize our contributions to keep motivating us so that we might keep working hard, and most importantly, to stay with the company longer. He might have asked others. When he asked my recommendations, I gave him two suggestions for his consideration.

I thought that the majority of my fellow immigrants would like to stay in the US a little longer once their student visa expires. Of course, there were some who cannot wait to finish their study and return to their family. I suggested that those who would like to stay in the US would appreciate and remain motivated if the company sponsors them for a working visa, H1B. The second group, I acknowledged, had been taking extra courses every semester to finish quickly that they might be struggling to pay their tuition fees. Reimbursing their tuition fees may keep them motivated until they leave the company.

The manager found the suggestions appealing. Hence, he proposed the two options. The majority including myself chose to be sponsored for a working visa. By the way, many of those sponsored stayed with the company for many years. Some of them are still working there. Those whose tuitions reimbursed too continued to perform great until they graduated and left the company. It was a win-win arrangement.

Providing relevant incentives to gain cooperation

Let me give you one more example. Between 2000 until I came to the US in 2005, I worked for an international research organization. I was part of a team of French scientists. The project we were working on was designed to study a trans-boundary livestock disease called Contagious Bovine Pleuropneumonia in one of the rural parts of Ethiopia. The study required taking cattle blood samples every month for two years or so.

The French scientists knew how livestock are the livelihood of farmers. They recognized that we need the cooperation of the farmers. However, rather than bringing some expensive gifts from Europe to gain cooperation, they decided to go and figure out what motivates the peasants.

The overwhelming majority of farmers cared about their cattle. They suggested, "Bring mineral salts for our livestock whenever you come to take blood samples." Every month, our data collectors went with the blocks of salts purchased from the capital city, Addis Ababa. We had outstanding cooperation from the farmers throughout the lifespan of the project.

The moral of the story is that rather than the Europeans or myself, who didn't have any clue about the needs of rural farmers, deciding what motivates the rural farmers, we sought their inputs to understand the very thing that inspires them to collaborate. It worked. They collaborated for the success of the study.

Rather than motivated, someone was pissed off!

I heard so many hilarious recognitions that went wrong. These recognitions rather than invoking motivation, they pissed off recipients. One of my trainer friends once shared a fascinating story on how a company recognized an employee, who didn't have a car at all, as 'Employee of The Month.' Accordingly, they awarded him a front row parking spot for a month.

The employee was an environmental activist who didn't drive. He resented people who drive. He was mad because the management didn't take time and made reasonable efforts to understand what mattered to him. Rather than inspiring him, they pissed him off.

One size doesn't fit all

Rafael concluded this section by remarking, "When it comes to recognizing and inspiring people, one size doesn't fit all. Each individual has unique preferences when it comes to things that motivate him or her to do extraordinary things. This requires the leader to tailor her motivational approaches. She should know what inspires each team member to go the extra mile."

II. Assessments, Processes, and Tools
2.1. MBTI

The class didn't take a specific assessment concerning motivation. However, Dan believed that MBTI was still very relevant since he decided to tailor his motivation and recognition approaches to each team member. Dan explained, "The principle behind MBTI is that each person has unique preferences of needs, interests, aspirations, and so on. I should find out their preferences and customize my recognitions accordingly."

Rafael agreed with Dan's idea but reminded him that first, his team should take the assessment, and most importantly, he has to get their willingness to share their results. "Otherwise, you shouldn't assume these things. The first step is for them to take the assessment. Even then, you shouldn't force them to share their results." They talked about some strategies, based on Rafael's personal experience, on how he might gain the cooperation of his team members to reveal their preferences and aspirations.

2.2. Abraham Maslow's Hierarchy of needs theory

Dan found the motivational theories discussed in the class very helpful. Among the theories covered, he liked Abraham Maslow's theory. "This theory allowed me to recognize that there are hierarchies of needs. I also realized that met needs don't motivate."

Upon Rafael's request, Dan elaborated the theory:
- "At the bottom of Maslow's pyramid are **physiological needs** that are necessary for survival such as food, water, air, sleep, rest, etc.
- **Safety** needs are on the second tier such as well-being, safety, and financial security.
- **Belonging** is the third hierarchical need like friendship, belongingness, love, and so on.
- The forth hierarchy is **esteem** such as the need for recognition, status, confidence, etc.
- **Self-actualization** is the last layer. Once lower level needs are satisfied, one may seek personal fulfillment to tap into his/her full potential."

Rafael pointed out that Maslow added another top end layer called self-transcendence. He also expressed his point of views about theories in general,
- "Theories are just theories.

- There is no one perfect theory that explains every thing.
- Maslow's theory is not exceptional."

"By the way, Maslow's theory has been criticized for failing to explain cultural differences and individual exceptions," Dan mentioned what he figured out from his further reading. "Regardless," Rafael defended Maslow's theory, "Like every other theory, his theory gives us a framework to think about the hierarchical needs of humans. We can still use it regardless of its flaws. We just need to complement it with other theories to compensate its shortcomings."

Rafael was curious to know how Dan was going to apply the theory, "How and where do you plan to use Abraham Maslow's Hierarchy of Needs?" Dan was quick to reply, "To align my recognitions with personal needs. The needs of my team members vary according to where they are professionally and in life. That is why I should align my recognitions with the needs of each member."

After appreciating Dan's point, he commented, "If someone is struggling to make ends meet, it is unlikely to motivate that person with incentives that don't address his/her lower level concerns. Likewise, if someone has been already at the top of the pyramid, it is futile to use incentives at lower levels to motivate that individual."

III. Action item

Including removing things that had been demotivating his team, Dan was armed with so many great ideas to motivate his team. He began unloading his action items, "While working on those dissatisfactory factors, I should come up with some words to use, behaviors to demonstrate, and measures to take that aim at inspiring my team to believe that they can do extraordinary things they haven't thought possible before." His enthusiasm was palpable from his facial expression, gestures, and body language. Rafael didn't miss Dan's genuine desire to become an inspirational leader.

However, he was concerned about the timing. Rafael's worry wasn't just whether Dan could do it right away or not. "I'm afraid that the team might not immediately buy into your abruptly changed mannerism even if your intention is good and genuine." He advised him to take it slowly. And thus, he asked, "What is that one thing that you can do right away that may lay the foundation to motivate your team and take them to the next level?"

Dan suggested, "I think I can start being positive and enabling in my next one-on-one conversations with each team member." Dan paused and asked, "What do you suggest for me?" Rafael recommended, "Don't forget to acknowledge what they have been doing great so far and express your genuine appreciation. Some people may not expect a lot from their leaders to get motivated. They are happy and driven enough if what they do is recognized by their leaders."

"What you're saying is that, until I understand the real motivation of my team members and the corresponding recognitions, I should appreciate their unique contributions thus far." Dan wanted to make sure that he understood Rafael's point. Rafael nodded to confirm. He then smiled broadly and indicated, "This buys time for you until you roll out your long-term plan to keep motivating your team." Dan nodded, and they concluded the mentoring session.

Summary

Unlike in the past, leaders in the 21st C cannot just demand their people to do what they want using manipulation, intimidation, and other dishonest tricks. The stake is high; a lot is expected from today's leaders. The 21st C leaders are expected to motivate their people to tap into their unlimited potential. However, motivating others should begin by motivating self constantly, and demonstrating consistency. It also requires removing those factors that demotivate team members. But, the absence of these factors alone cannot elevate people's motivation. Leaders must meet the needs of their people to inspire them continually. Motivating people on a consistent basis involves understanding the unique preferences of individuals, their unmet needs, aspirations, and tailoring motivational approaches accordingly. Leaders should also customize their recognitions to motivate their people consistently.

Soft Skill 10: Coaching & Mentoring to Empower Others

"Before you are a leader, success is all about growing yourself. When you become a leader, success is all about growing others." **Jack Welch**

Leading demands empowering others

- The Leading Others process has three stages.
- The first stage is motivating.
- When a leader is assigned to lead a team of people, the leader is expected to inspire them to aim high.
- Without motivation, a leader cannot tap into her people's untapped potential and materialize the vision.
- Workshop nine covered the first soft skill- Motivating others to aim high.
- The mere ability to motivate others, however, doesn't enable a leader to achieve extraordinary results.
- The leader should develop three more soft skills that empower her to transform each member, other stakeholders, and finally the team/organization as a whole if her desire is to influence others and finally succeed in meeting the shared goals.
- Transforming each member to carry out their job description requires developing the soft skill- Coaching and Mentoring, which was covered in Workshop ten.
- Transforming each person through coaching and mentoring could be done by the leader herself and other in-house and external coaches and mentors.
- Empowering also involves, on top of coaching and mentoring, many other methods such as delegating, giving them autonomy, and sending them to training, etc. Here, however, we only talk about what leaders can do by himself/herself to empower each team member.
- The goal is to take your people to the place where they can accomplish those things you are influencing them to do by sharpening their skills; modifying their mindset and behaviors; and providing them what they need to maximize their full potential.
- Leaders also need this soft skill to raise their and some of their team members' successors.

Going beyond motivating

Recognizing, incentivizing, giving bonuses, using powerful inspirational words, and other means of motivation to continuously enthusing your people are important as you influence others to do extraordinary things. Great leaders, however, don't stop there. They transform their people to translate the motivation into tangible results by giving them one-on-one attention. By investing their scarce time and resources, they use coaching and mentoring to empower their team members.

Unfortunately, many leaders think that their great personality is enough to continually inspire, transform, and influence so that their people to do extraordinary things. Peter Drucker disagreed when he said, *"Leadership is not magnetic personality, that can just as well be a glib tongue. It is not making friends and influencing people, that is flattery."* He clarified what authentic and empowering leadership is. *"Leadership is lifting a person's vision to higher sights, the raising of a person's performance to a higher standard, the building of a personality beyond its normal limitations."*

Extraordinary leaders tap into the potential of individual team members' strengths and work on their limitations by giving them one-on-one care. And coaching and mentoring are the two critical approaches that could help leaders accomplish just that. This soft skill indeed enables leaders to raise extraordinary team members that add unique values toward the success of the team, and in turn to the larger organization. John D. Rockefeller was quoted as saying, *"Good leadership consists of showing average people how to do the work of superior people."*

What do you get paid for?

Leaders must do many things at the same time to lead others and succeed in their leadership. Among these, empowering their people to do extraordinary things differentiate great leaders from mediocre. That is why Ferdinand Fournies, the author of 'Coaching for Improved Work Performance' wrote, *"Your ability as a manager is measured by what your employees do, not by what you do."* He underlined, *"The facts of life dictate that, as a manager, you don't get paid for what you do, you get paid for what your employees do."* For your people to perform amazingly, you need to coach and mentor your people to do their jobs superbly.

I. Key lessons
1.1. Similarities and differences between coaching and mentoring

Dan used to use the two words interchangeably. He hadn't understood their similarities and differences. He confessed, "I hadn't known their differences, and most importantly which one to use when and where. This workshop allowed me to understand the similarities and differences between the two."

Rafael asked Dan to clarify the main difference between the two. Dan began. "Coaching is used mainly to improve performance. Mentoring, on the other hand, is a necessity for the long-term health and performance of the organization such as raising successors, for instance."

Rafael nodded and added, "Here is another way to look at it. Coaching is to help coachees develop 'hard skills', so to speak, to improve performance while mentoring is aimed at helping mentees develop soft skills such as how to make smart decisions, handle objections, resolve conflicts, and so on based on the mentor's personal experience." He further underlined, "The two supplement one another. Sometimes, the line between the two may become blurred."

Coaches and mentors- Difference makers?
"By the way, I hadn't considered having coaches or mentors, let alone to be one," Dan disclosed.

Rafael remarked, "Coaches and mentors are difference makers in the lives of others. The giants that we see in various fields today have coaches and mentors. Many of them publicly share who helped them to reach where they are today."

For instance, one of the richest men in the world, Warren Buffet credited his success to his mentor Benjamin Graham. One of the world's renowned motivational speaker, Tony Robbins, regularly mentions the name of his mentor- Jim Rhon- for his success. Another great motivational speaker, Les Brown talks about Mike Williams who stretched and inspired him to become a motivational speaker back when Brown did not believe in his ability to inspire others.

Richard Branson of Virgin Group attributed his airlines business success to his mentor Freddie Laker. He said, *"Freddie Laker, was integral to Virgin Atlantic succeeding in the airline business."*[100] A survey by ASTD (American Society for Training and Development) revealed, *"75% of private sector executives said that mentoring had been critical in helping them reach their current position."*[101]

1.2. Feedback giving and receiving
Reminding Rafael that they had already talked about feedback giving and receiving when they talked about playing teamwork, Dan informed him that the theme also resurfaced in this workshop.

"For me to succeed either as coach and mentor or coachee and mentee, I need to be a skillful feedback giver and receiver." Dan recognized. "These relationships require soliciting and providing honest and constructive feedback. It's great that you got additional insights from this workshop too." Rafael expressed his gladness. "Yes. By now, I have enough understanding of the process of receiving and giving feedback. What I need is practicing it in coaching and mentoring." Dan spoke enthusiastically.

"Tell me more." Rafael inquired. Dan stopped and took a deep breath. He then responded with a visible conviction. "I should ask questions to get feedback from my coaches and mentees than telling them what went wrong and what they should do to fix it." "Are you saying that coaches and mentors should know how to ask probing questions than assuming what went wrong, and prescribing things to their cochees and mentees before seeking feedback first?" Rafael double checked. "Exactly!" Dan confirmed.

Max Landsberg in his book entitled 'The TAO of Coaching' advised coaches to ask their coachees feedback than telling them what they did wrong and what to do next. He wrote, *"Coachees can often learn more if the coach asks them how well they're performed a particular task than from being told, 'Here's what you did wrong, and here's what to do next time.'"*[102]

Dan moved on. "To succeed in getting along with and leading others, especially to succeed in my new roles as coach and mentor, I need to be skillful in providing feedback, especially tough feedback. Unfortunately, this task is easier said than done. Giving feedback about what they do great is easier. What about giving feedback about their weaknesses and limitations? How do you do it?" Admitting that he isn't yet in the position to provide difficult feedback neither to his team nor his boss/peers, he solicited Rafael's advice.

"It's a very tough challenge," Rafael acknowledged and advised. "However, it's possible to develop and continually fine-tune this soft skill. It's within your reach to remain nice while at the same time giving honest and strong feedback to the people you love and care about." Dan double-checked. "You're encouraging me to be direct when I provide tough feedback but to make sure that I do it nicely." Rafael nodded.

Next, Rafael shared the process he uses when he gives strong criticisms. He then gave him a simple example. "For instance, let's say that one of your team members came to an event you organized with a wrong tie. You decided to coach him. Be direct. Of course, first, create a positive atmosphere. Tell the person 'Your tie looks great on you.' And ask, 'Are you aware that this tie doesn't match the occasion?' Remember, before you reach any conclusion and tell the person that 'his tie doesn't match with the event'; it's wise to ask first. The person may already know about it. Or he didn't know about it and was not sure what kind of tie he should have chosen. The latter gives you an opportunity to provide more explanation, and offer some options for future considerations." Dan loved the example.

Rafael offered his final advice. "Of course, you don't need to implement this process strictly. You may customize and use it as it fits your objective condition on the ground. The most important thing is to understand the place of giving tough feedback as you empower your people to succeed in what they do. By the same token, seek tough feedback if your desire is to grow as a leader continually."

The last advice of Rafael is important to note. Kevin Cashman declared, *"Sometimes other people hold keys to unlocking self-knowledge."* He recommended, *"Rather than spending energy resisting feedback, look for the seeds of learning contained in people's perceptions. Leaders grow proportionally to their openness to input."*[103] Soliciting feedback is our responsibility. Max Landsberg too advised, *"It's up to you to obtain feedback from others."*

1.3 Benefits of coaching and mentoring
"On top of personal growth that leads to improved performance, coaching and mentoring also have corporate level benefits." Dan shared the third lesson he learned. Rafael nodded and signaled him to continue. Dan enlisted the following advantages:
- To increase productivity,
- To exchange valuable information,
- To grow together,
- To impart the corporate values, and
- To align with corporate culture.

Coaching for performance
Rafael wanted to know how Dan is going to tap into the first benefit. "How do you plan to use coaching to improve productivity?" Dan explained, "Some of my team members may have blind spots that have prevented them to improve their performance. They may need my coaching to uncover these blind spots that sabotage their ability to perform well continually."

After listening attentively, Rafael advised, "I see. If some of your team members are not performing well. And if you observe what they say, behave, and/or do get in the way and derail their performance and in turn the bottom-line of the team, they need your coaching desperately. Coach them so that they may continue to do what they do well, and improve those things that are not working in their favor."

Mentoring to raise successors

"Dan, you need also mentoring to raise as many great leaders within your team as possible who complement, support, and at the end of the day succeed you and other team members when the need arises." Rafael recommended.

Rafael's advice is precious. There is a famous saying: *'Success without a successor is a failure.'* As leaders, we shouldn't wait until we are incapacitated or leave our office to worry about our successors. We should have enough people in our team who could do great jobs in our absence. That is why Patrick Lencioni said, *"As a leader, you're probably not doing a good job unless your employees can do a good impression of you when you're not around."*

1.4. Selecting the right coaches and mentors

Even if Dan decided to become a great coach and mentor, he determined to find the right coaches and mentors for himself. He wanted to learn how it is done first before he begins this duty himself. They took several minutes to talk about the kinds of questions Dan should ask to select his coaches and mentors.

Dan also expressed his interest in retaining Rafael as his mentor after the Soft Skills Development program is over. Rafael agreed, "I don't mind to continue the relationship after the program is complete." Dan thanked him and stretched his hand to shake Rafael's hand to show his appreciation. They shook hand while smiling and laughing. They looked at each other's eyes and could see that the two were enjoying each other's company.

Multiple coaches and mentors

Next, Rafael suggested Dan to consider having multiple coaches and mentors depending on his needs. He shared his personal experience, "I need to grow as a leader, mentor, and coach. Accordingly, I've multiple mentors who give me one-on-one opportunities and chances to shadow them and in the process grow. Others bring me to their ad hoc team and allow me to learn by participating."

Dan sought Rafael's advice. "What is one thing that I should pay close attention as I choose my coaches and mentors?" Rafael took the time to think for several seconds and underscored, "One temptation when we choose our coaches and mentors is to look for individuals we like. For that, we already have friends and colleagues. What we need is those who would give us honest feedback, the ones who stretch and help us achieve our growth goals."

Great advice. Steven Stowell and Matt Starcevich, in their book 'The Coach: Creating partnerships for a competitive edge', wrote: *"When you go looking for a coach, you are not looking for a clone of yourself- you're already got you. you are looking for someone who has experience or insight you don't have in dealing with a particular subject."*[104]

Attributes of effective coaches and mentors

Dan exclaimed, "Got it!" And he moved to his next question. "What kind of attributes should I look for when I choose my coaches and mentors?" "From my experience, there are three essential characteristics of great coaches and mentors: Trust, authenticity, and flexibility." He briefly explained each attribute:

1. **Trust** has a central role for successful coaching and mentoring relationship.

   Chip Bell in his book 'Managers as Mentors' noted, *"A mentor with only modest mentoring skills can be successful if the protégé experiences a high level of trust."*[105]

2. **Authenticity**, being real and honest, is one of the marks of successful coaches and mentors.

   The author of 'The Heart of Coaching' Thomas Crane noted, *"The greatest gift you can bring to your coachees is to be true to your innermost thoughts and deliver authentic messages honestly and directly."* He continued, *"Caring about people is one of the basic reasons many of us choose to become a coach. Coaching is a path of service and can only be traveled out of genuine honesty with others."*[106]

3. **Flexibility**, the ability to accommodate and adjust with the needs and personality of the coachees and mentees, is required from outstanding coaches and mentors.

   Steven Stowell and Matt Starcevich in their book 'Win-Win Partnerships: Be on the leading edge with synergistic coaching' wrote, *"A coach, no matter how effective, cannot force a team member to participate in the coaching process."*[107]

II. Assessments, Processes, and Tools
2.1. Coaching model

"We reviewed a couple of coaching models," Dan explained, "However, I found one of them very easy and straightforward to guide me in my coaching efforts." Rafael reminded Dan that there are many coaching models out there to choose from. Next, he shared his favorite model and asked Dan to talk about his briefly.

Dan shared his favorite coaching model. Rafael asked him a couple of follow-up questions why he chose this model, and also to describe each step. Let me share with you one of the coaching models that I like. The 8-step model of Steven Stowell and Matt Starcevich:

1. Be supportive
2. Define the topic and needs
3. Establish impact
4. Initiate a plan
5. Get a commitment
6. Confront excuses/resistance
7. Clarify consequences, don't punish
8. Don't give up[108]

IV. Action item
Working on relationships

Dan revealed his immediate area of focus, "My first action is to find the right coaches and mentors. I'm convinced that getting proper coaching and mentoring contributes to my success as a leader. I've already learned from you a lot. I'd like to continue to learn from you, and also find a coach. These opportunities will definitely give me chances to learn on how to coach and mentor my team properly. In both scenarios, the relationship is crucial, especially with my team members. Therefore, my first focus is to work on my relationship with the team, and become a trustworthy partner."

Rafael remained silent. After a brief pause, Dan pointed out, "But, it won't be that easy considering that some of my relationships have been already damaged. I haven't yet created the kind of relationship that requires to being a successful coach and mentor."

That was a valid concern. John Whitmore, in his book 'Coaching for Performance' wrote, *"Coaching to work at its best the relationship between the coach and the coachee must be one of partnership in the endeavor, of trust, of safety, and of minimal pressure."*[109]

Rafael understood Dan's challenge. He realized that becoming a trustworthy partner takes time and lots of efforts. Thus, he proposed, "If you think that you don't have the relationship in place with some of your team members yet, why don't you delay it a little longer? If you need to begin empowering your people immediately, you may consider using coaches and mentors from other projects and even from outside of GHR." Dan found these options useful. He took it as an assignment to further think and choose one of the options.

Before they concluded this mentoring session, Rafael alerted Dan, "Coaching and mentoring others and the willingness to get mentoring has become mandatory in many successful organizations. And, GHR is also heading in this direction. Therefore, take this soft skill seriously so that you may find yourself ahead of the curve by the time it becomes mandatory."

Several organizations are redefining the term boss. Organizations are demanding their managers to transform themselves from being in charge and giving orders to coaching and mentoring their people to do excellent jobs. Many Fortune 500 companies such as General Electric, Intel, Caterpillar, Google, and Time Warner Cable offer formal mentoring programs.[110]

Summary

Leading others entails transforming team members by empowering them using coaching and mentoring. This soft skill allows leaders to give one-on-one attention to each member. It enables leaders to work on their people so that the latter could be able to carry out their job descriptions successfully. Coaching and mentoring could also be used to improve performance, increase productivity, impart corporate values, and raise successors. As much as coaching and mentoring to empower others is critical, leaders at all levels should also find their own coaches and mentors to grow and lead their people continually. The three most important attributes to look when leaders choose their coaches and mentors include trust, authenticity, and flexibility.

Soft Skill 11: Negotiating With Others for Win-Win Deals

"Human beings are born solitary, but everywhere they are in chains - daisy chains - of interactivity... And in a way, every social action is a negotiation, a compromise between 'his', 'her' or 'their' wish and yours." **Andy Warhol**

Leading others involves engaging others

- Leading Others is a process.
- Motivating is the first stage, which was covered in Workshop nine.
- The second stage is transforming.
- Out of the three soft skills necessary to transform all stakeholders, Workshop ten covered Coaching and Mentoring.
- The second soft skill is negotiating with others for win-win deals to increase the leader's chance to engage and ultimately influence all stakeholders to attain success.
- Workshop eleven covered Negotiating with others for win-win deals.
- Many of the conflicts that we experience in our organizations could have been easily avoided or at least resolved quickly if all involved parties engage in win-win negotiations.
- Leaders cannot lead without influencing. It's an uphill battle to influence diverse stakeholders without becoming a skillful negotiator.

Everyone negotiates

When people think of negotiation, they mainly consider formal and large-scale negotiations such as between nations (Egypt vs. Israel) or political parties (Democrats vs. Republicans), corporate management vs. labor union leaders, and so on. People neglect the fact that we all negotiate on a consistent basis at home, on the road, office, marketplace, almost everywhere whether we would like to admit it or not.

Besides, many people think that negotiation is for lawyers and politicians. Accordingly, they refrain from honing their negotiation skills, and in turn, leave great stuff on the 'negotiation table.' Many leaders fall short of developing and refining their ability to negotiate for win-win deals.

Mandatory for leaders

Unlike in the past, today's leaders cannot accomplish anything meaningful without engaging in constant negotiation. The days where leaders just give the order to achieve their goals are literally over. In the 21st C:

- As they set goals,
- Assign tasks to their team members,
- Interact with their peers, superiors, and other stakeholders within and outside of their organizations,

- They need to excel in negotiating for win-win deals.

Negotiation: A two-way street

As Andy Warhol depicted in the above leading quote, negotiation is a social interaction among diverse parties, which requires giving and taking. To get what we want, we need to give by way of meeting the needs of others. As much as we would like to influence others, we also need to be willing to be influenced, which involves negotiation. Negotiation is a two-way street.

Be positive and don't take things personally

Negotiation also necessitates having a positive outlook about the other party, refraining from taking things personally. Brian Koslow, best-selling author, speaker, international businessman and investor advised, *"During a negotiation, it would be wise not to take anything personally. If you leave personalities out of it, you will be able to see opportunities more objectively."*

Also, contrary to popular belief, most people really want to make deals. The majority of negotiators are not inherently stubborn. They desire to make deals. The 51st Secretary of State of the US, Dean Acheson, who had hands-on experience when it comes to negotiation, remarked, *"Negotiation in the classic diplomatic sense assumes parties more anxious to agree than to disagree."*

I. Key lessons
1.1. Preparation determines the level of success

One of the eye openers Dan got from the workshop was the significance of preparation for win-win deals. "We learned that many well-intentioned leaders think that negotiation begins when they ask and make concessions at the negotiation table. Successful negotiators, on the other hand, do their homework well before they enter the negotiation room."

"What are the key considerations to get what you need from a win-win negotiation as you prepare for both formal and informal negotiations?" Rafael probed. Dan looked at the roof while thinking and came up with a few factors. "I should spend enough time ahead to know about mine and my counterpart's:

- Strengths and weaknesses,
- Wants and needs,
- Best and worst case scenarios, and
- Walking away points."

"These are significant areas of focus during preparation!" Rafael recognized and emphasized. "If leaders fail to answer these questions adequately before they arrive at the negotiation table, they are planning to fail. They are allowing themselves dragged into the room blindfolded."

Avoiding poor negotiation

Rafael underscored, "Nonetheless, these are bare minimums. We should take each potential talk seriously and be aware of our counterparts' options to maximize our success from each negotiation."

Reading from Dan's facial expression, Rafael decided to make his point explicit, "We need to understand our relative position in any negotiation. We need to know the leverages we have about the other party. Our approach must be different when we negotiate with someone who has all the leverages and with someone who has less or no leverage at all."

Dan took a trip down memory lane and remembered his negotiation with Susan and Paul. He didn't have strong leverages. Dan learned at one point that he was negotiating with his superiors who had better advantages than he had. That was why he didn't get what he wanted and settled for a compromise. Dan's position, in the beginning, was to keep leading the project without bothering about his soft skills. That didn't happen. He compromised to work on his soft skills by attending the Soft Skills Development program to keep his leading role.

"Awareness about who has the most leverage empowers us to avoid negotiating poorly." Dan pinpointed. "We talked in the class about the importance of knowing ours and the other party's Best Alternative To a Negotiated Agreement (BATNA), Worst Alternative To a Negotiated Agreement (WANA), Walk Away Price (WAP), and Zone Of Possible Agreement (ZOPA)."

Let me just pick BATNA and share with you what the authors of 'Getting To Yes' wrote about it, *"The reason you negotiate is to produce something better than the results you can obtain without negotiating."* They continued, *"[BATNA] is the only standard that can protect you both from accepting terms that are unfavorable and from rejecting terms it would be in your interest to accept."*[111] John Bolton, the 25th US Ambassador to UN, agrees, *"Negotiation is not a policy. It's a technique. It's something you use when it's to your advantage, and something that you don't use when it's not to your advantage."*

1.2. Shunning win-lose negotiation

"I was surprised to realize that winning negotiations all the time is not always the best scenario," Dan disclosed and continued, "I used to think that negotiation is all about vouching for your best interest and get as much as you could get from any deal." Rafael expressed his delight. "I'm glad that you figured out this vital truth." He then pointed out the consequences of pursuing winning at any cost approach. "Seeking win-lose backfires, and hurts the long-term interest of the organization." Dan consented. "Yes, win-lose damages relationships."

"Why win-lose approach is still popular regardless of its side effects?" Dan wondered and solicited Rafael's take on this. "Many organizations directly or indirectly encourage their leaders to win at any cost. They recognize, reward, and promote those who win for their organizations. Because of that, their leaders use everything at their disposal to win." By the way, Stephen Covey enlisted some of the tools such leaders use: *"Win/Lose people are prone to use position, power, credentials, possessions, or personality to get their way."*[12]

"What about those negotiators whose companies don't encourage win-lose? Why leaders in such organizations continue to use it?" Dan marveled. Rafael shared his perspective about why many leaders still use win-lose negotiation approach. "You're right. Many negotiators still go for win-lose approach without being pressured to do so. In my view, the main reason is a lack of awareness. They may not know the long term consequences of this tactic."

Looking for a solution, Dan inquired, "How can organizations discourage such negotiators?" "They should put in place some boundaries to dictate how their leaders negotiate," Rafael quick replied. "What about our organization?" Dan asked a follow-up question. Rafael responded, "GHR doesn't have a formal policy or guidelines in this regard. However, there is an unofficial common understanding that encourages win-win negotiations both within the organization, and as our leaders interact with the outside world."

Based on his own experience, Brian Tribus suggested that organizations should set boundaries on how to operate during negotiations. In 'Influencing Your Organization's Moral Philosophy', he warned: *"In the absence of proactive measures, members of an organization may be left to make critical, strategic decisions on their own. Good intentions aside, they may make decisions that the organization will later regret."*[13]

1.3. Encouraging Win-Win Negotiation
"I liked the story Joe told us that encouraged me to seek win-win negotiation all the time." Dan was talking about the tough negotiation between Egypt and Israel that was concluded with a win-win deal on March 26, 1979, at Camp David. The two archenemies were in a deadlock. Both

sides had strong positions, and they were unwilling to compromise initially, though they finally reached a win-win agreement.

Rafael asked. "Tell me a couple of lessons you learned from this negotiation?" Dan decided to share three factors that contributed toward the successful conclusion of this negotiation brokered by former President of the US- Jimmy Carter:

- **Creating a trust-filled environment**. "Though Jimmy Carter had influence over both leaders of the two countries, he didn't rely on his statesmanship to break the stalemate. He assumed a neutral role and brought the two leaders to the negotiation table and created a trust-filled environment."

- **Focusing on interests**. "Both had emotional attachments to their strong positions: Israel wanted to keep part of the Sinai Peninsula while Egypt's position was to get back all of the Sinai desert, which had been part of the country from the era of the Pharaohs though she lost it following the Six Day War of 1967. They hadn't agreed based on their positions. On the other hand, Egypt's interest was sovereignty while Israel's was security. Once they realized each other's interest, they could reach a win-win deal that satisfied their respective interest." This famous Egyptian-Israeli Peace Treaty was signed because President Sadat of Egypt and Prime Minister Begin of Israel *"agreed to a plan that would return the Sinai to complete Egyptian sovereignty and, by demilitarizing large areas, would still assure Israeli security. The Egyptian flag would fly everywhere, but Egyptian tanks would be nowhere near Israel."*[114]

- **Going the extra mile.** "Another thing to consider as we seek win-win negotiations is to go the extra mile. Anwar Sadat decided to pay a visit to Israel in the middle of hostility." Dan recognized one of the reasons this high stake negotiation succeeded. Rafael interjected, "By the way, Anwar Sadat's move, defiling all odds, could have cost his life but he determined to demonstrate how much he was willing to go to reach a win-win deal." Eli Broad, entrepreneur and philanthropist known for building two Fortune 500 companies in different industries, said it very well: *"The best move you can make in negotiation is to think of an incentive the other person hasn't even thought of - and then meet it."* Negotiators with the right mindset are the ones who are willing to go the extra mile.

Negotiation (more specifically, win-win negotiation) is a soft skill that can be developed, refined, and fine-tuned. But, the impetus to pursue win-win negotiation is having the right mindset and attitude. Stephen Covey emphasized, *"Win/Win [negotiation] is a frame of mind and heart that constantly seeks mutual benefit in all human interactions."*[115]

1.4. Honesty in negotiation

"Honesty is always the best policy, especially in negotiation," Dan stated. "Why is so?" Rafael wanted to know more. Dan explained, "This is our responsibility, to be honest with our counterparts. Sometimes the other party may not be at its best and may momentarily think that it has got a win-win deal while what happened was win-lose. If they feel cheated, manipulated, maneuvered, or took advantage of after the fact, we lose their trust, and therefore, the relationship suffers."

Rafael double checked, "What you're saying is that even if we may win a negotiation temporarily, once they find out later on that we were dishonest, we lose trust." Dan concurred and further remarked, "Once we lose trust, it is tough to regain it. Afterward, we may not be able to continually engage in a win-win negotiation with them in the future."

Overcoming tricky negotiators
"Going forward, I'd like to play fair, seek win-win, and deal honestly," Dan promised. "But, what should I do if the other party doesn't have a moral compass?"

Rafael answered Dan's question with another question, "What do you do? Do you quit or pay back in kind or should you just ignore it and play along as far as you get a satisfactory deal?"

It took Dan several seconds to respond. "If I find myself in this position in the future, I most probably play along as far as I get a satisfactory deal." With further probing questions, Dan understood that his approach may be okay for a onetime deal and if he doesn't care about the relationship. Rafael shared what he had done in the past when he found himself in such tricky situations. Dan liked Rafael's approaches and planned to apply some of them.

The authors of 'Getting To Yes' book suggested three steps to take whenever we deal with those who use illegal, unfair, and unethical tactics:
- *"Recognize the tactic,*
- *Raise the issue explicitly, and*
- *Question the tactic's legitimacy and desirability- negotiate over it."*[116] What they are suggesting is to stop the ongoing negotiation, be upfront, and start another negotiation within a negotiation.

Don't reveal everything at the outset of a negotiation
Speaking of being honest, I'd like to interject here to share my perspective. Yes, it is great, to be frank. But, we should be careful not to reveal our BATNA, WANA, WAP, and ZOPA at the wrong time. Negotiation is an

art and requires being strategic in our approaches and timing.

You might have already read or watched the news about Mexico's President, Enrique Pena Nieto, canceling a meeting with US President Donald Trump. If you review the events leading to the cancellation, you wouldn't be surprised. On Wednesday, January 25, 2017, Donald Trump signed an Executive Order to build the wall on the southern border of the US believing that Mexico will pay the cost in one form or another.

This decision was unilateral and was made without the consent of Mexico's government. The Executive Order offended members of Mexico's delegate who were in the US at that time to have some forms of negotiations with Trump's administration. Following the signature, the high-level representatives called their President to cancel the scheduled meeting with Trump.

On Thursday, while this was still going on, Trump tweeted saying: *"If Mexico is unwilling to pay for the badly needed wall, then it would be better to cancel the upcoming meeting."* It didn't take long for Mexico's President to just do that- he canceled the planned meeting on Tuesday the following week, like Trump, via Twitter: *"This morning we have informed the White House that I will not attend the meeting scheduled for next Tuesday with the POTUS."*

Why he canceled the meeting, you may ask, especially knowing that Mexico is going to lose the most? For your information, according to US Census Bureau, Mexico is US's 3rd largest trading partner. Not only that, reports show that Mexico exports more than it imports- $63 billion dollars in deficit.

It is simple. In any negotiation, if you give your counterpart an ultimatum with your walking away price upfront and honestly (in this case, Trump revealed that he walks away if Mexico doesn't agree to pay for the wall), your counterpart immediately realizes your best and worst scenarios. And, if they figure out that they won't get a satisfactory agreement from a negotiation and somehow they could be able to live with the worst scenario, they walk away. That is what Mexico's President just did.

Valuable lessons from the above episode:
- **Don't give ultimatum upfront before the start of any negotiation.** This applies to you even if you have the upper hand as you enter into any negotiation. Of course, if your desire is a win-win deal. I'm not sure whether Trump was making a tactical move to begin the negotiation from a strong ground or whether that was a misstep and oversight or

brutal honesty. Otherwise, you shouldn't reveal your position honestly at the wrong time; most importantly, you shouldn't demand concessions before the start of a negotiation. You should wait for the right time to demand concessions, and if necessary to make some concessions.

- **Don't reveal the bottom-line too soon.** This is especially important during negotiations between two nations. Negotiations in business are entirely different than negotiations between nations, especially those from different cultures. In the case of business negotiations, as far as the negotiators get a deal acceptable by the majority of the shareholders, they may be considered successful. Unfortunately, negotiations between countries are complex. There are many stakeholders with diverse, sometimes irreconcilable, interests and priorities. Trump attempted to negotiate on Twitter and revealed his bottom lines honestly for all stakeholders too soon. Sensitive negotiations should be done behind closed doors, at least, at the initial stage. There should be an agreement from both parties on how and when to communicate the progress of the negotiation to their respective stakeholders.

- **Don't undermine emotions**. Negotiations should consider both positive and negative roles emotions play. In their book 'Beyond Reason', Roger Fisher and Daniel Shapiro discussed the critical roles emotions play[117]. They believed that people experience both positive and negative emotions as they negotiate. The authors claimed that people have difficulty to deal with their own and the emotions of others, and that affect the success of negotiations. His inner circle and thousands of ordinary citizens pressured Enrique because they felt that Trump's publicly displayed tweets did hurt their national pride! According to news from Mexico, the President was forced to cancel the meeting because citizens felt that their country and its people are bullied, and therefore, regardless of the economic consequences of walking away from the negotiation, they demanded their President cancel the meeting. *"Emotions of the negotiating parties play critical roles for the success of a given negotiation. Recognizing my emotions and the message they may send, and also reading the emotions of others to recognize where they are in the negotiation."* In this regard, Daniel Goleman also acknowledged, *"Without the ability to sense our own feelings- or to keep them from swamping- we will be hopelessly out of touch with the moods of others."*[118] Sharpening one's negotiation skills requires understanding our emotions and regulating them so that we may not send inadvertent messages that may be used against us. And also the ability to read our counterparts' emotions and tap into that knowledge to lead the other party where we want to take them without manipulating.

- **Don't damage long-term relationships**. Neighboring countries like the US and Mexico shouldn't just negotiate to get a better financial deal. They need each other for other collaborations that are critical to their countries, people, and the region. That doesn't mean they shouldn't aim at getting better deals for their respective countries, but this shouldn't come at the expense of permanently damaging their relationship. Win-lose negotiations always burn bridges and also injure healthy relationships. For Sunil Mittal- billionaire Indian telecom tycoon, *"Relationship is very important. I can lose money, but I cannot lose a relationship. The test is, at the end of a conversation or a negotiation, both must smile."*

At the time of this writing, it's too early to reach any conclusion, too premature. However, going forward, I'm sure that the two nations may keep working on a win-win deal, at least, behind the scene… I guess they have already realized that negotiation doesn't succeed on Twitter.

II. Assessments, Processes, and Tools
2.1. The four steps of negotiation
Dan found the four stages of negotiation Joe shared based on the work of Fisher, Ury, and Patton very helpful:
1. Separate the People from the Problem,
2. Focus on Interests, Not Positions,
3. Invent Options for Mutual Gain, and
4. Insist on Using Objective Criteria.

Firmly, Dan decided to follow this process whenever he engages in any negotiation, formal or informal, small or big. Rafael is well aware of this process. He shared one personal story for each step to show Dan the critical role each stage plays toward win-win negotiations.

III. Action item
Dan was going to have a negotiation, in two weeks, with his real estate agent to sell his current home and buy a new one. He wanted to use the opportunity to practice what he learned from this workshop. After giving Rafael the background, he asked Rafael to give him some negotiation tips that may help him succeed in the upcoming negotiation.

After Rafael had given him some tips, they talked about Dan's:

1. BATNA,
2. WANA,
3. WAP, and
4. ZOPA.

Summary

Whether we admit it or not, we all negotiate. Formally, or at least informally, we all negotiate on a consistent basis. This awareness is very vital, especially for leaders. We cannot lead without the ability to negotiate for win-win deals. When we realize the fact that we negotiate more than we would like to admit and the critical role negotiation plays to lead others successfully, we become proactive and invest our time and resources to develop and continually improve our ability to negotiate for win-win deals. If we make enough efforts, there are always mutual gains in any negotiation. Our long-term success as negotiators, however, is determined by our mindset that honors win-win deals. It's also dependent on the time we spend to prepare before each negotiation to fully understand ours and the other party's strengths, weaknesses, wants and needs, best and worst case scenarios, and walking away points. Emotions also could make or break a negotiation. As leaders, we should have the full awareness of our own feelings, and the emotions of those who are involved in a negotiation.

Soft Skill 12: Leading Others Through Change Smoothly

"The world hates change, yet it is the only thing that has brought progress."
Charles Kettering

Leading others takes leading change

- Leading Others is a process.
- This process begins by motivating others, which was covered in Workshop nine.
- The second stage is transforming others.
- One of the soft skills in the second stage is coaching and mentoring others, which was covered in Workshop ten.
- The other soft skill essential in the second stage is negotiation.
- Unlike in the past, leaders of the 21st C cannot command and make things happen. They are required to engage stakeholders in constant negotiations to make win-win deals and also to build coalitions, which was covered in Workshop eleven.
- The third soft skill in the second stage is leading change.
- Workshop twelve covered leading others through change smoothly.

Change, the only constant

Everything in life and nature changes except change itself. It remains the only constant that doesn't bow down to the course of nature. Change has been with us since the beginning of history. The only thing that changed is the pace of change that has been quickened especially nowadays.

John Kotter projected, *"The rate of change is not going to slow down anytime soon. If anything, competition in most industries will probably speed up even more in the next few decades."* That is why, in the 21st C, the ultimate success of a leader is determined by his/her soft skill ability to transform his team and organization by developing the capacity to initiate, implement, and sustain change.

Change to experience progress and innovation

Unfortunately, the task of leading change is not easy. The main reason is our hostility toward change in general. Dennis O'Grady lamented, *"Change has a bad reputation in our society."* We hate to change more than we would like to admit. Unlike the popular belief that only some people are inherently resisters of change, we all find ourselves in this category more than once.

Fortunately, change has been surviving throughout the years to benefit humanity regardless of being treated unfairly by the majority of us. In the leading quote above Charles Kettering- a prolific inventor, credited change for being the author of the progress humanity has experienced. George Bernard Shaw agreed, *"Progress is impossible without change."* Particularly in this competitive era, it's difficult to advance and innovate without saying yes to lots of changes at many fronts and levels.

Winston Churchill observed, *"To improve is to change; to be perfect is to change often."* Individually and collectively, if our desire is to advance and experience progress, enjoy innovation, and ultimately succeed in what we do; we need to develop the soft skill that empowers us to lead others through change smoothly. Dennis O'Grady recognized, *"Change is necessary in life – to keep us moving ... to keep us growing ... to keep us interested ... Imagine life without change. It would be static ... boring ... dull."*

Dan is super excited about the last workshop
This is the last workshop of the Soft Skills Development program at GHR. Though Dan had been enthusiastic about each workshop, this theme was unique to him. This workshop was the last in the program, and therefore, he decided to give it his best to finish the program strong. Moreover, GHR is in the middle of an enormous organizational level change where attending this workshop on the theme change equips him to play his share successfully.

An entirely different attitude
Remember, three months ago, he was resentful for being forced to attend this program. As he drove to attend this last workshop, nonetheless, he had a different attitude. He felt great because he learned a lot. He has become a better person not only at work but also in his personal space as he interacts with his wife, family members, and friends because of this program.

I. Key lessons
1.1. Leading change is the toughest soft skills to develop
Dan considered leading change is the hardest soft skill to develop. Rafael probed to find out why Dan reached this conclusion. Dan expanded, "Leading change takes boldness, confidence, risk taking, discernment, and so on. It also takes to sense change ahead, courageously initiate it ahead of the curve, and chart ways for your team in uncharted water. As a change agent, if you don't grab change by its tail, if you hesitate, you may miss the boat."

Rafael pondered a little while, and then he emphasized, "I completely agree with your assessment. The challenge with this soft skill, unlike other soft skills, is that you aren't just changing the organizational structure, systems, and workings of your company. You are required to change not just yours but also the attitude, mindset, and behaviors of your people by changing their heart."

Rafael was on the mark. Marshall Goldsmith, in his latest book 'Trigger', admitted that behavioral change is hard, *"Even harder to stay the course, hardest of all to make the change stick. I'd go so far as to say that adult behavioral change is the most difficult thing for sentient human beings to accomplish."*[119] Systems Scientist-Peter Senge, also said, *"People don't resist change. They resist being changed!"*

With a frustrated voice, Dan bluntly inquired: "How can I change the heart of my team?" Admitting that it's a tough question, Rafael shed some light based on his personal experience. "Personally, I found it very helpful first to know what matters the most to my team members. Then, I take the time to figure out how the change contributes toward advancing what is valuable to the team as a whole and individually. I found this working in most cases. People want to know 'what is in it for them' in a particular change situation before they buy into the change agenda and commit themselves." Dan nodded and remarked, "It gives sense. I'll try it."

Rob Lebow and William Simon- the authors of 'Lasting Change', suggested using values to gain the cooperation of stakeholders. They warned, *"Trying to "fix" the behaviors of people leaves a company's people bewildered and discouraged, unprepared to meet the different climates and challenges of the rapidly changing enterprise jungle."*[120] They recognized, *"People respond and relate to values."*

In order leaders to bring behavioral changes and in turn lasting transformation, they need to tap into the power of values. Leaders should work with the major stakeholders to create shared values and align their people alongside these values. People are willing to make behavioral changes as far as they could see that these changes contribute toward advancing and protecting the shared values.

Of course, behavioral changes alone don't bring lasting transformation unless backed by altering the underlining organizational culture. In the latter case, the involvement of the top leadership is crucial. The latter should have excellent ability to lead change smoothly. Research shows that *"The single most visible factor that distinguishes major cultural changes that succeeded from those that fail is competent leadership at the top."*[121]

1.2. Change or die

Dan was surprised to hear that the mantra, which says 'if you don't change you stagnate', is outdated. Enthusiastically, he announced, "In the 21st C, the motto is either you change- flow with the current, or die." "That is so true!" Rafael further noted, "Some individuals and organizations learned that the hard way. They hesitated to change, and as a result unable to survive to tell their side of the story."

"What does that mean to you and your team?" Rafael asked. Dan had a ready-made answer as he had taken the time to think about the implication of this new reality. "Even if we don't like change or feel uncomfortable about it or angry at what is changing; we shouldn't waiver to make changes on time. We need to befriend with change and embrace it. And I'm glad that I attended this workshop." "Absolutely." Rafael exclaimed, and further stressed, "Even if, unlike the death in humans, team and organizational deaths may not be drastic. Surely, those who fail to make deep changes as frequently as they should experience a slow death."

Robert Quinn, in his book 'Deep Change', pointed out that slow death starts when someone faces *"the dilemma of having to make deep organizational change or accepting the status quo, rejects the option for the deep change."* He concluded, *"This decision results in the gradual (and occasionally not so gradual) disintegration of an organization, business, or industry."*[122]

Dinosaurs did extinct for their uncooperativeness to change

"Think about Dinosaurs," Rafael thought giving Dan an illustrative example. "They failed to adapt to change and ended up vanished. This the same principle works in the work and marketplaces. I can give you many known brands that hesitated to change and died."

Kodak hesitated to change and paid a terrible price...

Dan listened quietly and expressed his eagerness to hear more about stories of those companies that did extinct like Dinosaurs. Rafael enumerated some organizations that paid dire prices for their tardiness.

"First, Kodak. It overstayed in the industry that was dying and lost its leading status. As a result, it struggled and finally unable to survive. On the other hand, it's counterpart- Fuji Film- quickly recognized the change that was coming in the print photography industry. It swiftly embraced digital photography. It also diversified its portfolios and began producing healthcare products and Information Technology services to adapt to change, survive, and eventually thrive."

Xerox waited too long...

Rafael paused for a couple of seconds to give Dan a chance to ask or comment. Dan was intensely listening. Rafael then moved to his second example, "Xerox was unable to see the change that was coming as fast as it should. It stayed too long, failed to discern the timing for the coming of the personal computer revolution. Steve Jobs sensed the season and the readiness of the market for personal computers. He asked to visit Xerox's lab. This visit allowed Jobs to make a quantum leap forward that changed the computer industry forever. You already know the unparalleled current worth of these two companies."

Blockbuster gave way to Netflix...

"At the turn of the century, Reed Hastings approached Blockbuster to acquire the business he co-founded in 1997, Netflix, only for 50 million dollars. The then CEO of Blockbuster- John Antioco couldn't see the coming of online streaming and on-demand movie service ahead of the curve that he declined to purchase Netflix."

By the way, in 2015, the market value of Netflix was almost 40 billion. As it is stated in its website Blockbuster's assets were acquired by DISH Network in April 2011. Before the bankruptcy, in 2010, the company's value was 37 million. Blockbuster's value was 5 billion US dollars around the time Netflix was founded.

Nokia's CEO crying was too late...

The last story Rafael shared was the sad story of Nokia, one of the most respected companies for decades. He quoted the CEO of Nokia who said *'We didn't do anything wrong, but somehow, we lost'* while crying like a baby during the press conference that was arranged to announce Nokia's smartphone division being acquired by Microsoft. Rafael remarked, "What Nokia's CEO didn't realize was that they didn't just lose when Microsoft bought them. They had failed to sense the change that was coming on time. And, that negligence had a terrible price."

After listening to these dramatic stories of defeats, Dan asked a couple of follow-up questions. Rafael answered these questions. They finally concluded that it's imperative to discern change ahead, prepare the organization for transformation, and make the change before it becomes too late- before paying dire prices for being reluctant to change.

Complacency: Success is the enemy of change

Dan asked one afterthought question, "By the way, I'm wondering why these once gigantic companies failed to make the change on time and when it mattered the most?" Rafael responded decisively, "They became complacent. By the time they attempted to change, it was too late."

Yes, we must make changes as fast as possible and proactively before they become mandatory. That was why Jack Welch advised, *"Change before you have to."* Mark Sanborn- leadership expert and keynote speaker, blatantly said: *"Your success in life isn't based on your ability to simply change. It is based on your ability to change faster than your competition, customers and business."*

We shouldn't hesitate to change on time. Reluctance to change predisposes us to miss the boat that would take us to our envious future. John F. Kennedy famously remarked, *"Change is the law of life. And those who look only to the past or present are certain to miss the future."*

By the way, there is a common misunderstanding concerning why the above once giant companies and similar others vanished or became insignificant. Mistakenly, many people think that these once leading companies were stubborn and refused to change at all. That is not accurate. Most of them made so many desperate moves to catch up with the change they had just missed. Unfortunately, their past success blinded them and felt that they were too big to lose to Change. They waited too long to change.

Yes, complacency was the main reason!!! Otherwise, almost all of them awakened at one point, stopped resisting, and desperately attempted to save their capsizing ship by making some desperate change moves. It was too late. They missed the boat that would have taken them to a glorious future. The initial misstep denied them from transforming their people and organization to the next height.

1.3. Responses to resistances are the main reason why changes fail

"I had been resisting many changes without spending enough time to evaluate their merits," Dan recalled. "The majority of us, at home, work, and in the marketplace, resist change knowingly or unknowingly." Rafael acknowledged and pointed out, "Of course, individuals aren't the only resisters of change. Teams and organizations too, they resist change."

The latter statement of Rafael shouldn't surprise us. By design, organizations are configured to maintain stability, not to promote change. In his book 'Deep Change', Robert Quinn reminded us that *'It is natural for organizations to discourage transformation. Organizational structures and processes encourage equilibrium, not change.'*[23]

"I had been asking myself for a very extended period why many of the changes implemented at GHR failed," Dan disclosed his assumption. "It seems to me that these changes failed not because of technologies, methods, or lack of funding. Now, I see that they were unsuccessful mainly because of the resistances they faced." Rafael quickly interjected to second Dan's point of view, "I concur with you. Many researchers reported that two-thirds of changes failed miserably, and GHR isn't exceptional."

Yes, the overwhelming majority of changes fail but why? Rick Maurer found out that Fortune 500 executives acknowledged that resistances to change had been the primary reason their change agendas were unsuccessful. He wrote, *"And 80 percent of the chief information officers said that resistance – not a lack of technical skills or resources – was the main reason why technology projects failed. It's that soft, touchy-feely, human reaction of resistance that matters."*[24]

Dan was surprised to discover the fact that many change agendas failed not just because of resistances. But rather, due to the leadership's responses to resistances. In the next several minutes, they went back in retrospect to identify some changes that failed and those inappropriate responses that contributed toward the demise of those change agendas.

Yes, responses to resistances were the main reason many change agendas failed. Rick Maurer, in his book 'Beyond The Wall of Resistance', wrote, *"New ideas often fail, not on their relative merits, but on how well we are able to handle resistance."*[25]

1.4. Overcoming resistances to change

"The workshop equipped me to overcome resistances to change. I learned that we should go beyond the surface and understand the root causes why people resist change and respond accordingly." Dan shared the fourth lesson he got from the last workshop.

"How do you plan to overcome resistances to change?" Rafael gave Dan the opportunity to share his plans to tackle future resistances. Accordingly, Dan came up with a couple of suggestions:
- Changing my attitude,
- Understanding the sources of resistances and responding appropriately,
- Dealing with resistances right away, and
- Involving all stakeholders at the early stage.

Changing our attitude

"How changing your attitude enables you to overcome resistances?" Rafael probed. "The starting place to overcome resistances to change should be changing our very attitude. Most of us think that our resistances to change are justifiable when we do it, but we don't give that same room for others. We question their motives without even giving them a fair chance to explain why they resist a given change in the first place." Dan elaborated.

Understanding the sources of resistances & responding appropriately
Rafael inquired, "Have you identified the common sources of resistances you've been facing thus far?"

To give Rafael a little background before answering this question, Dan talked about the three levels of resistances based on the work of Rick Maurer:
- **Level 1** (I don't understand it),
- **Level 2** (I don't like it), and
- **Level 3** (I don't trust you).

Rafael asked him to explain the appropriate responses for each level of resistance. Dan expounded:
- "Level 1 resistance requires giving more info, statistics, and examples to help people understand the very nature of the change itself.
- Level 2 resistance demands addressing people's fear toward the change and its impact.
- Level 3 resistance calls for generating trust."

"Which one is the toughest resistance?" Rafael queried. Dan pondered for a couple of seconds and responded, "For me, the last level of resistance is the most challenging than the other two levels of resistances." Agreeing with Dan's selection, he gave Dan some examples to show the difference between these three resistances.

"By the way, Level 1 resistance is at intellectual level while level 2 is at emotional, and level 3 is at heart level," Rafael rationalized. He further clarified, "We cannot overcome level 2 resistance by bombarding those resisting at this level with more data. They already understood the change. They already passed level 1 resistance. We need to address their fear and show them what is in it for them to get their cooperation. Level 3 resistances are the most entrenched of all resistances. Since it's to do with lack of trust, it takes more time, and generating or regenerating trust by taking some measures."

Be influenced in response to Level 3 resistances
I was invited by a colleague of mine to attend a press conference on the eve of Ethiopian New Year in 2016 in Arlington, VA. My colleague is one of the well-respected community leaders among our community. He wanted well-known Ethiopian community leaders to come together and release a

timely press release to show solidarity to the people of Ethiopia back home.

The occasion brought some of Ethiopia's best children from diverse backgrounds into one room. Some of the participants conferred with me in private that they wouldn't have come that close with some of the participants if it were not because of the person who organized the session. Many of these individuals have many of followers and have their own unique brands. They're smart and completely recognized the importance of the occasion. They also liked the idea and the person who invited them.

My colleague tried his best to create a consensus and hoped the group would deliver something at the end of the brainstorming session. Time ran out and it seemed impossible to bring them into one accord. It looked like this group- consisted of high profile Ethiopian leaders in the diaspora- wouldn't be able to use that critical moment to issue a strong message of solidarity.

I was invited to this event as an attendee, as an observer. I was carefully analyzing the situation from the back of the room. When the session was on its last legs- ten or fifteen minutes before it ends- my colleague asked me to come forward and lead the remaining brainstorming session. To be honest, though I'm a trainer and speaker and don't have stage fright, it was quite frightening to stand in front of leaders I admire and respect a lot without preparing myself, especially while it looked like things were going south. Fortunately, my trainer, coach, and consultant instinct kicked in and I thought on my feet on how to break the deadlock.

Coincidently, I was preparing to lead a change management workshop the following week, and the materials were fresh in my mind. I quickly recognized that these people don't need further data (it wasn't a level 1 resistance) or more convincing arguments about its timeliness and relevance (it wasn't a level 2 resistance). I believed that the resistance was level 3. And thus, I decided to be influenced, and thus, allowed them to have control over the outcome of the meeting.

I said, "I believe that you all understand the relevance and timeliness of sending this solidarity message today- on the eve of Ethiopian New Year. However, if you guys don't want to give the press release, fine, let's call it quits. Or, you are already here, and you believe in the message and the urgency of the matter, and therefore, you may please take 10 minutes and prepare yourself to say whatever you want in front of the camera."

The room was quiet for a while, and it felt forever. I didn't know what to expect. Within those few seconds, some thoughts crossed my mind though. I wondered what the host would think of me if they take the first option, and walk away from that room after he spent days and days in preparation and investing lots of money in renting the room and coordinating the event? Would he forgive me for giving them a way out?

Well, when they knew that they had control over the outcome and could walk away if they wanted to, they felt in charge. The willingness to be influenced generated trust. And thus, they were willing to deliver right away what they were asked.

Dealing with resistance right away

Dan and Rafael further talked about some more approaches that help overcome resistances to change. They also talked about the importance of addressing resistances while they are still infants before they grow and become monsters. Ed and Doug noted, *"Trying to overcome resistance late in a change process is like the antiquated and expensive method of fixing a bad product at the end of the manufacturing process."*[126]

Resisting change, not always a bad thing

Before they moved to the next section, Rafael pointed out that resisting change is not always a bad thing. "In some cases, resisting change is a good thing." He gave some examples from his experience how, in the past, some bad changes were accepted without resistance and in turn harmed GHR. "You should be very careful and walk the delicate line between change that comes to harm your team and organization, and that comes to transform and take your team to the next level."

What Rafael was saying is that as much as we should recognize what must change, we should also know what must not change. Great change agents have developed discernment to make the right call. Rick Maurer reminded us, *"Resistance protects us from harm... It keeps us safe. Resistance can be a sign of health, a way to navigate in a complex and rapidly changing world."*[127]

II. Assessments, Processes, and Tools
2.1. William Bridges Transition model

"We were introduced to three change models," Dan revealed and briefly talked about them. "Which one do you like the most?" Rafael inquired. "William Bridges' transition model," Dan answered.

"Why do you like it over the other models?" Rafael further probed. Dan explained, "People don't fear change but the transition. And, this model explains the three phases of change, and how to move people from one stage to another." "What are the three phases," Rafael asked. Dan enumerated the three phases and described them briefly:

- **Letting Go**. Ending the old way of doing things.
- **The Neutral Zone**. The Transition.
- **The New Beginning**.

Rafael inquired, "Which phase is critical?" Dan pointed out that all of the three phases are important, but he found out that many leaders fail during the transition stage where the actual change happens.

Rafael consented and further noted, "That is true. The Neutral Zone is the difference maker. It's where heroes are made. The transition is where goliaths are slain. The transition is where change dies or thrives. Leaders are not tested in the first or last phase. True change agents are tried and made during the transition phase."

Leading change successful involves developing all the hard and soft skills necessary to succeed in all three phases. But, the soft skills essential during the transition period are lacking in many leaders. Jon Katzenbach said, *"Real change leaders learn how to survive and win in the delta state [transition], while traditional managers can only survive in the current state or the future state."*[128]

2.2. Appreciative inquiry model

Rafael found it appropriate to share with Dan one additional model, Appreciative Inquiry (AI). He described, "AI is a relatively new change model, and many organizations haven't yet adopted it. However, some organizations have used it, and found it very helpful."

Since this is the first time Dan heard about this model, he was curious to learn, "What makes it different than the other models we covered in this program?" "AI facilitates change based on what worked in the past and where the organization would like to go. It doesn't focus on problems that occurred in the past." Rafael answered briefly.

The author of 'The Think Book of Appreciative Inquiry' Sue Hammond wrote, *"The traditional approach to change is to look for the problem, do a diagnosis, and find a solution. The primary focus of on what is wrong or broken; since we look for problems, we find them."*[129] According to the author, the justification for using AI is: *"people know how to repeat their success."*[130]

The explanation, rather than answering Dan's question, created further confusion. "I don't get it. The whole idea of change is to address problems and bring change. So, how can we just ignore what went wrong?"

"The main thesis of this model is that some things are already working. Any future change should tap into these things that have been already working. It discourages spending countless hours on those things that have not worked. It also emphasizes on strengths rather than on weaknesses. Another important premise of this model is that people will have more confidence to join a change agenda that carries some parts of the past they are familiar with."

"Are you saying that," Dan began understanding the concept of AI, "People feel less threatened when their past is incorporated in their future?" Rafael confirmed and further indicated that in any change, the most important thing that we should pay close attention is not what must change but also what must not change.

"What are some of the things that must not change?" Dan probed. "For instance, the very mission of the organization, its vision, and shared values are some of the things that must not change," Rafael responded.

AI isn't a problem-solving tool
One of the questions that I frequently get when I bring up AI as one of the processes of leading change is: How can we directly go and talk about what went well without acknowledging the problem at hand? My quick response is to let them know that AI isn't a problem-solving tool. It is a change management tool. By the way, there are two types of changes:
- Unplanned
- Planned.

Unplanned change
Unforeseen changes happen all the time. Things happen and cause problems. Such happenings may demand to understand the underlining problem and make changes to fix it. For example, if an organization is losing market share and its profit margin is declining, and the problem (s) isn't obvious yet, the first step is to research and critically analyze the problem to figure out what went wrong. In this case, what you need is a problem-solving tool, not AI. Once the problem is identified, you may then consider using AI though.

Planned change
If an organization already knows the problem it's facing, no need to spend any time to talk about it. For example, if a company already knows that its customer service failed and would like to transform its customer service;

the problem is already being identified. No need to talk about what went wrong. Rather, the team should use the process of AI to appreciate what has been working in the past in making customers happy, and then further inquire on how these things from the past could be duplicated in the future to improve customer satisfaction, and in turn, increase customer retention.

For your information, AI uses a process called 4-D cycle:

- Discovery,
- Dream,
- Design, and
- Destiny. The author of 'The Power of Appreciative Inquiry' suggested, *"The 4-D Cycle can be used to guide a conversation, a large group meeting, or a whole system change effort... Whatever the purpose, the Appreciative Inquiry 4-D Cycle serves as the foundation on which change is built."*[131]

However, there is one prerequisite for AI to work properly and enable you to achieve lasting change. Change in mindset and organizational culture is a necessity. Sue Hammond wrote, *"One measure of success for an Appreciative Inquiry initiative is whether an organization has enhanced its capacity for positive change. Has the organization's inner dialogue transformed from problem-oriented, deficit discourse to strength-oriented, affirmative discourse?"*[132]

III. Action items
Dan declared, "Leading change begins first with me. I must be ready and make some changes to become an effective change agent." By quoting Gandhi who said *'Be the change that you would like to see in the world'*, Rafael encouraged Dan to start the change from within.

Dan had been trying to change others. Now, he began taking responsibility to change himself for whom he has control. Jim Rohn underscored, *"You must take personal responsibility. You cannot change the circumstances, the seasons, or the wind, but you can change yourself. That is something you have charge of."*

Wondering the kind of changes Dan planned to implement, Rafael asked: "Do you mind to share with me the kind of changes you're planning to make?" Dan didn't mind. He enlisted some of the personality traits that hadn't helped him that must change. He also enumerated those characteristics that he would like to develop to become an effective change agent. They then talked about what Dan should do to develop those critical traits necessary to empower him to lead change smoothly and successfully.

If you're interested to know some of the characteristics of real change agents, below are the top five traits that are identified by Jon Katzenbach, which he enlisted in his work 'Real Change Leaders':

1. Commitment to a better way
2. Courage to challenge existing power bases and norms
3. Personal initiative to go beyond defined boundaries
4. Motivation of themselves and others
5. Caring about how people are treated and enabled to perform[133]

Jon also suggested that real change leaders should adopt situational leadership style. He wrote, *"They [Real Change leaders] are becoming very adept at matching their leadership styles and skill balances to the situation at hand."* He further suggested, *"The best Real Change Leaders develop a unique combination of skills, values, attributes, and attitudes for a wide variety of change and performance situations."*[134]

Summary

We live in a fantastic century filled with constant change. In this very exciting but at the same time challenging era, teams, organizations, and communities need transformational leaders. These leaders should have the mindset, attitude, and discernment to sense change ahead of the curve and transform their people to adapt to change on a consistent basis. They should be skillful in initiating, implementing, and sustaining change successfully. They should also understand resistances of change and respond appropriately. More than the resistances, the responses to the resistances make or break the success of a given change agenda. The 21st C change agents also need to use some of the well-tested change management models to lead stakeholders through change smoothly.

Conclusion

Dan finished the program with flying colors. He gained so many great insights that changed his mindset and perspectives. He got some useful processes, approaches, and tools that he has already begun using.

One week after the last workshop, Pat- the Senior Program Manager of GHR professional development program- arranged a final session that included a graduation ceremony. Some of the participants invited their family members and friends to join them during the graduation ceremony. Their immediate bosses and colleagues joined a few participants. Susan came to cheer Dan. His admin assistant too attended the ceremony and took some pictures.

The final session began at 9 am. Karen was the master of ceremony. With a big smile, she congratulated participants for finishing this rewarding program. Next, she briefly talked about the outline of the final session. Once that was out of the way, Karen invited Joe to the stage. He spent the next 90 minutes to:

- Summarize the main discussion points of the program,
- Review the assessments participants took,
- Recap the tools covered in the program, and
- Answer their questions.

Once Joe was done, Pat was introduced to make the final remark. At the center of Pat's speech was continual learning. He encouraged participants to take advantage of the available in person and online training courses at GHR to continue to develop their soft skills.

Pat shared some stories of alumni who kept a close relationship with him and the program long after they were done with the program. At the end of his speech, Pat encouraged them to reach out to him. "I've helped many alumni who finished this program ahead of you. Feel free to reach out. I'd love to support you in your continual growth."

Karen invited each participant according to their alphabetic order to receive their certification from Pat's hand. The ceremony was very successful.

Susan and Dan walked out together. With noticeable excitement and joy, Susan expressed her feeling, "I'm happy the way things have turned out. Dan, I'm impressed by the progress you have made. I've already got great feedback from some of your team members and colleagues. This is an amazing turnaround, and I'm glad that we worked on a compromise. I'm happy that things worked out all right."

Dan in his part appreciated Susan for pushing him to change. "It turned out one of the best things that happened in my professional life. I've learned a lot, got so many insights, and tools to use. Most importantly, I've developed some soft skills that would help me succeed in my personal life, relationships, and career. Above all, I've become a better person. Thanks for your patience and continued support including covering for me during my absence."

They chatted a little more about Dan's personal development plan. And then, they finally said goodbye to each other and went their separate ways.

After completing the program, Dan continued to work on his soft skills. His personal mastery improved tremendously. He has been getting along with Susan, his peers, other stakeholders, and also leading his team successfully. As a result, for the last three years, his team has been functioning like a well-oiled machine. The team and Dan himself received a few program level and companywide awards and recognitions for their extraordinary performance. Not only that, early this year, Dan began mentoring a couple of junior scientists who enrolled in the Soft Skills Development program.

I'm sure that Dan's story inspired you. I believe that you gained some insights, processes, and tools that could empower you to attain extraordinary success in what you do. This is my hope that you'll continue to grow and finally achieve the success that you have been dreaming, the success that you deserve. Good luck to you!

Disclaimer

Before I conclude this book, I have a confession to make. This stand-alone book isn't enough to demonstrate the turnaround Dan has shown. The goal of this book is to function as a reference, to show you the importance of the 12 soft skills that make or break your success. I don't believe that reading this book alone enables you to master self, get along with, and lead others successfully.

When I decided to write this book, my intention wasn't to provide readers a silver bullet to succeed in their lives, professions, and their other endeavors. This book is a starting place. I encourage you to find additional resources and programs to supplement this reference book if your desire is to achieve extraordinary success in your life, career, and business.

We're here to help

I'm not suggesting that we are the only ones to help you develop these soft skills and grow continually. But, if you choose to continue developing yours (your team's) soft skills, and if you prefer Success Pathways, LLC as a partner, we're more than happy to serve you.

Below are some of the follow-up services we have to complement the book:
- Keynotes for your events
- Individual coaching for you and group-coaching for your team
- Soft Skills Development program, like the one Dan attended
- Individual workshops of your choice from the twelve soft skills
- Online course

For the above services, this book is going to be a reference. On top of this text book, we have a well-developed workbook for each session.

Our workshops are designed based on adult learning principles, and thus, the workshops are dynamic, engaging, and very interactive.

Our program can be carried out for:
- One year, one workshop per month, or
- Six months, two workshops per month, or
- Three months, one workshop per week like in the case of GHR, or
- Six weeks, two workshops per week.

We leave the above decision to you. Not only that, you may choose not to take the entire program at all if you believe that your people have already developed some of the soft skills or if you find some of the soft skills aren't directly relevant to your people.

In any case, the program is going to be:

- **Interactive**. The trainer acts as a facilitator, not as a lecturer. Except providing a brief background before the start of each section followed by one or two stories, metaphors, and/or analogies, each workshop is designed to put participants at the center allowing them to interact with the facilitator and other fellow participants.
- **Engaging**. Each session allows participants to discuss in pair; small and large groups so as to learn from one another through well-designed activities, exercises, and role-plays.
- **Reality-checks**. Participants will take some relevant assessments wherever applicable prior to coming to some of the workshops, and results will be discussed in the classroom with the trainer and other participants to get feedback.
- **Practical**. Each workshop is designed to be practical where participants get processes, models, methods, and tools they can use in the workplace right away.
- **Assignments**. Participants will be given practical assignments at the end of each workshop to keep the momentum going long after the end of each workshop.

Hope, you enjoyed reading this book. If there is anything we can do to help, please don't hesitate to reach out. Below is my contact info:

P.O. Box 10136
Silver Spring, MD 20914

Email: Assegid@successpws.com or
Assegidh@gmail.com

Tel: 703-895-4551

[1] National Soft Skills Association (February, 2015). The Soft Skills Disconnect. Retrieved on October 25, 2016, from http://www.nationalsoftskills.org/the-soft-skills-disconnect/ **Note**: Though this research was conducted long time ago, it still stands. In my research thus far, I've not found a single research that came up with a different conclusion that attributes the lion share of success to technical skills.

[2] Schawbel, D. (2013). The Soft Skills Managers Want. Retrieved on October 24, 2016, from https://www.bloomberg.com/news/articles/2013-09-04/the-soft-skills-managers-want

[3] Anonymous (2014). 1 Million People cannot be wrong. Retrieved on October 25, 2016, from http://cafepharma.com/boards/threads/1-million-people-cant-be-wrong.565988/

[4] Green, M. & DeSandro E. (2011). The 2011 State of the Industry: Increased Commitment to Workplace Learning. Retrieved on October 26, 2016, from https://www.td.org/Publications/Magazines/TD/TD-Archive/2011/11/The-2011-State-of-the-Industry-Increased-Commitment-to-Workplace-Learning

[5] National Soft Skills Association (February 2015).

[6] NACE (2016). NACE's Job Outlook 2016. Retrieved on May 12, 2016, from https://www.naceweb.org/about-us/press/2016/verbal-communication-most-important-candidate-skill.aspx

[7] Goldsmith, M. (2007). *What Got You Here Won't Get You There*. New York: Hyperion Books. p. 79.

[8] Senge, P. M. & Smith, B. J. & Ross, R. B. & Roberts, C. & Kleiner, A. (1994). *The Fifth Discipline Fieldbook*. New York: The Crown Publishing Group. p. 193.

[9] Covey, S. (2005). *The 8th Habit: From effectiveness to greatness*. New York: Free Press. p. 15 - 16.

[10] Oakley, E. & Krug, D. (1991). *Enlightened Leadership: Getting to the heart of change*. Palmer, AK: Fireside Books. p. 10.

[11] Ziglar, Z. & Ziglar, T. (2012). *Born To Win: Find your success code*. Success Books. p.19.

[12] Cashman, K. (1998). *Leadership From The Inside Out: Becoming a leader for life*. Oakland, CA: Berrett-Koehler Publishers. p. 137.

[13] Maxwell, J. (2008). *Leadership Gold: Lessons I've learned from a life time of leading*. Nashville, TN: Thomas Nelson. p. 11.

[14] Koch, K. (1999). *The 80/20 Principle: The secret to success by achieving more with less*. New York: Crown Business. p. 4.

[15] Adams, M. (2009). *Change Your Questions, Change Your Life*. Oakland, CA: Berrett-Koehler Publishers. p. 8.

[16] Helmstetter, S. (1982). *What to say when you talk to your self*. New York: Pocket Books. p. 17.

[17] Helmstetter (1982). p. 138.

[18] Drucker, P. (1993). *The Effective Executive*. New York: Harper & Row Publishers.

p. vii.

[19] Hedge, J. (2013). *The Essential DISC Training Workbook: Companion to the DISC Profile Assessment*. DISC-U.org p. 3.

[20] Hedge (2013). p. 3.

[21] Covey (2005). p. 84.

[22] Covey, S. & Merrill, R. & Merrill, R. (1996). First Thing First. New York: Free Press p. 45.

[23] Welch, J. & Byrne, J. (2003). *Straight from Gut*. New York: Grand Central Publishing. p. 6.

[24] Luft, J. & Ingham, H. (1955). The Johari window: a graphic model of interpersonal awareness. *Proceedings of the western training laboratory in group development* (Los Angeles: UCLA).

[25] Goleman, D. (1994). *Emotional Intelligence: Why it can matter more than IQ*. New York: Bantam Books. p. 55.

[26] Goleman, D. (1998). *Working with Emotional Intelligence*. New York: Bantam Books. p. 54.

[27] Bradberry, T. & Greaves, J. (2009). *Emotional Intelligence 2.0*. San Diego: TalentSmart. p. 7 - 8.

[28] Bradberry & Greaves (2009). p. 8.

[29] Bradberry & Greaves (2009). p. 8 & 13.

[30] Bradberry & Greaves (2009). p. 20 – 21.

[31] Bradberry & Greaves (2009). p. 21 – 22.

[32] Goleman, D. & Boyatzis, R. & McKee, A. (2002). *Primal Leadership: Realizing the power of emotional intelligence*. Boston, MA: Harvard Business Review Press. p. 250.

[33] Goleman, D. (1994). p. 56.

[34] Daniel Goleman (2006). *Social Intelligence: The new science of human relationships*. New York: Bantam Books. p. 83.

[35] Goleman, D. (1998). p. 27.

[36] Goodwin, D. (2005). *Team of Rivals: The political genius of Abraham Lincoln*. New York: Simon & Schuster. p. 104.

[37] Goleman (1998). p. 135.

[38] Both, B. (2015). *The Achievement Habit: Stop wishing, start doing, and take command of your life*. New York: Harper Business. p. 15.

[39] Bradberry & Greaves (2009). p. 6.

[40] Bradberry & Greaves (2009). p. 6 – 7.

[41] Goleman & Boyatzis & McKee (2002). p. 29.

[42] Sherod Miller, Phyllis Miller, Elam W. Nunnally, and Daniel B. Wackman (1991). *Couple Communication I: Talking and Listening Together*. Evergreen, CO: Interpersonal Communication Program. p. 15.

[43] Peter Drucker (1993). p. 26.

[44] Peter Drucker (1993). p. 26.

[45] Mackenzie, A. & Nickerson, P. (2009). *The Time Trap (4th edition): The classic book on time management*. New York: AMACOM. p. 27.

[46] Drucker (1993). p. 2.

[47] Covey, S. & Merrill, A. R. & Merrill, R. R. (1994). *First Things First*. New York: Free Press. p. 44.

[48] Mackenzie & Nickerson (2009). p. 101.

[49] Temme, J.(1993). *Productivity Power: 250 great ideas for being more productive.* Mission, KS: SkillPath Publications. p. 74 – 80.

[50] Loehr, J. & Schwartz, T. (2003). *The power of full engagement: Managing energy, not time, is the key to high performance and personal renewal.* New York: Free Press. p.6.

[51] Allen, D. (2001). *Getting Things Done: The art of stress-free productivity.* New York: The Penguin Books. p. 138 – 139.

[52] Drucker (1993). p. 26.

[53] Drucker (1993). p. 167.

[54] Reynolds, H. & Tramel, M. E. (1979). *Executive Time Management: Getting 12-hours' work out of an 8-hour day.* Upper Saddle River, New Jersey: Prentice-Hall. p. 54.

[55] Gary, A. (2016). The 10 skills you need to thrive in the fourth Industrial Revolution. Retrieved on March 25, 2016, from https://www.weforum.org/agenda/2016/01/the-10-skills-you-need-to-thrive-in-the-fourth-industrial-revolution/

[56] Reynolds & Tramel (1979). p. 28.

[57] Kidder, R. M. (1995). *How Good People Make Tough Choices: Resolving the dilemmas of ethical living.* New York: Harper Perennial. p. 4.

[58] Kidder (1995). p. 3.

[59] Reynolds, H. & Tramel, M. E. (1979). *Executive Time Management: Getting 12-hours' work out of an 8-hour day.* Upper Saddle River, New Jersey: Prentice-Hall. p. 54.

[60] Both (2015). p. 9.

[61] Soll, J. B. & Milkman, K. L. & Payne, J. W. (2015). Outsmart Your Own Biases. Retrieved on March 26, 2016, from https://hbr.org/2015/05/outsmart-your-own-biases

[62] Geoff, P. (2006). *Strange and Dangerous Dreams: The fine line between adventure and madness.* Seattle, WA: Mountaineers Books.

[63] Geoff (2006).

[64] Sanow, S. & Strauss, S. (2009). *Get Along: With anyone, anytime, and anywhere.* Hampton, VA: Morgan James Publishing. p. v.

[65] Sanow & Strauss (2009). p. 7.

[66] Seth Godin (2008). *Tribes: We need you to lead us.* New York: Penguin Publishing Group. p. 6.

[67] Lencioni, P. (2002). *The Five Dysfunctions of a Team: A leadership fable.* San Francisco, CA: Jossey-Bass. p. vii.

[68] Temme, J. (1996). *Team Power: How to build and grow successful teams.* Mission, KS: SkillPath Publications. p. 9 – 15.

[69] Lencioni (2002). p. 195.

[70] Maxwell, J. (2004). *Winning With People: Discover the people principles that work for you every time.* Nashville, TN: Thomas Nelson. p. 124.

[71] Kouzes, J. & Posner, B. (2012). *The Leadership Challenge: How to make extraordinary things happen in organizations.* 5th edition. Francisco, CA: Jossey-Bass. p. 219.

[72] Alessandra, T. Dr. T's Timely Tips. Retrieved on March 2015, from http://www.alessandra.com/timelytips/7.asp

[73] Covey, S. R. (2006). *The Speed of Trust: The one thing changes everything.* New York: Free Press. p. 3.

[74] Covey (2006). p. 223.

[75] Powell, C. (2012). *It Worked For Me: In life and leadership*. New York: Harper Perennial. p. 25.

[76] Temme (1996). p. 78.

[77] Kimsey-House, H. & Kimsey-House, K. & Sandahl, P. & Whitworth, L. (2014). *Co-Active Coaching: Changing Business, Transforming Lives*. Boston, MA: Nicholas Brealey Publishing.

[78] Mehrabian, A. (1971). *Silent Messages: Implicit communication of emotions and attitudes*. Belmont, CA: Wadsworth Publishing Company. p. 43.

[79] William B. Gudykunst and Young Yun Kim (2003). *Communicating With Strangers: An approach to intercultural communication*. Columbus, OH: McGraw-Hill Humanities. p. 1.

[80] Zweifel, T. D. (2003). *Culture Clash: Managing the global high-performance team*. Rheinfall, Switzerland: Swiss Consulting Group. p. 2.

[81] Brown, J. (2013). Use the STAR model for success in job applications and interviews. Retrieved on March 2015, from https://career-ready.blogs.latrobe.edu.au/2013/09/10/use-the-star-model-for-success-in-job-applications-and-interviews/

[82] Carneigie, D. (1962). *The Quick & Easy Way to Effective Speaking: Modern Techniques for dynamic communication*. New York: Pocket Books. p. 28 – 29.

[83] Maxwell, J. C. (2010). Everyone Communicates, Few Connect: What the most effective people do differently. Nashville, TN: Thomas Nelson. p. 3.

[84] Maxwell (2010). p. 7.

[85] Livermore, D. (2011). *The Cultural Intelligence Difference*. New York: AMACOM. p. xiii.

[86] Senge & Smith & Ross & Roberts & Kleiner (1994). p. 425.

[87] Zweifel (2003). p. 29.

[88] Hunt, V. & Layton, D. & Prince, S. (2015). Why Diversity Matters. Retrieved on March 2015, from http://www.mckinsey.com/business-functions/organization/our-insights/why-diversity-matters

[89] Liao, E. Y. (2015). Why You Need Cultural Intelligence (And how to develop it). Retrieved on December 6, 2016, from http://www.forbes.com/sites/iese/2015/03/24/why-you-need-cultural-intelligence-and-how-to-develop-it/#4ae083e43670

[90] Liao (2015).

[91] Isaac, M. & Chira, S. (2017). *David Bonderman Resigns From Uber Board After Sexist Remark*. Retrieved on June 16 2017, from https://www.nytimes.com/2017/06/13/technology/uber-sexual-harassment-huffington-bonderman.html?_r=0

[92] Loden, M. & Rosener, J. (1990). *Workforce America!: Managing Employee Diversity as a Vital Resource*. New York: McGraw-Hill Education.

[93] Fisher, R. & Ury, W. & Patton, B. (2011). *Getting To Yes: Negotiating agreement without giving in*. New York: Penguin Books. p. xiii.

[94] Peter G. Northhouse (2007). *Leadership: Theory and practice (4th edition)*. Washington, DC: SAGE Publications. p. 175-176.

[95] Ziglar (2015). p. 157.

[96] Ziglar (2015). p. 158.

[97] Huffingtonpost.co.uk (2012). Leonardo DiCaprio 'Not Motivated' By Oscars. Retrieved on December 23, 2015, from http://www.huffingtonpost.co.uk/2012/01/21/leonardo-dicaprio-not-motivated-by-oscars_n_1220547.html

[98] Burg, B. (2005). *Winning without intimidation: Mastering the art of positive persuasion.* Jupiter, FL: Samark Publishing. p. 17.

[99] Ferdinand F. Fournies (2000). *Coaching for Improved Work Performance.* Columbus, OH: McGraw-Hill. p. 9.

[100] Rose, G. (2015). Mentor Mondays- Richard Branson. Retrieved on December 23, 2015, from https://www.virgin.com/entrepreneur/mentor-mondays-richard-branson

[101] Sean Bryant (2015). The Best Fortune 500 Mentorship Programs. Retrieved on January 6 2016, from http://www.investopedia.com/articles/personal-finance/022315/best-fortune-500-mentorship-programs.asp

[102] Landsberg, M. (1997). *The TAO of Coaching: Boosting your effectiveness by inspiring those around you.* Santa Monica, CA: Knowledge Exchange. p. 14- 15.

[103] Cashman (1998). p. 61.

[104] Stowell, S. J. & Starcevich, M. M. (1998). *The Coach: Creating partnerships for a competitive edge.* Sandy, Utah: CMOE Press. p. 138.

[105] Bell, C. R. & Zaiss, C. (2002). *Managers as Mentors: Building partnerships for learning 2nd edition.* Oakland, CA: Berrett-Koehler Publishers. p. XXI.

[106] Crane, T. G. & Patrick, L. N. (2002). *The Heart of Coaching: Using transformational coaching to create a high-performance culture (2dn edition).* San Diego, CA: FTA Press. p. 78.

[107] Stowell, S. J. & M. M. Starcevich (1996). *Win-Win Partnerships: Be on the leading edge with synergistic coaching.* La Jolla, CA: Center for Marine Conservation. p. 58.

[108] Stowell, S. J. & M. M. Starcevich (1998). p. 44.

[109] Whitmore, J. (2009) *Coaching for Performance: GROWing human potential and purpose- The principles and practice of coaching and leadership.* Boston, MA: Nicholas Brealey Publishing. p. 20.

[110] Bryant, S. (2015). The Best Fortune 500 Mentorship Programs. Retrieved on January 6 2016, from http://www.investopedia.com/articles/personal-finance/022315/best-fortune-500-mentorship-programs.asp

[111] Fisher & Ury & Patton (2011). p. 102.

[112] Covey, S. R. (2004). *The 7 Habits of Highly Effective People: Powerful lessons in personal change.* New York: Free Press. p. 218.

[113] Brian Tribus (2007). Influencing Your Organization's Moral Philosophy. In Leadership Lessons from West Point (ed. Doug Crandall).

[114] Fisher & Ury & Patton (2011). p. 43.

[115] Covey (2004). p. 217.

[116] Fisher & Ury & Patton (2011). p. 132.

[117] Fisher, R. & Shapiro, D. (2005). *Beyond Reason: Using Emotions as You Negotiate.* New York: The Penguin Group.

[118] Goleman (1998). p. 135.

[119] Goldsmith, M. (2015). *Triggers: Creating behaviors that lasts-becoming the person you*

want to be. New York: Crown Business. p. 4.

[120] Lebow, R. & Simon, W. (1997). *Lasting Change: The shared values process that makes companies great*. New York: Van Nostrand Reinhold Company. p. 50.

[121] John P. Kotter and James L. Heskett (1992). *Corporate Culture and Performance*. New York: Free Press. p. 84.

[122] Quinn, R. E. (1996). *Deep Change: Discovering the leader within*. Francisco, CA: Jossey-Bass. p.18.

[123] Quinn (1996). p. 15

[124] Maurer, R. (2009). Resistance to change- Why it matters and what to do about it. Retrieved on January 21, 2016, from http://www.rickmaurer.com/wrm/

[125] Maurer, R. (1996). *Beyond The Wall of Resistance: Unconventional strategies that build support for change*. Austin, TX: Bard Books. p. 17.

[126] Oakley, E. & Krug, D. (1991). *Enlightened Leadership: Getting to the heart of change*. Chagrin Falls, OH: Fireside Books. p. 18

[127] Maurer (1996). p. 24.

[128] Katzenbach, J. R. & the RCL Team (1996). *Real Change Leaders: How you can create growth and high performance at your company*. New York: Crown Business. p. 5.

[129] Hammond, S. A. (1996). *The Thin Book of Appreciative Inquiry (2nd ed)*. Bend, OR: Thin Book Publishing. p. 6.

[130] Hammond (1996). p. 7.

[131] Whitney, D. & Trosten-Bloom, A. (2010). *The Power of Appreciative Inquiry: A practical guide to positive change*. Oakland, CA: Berrett-Koehler Publishers. p. 6 – 7.

[132] Hammond (1996). p. 6 – 7.

[132] Whitney & Trosten-Bloom (2010). p. 283.

[133] Katzenbach, J. R. & the RCL Team (1996). p. 13.

[134134] Katzenbach, J. R. & the RCL Team (1996). p. 312 – 313.

98766621R00126

Made in the USA
Middletown, DE
09 November 2018